I0902455

Floral Jewels

anemone • blossom • daisy • dandelion • lily of the valley • narcissus • pansy • ivy • tulip • violet • calla lily • foxglove

• heliotrope • iris • lily • lotus

morning glory • poppy • rose • sunflower • vanilla flower • sweet pea • thistle • weeping willow

snowdrop • winter plum • dandelion • lily of the valley • chrysanthemum • hawthorn • hydrangea • orchid • wild oats • camellia • edelweiss • hellebore • holly • ivy • mistletoe •

FROM THE WORLD'S LEADING DESIGNERS

peony • tulip • violet • calla lily • foxglove • heliotrope • iris • lily • sunflower

mistletoe • snowdrop • edelweiss • orchid • foxglove • iris • poppy • rose • thistle • ivy

sunflower • lotus • iris

edelweiss • hellebore • tulip

weeping willow • chrysanthemum • hawthorn • hydrangea • orchid • rose • anemone • blossom • daisy • lotus • lily of the valley •

anemone • blossom • daisy • dandelion • lily of the valley • narcissus • pansy • peony • tulip • violet • calla lily • foxglove • lotus • morning glory • poppy • rose • sunflower

sweet pea • thistle • vanilla flower • hawthorn • hydrangea • orchid • wild oats • camellia • edelweiss • hellebore • peony

• anemone • blossom •

morning glory • poppy • rose • sunflower • vanilla flower • sweet pea • thistle • weeping willow

by CAROL WOOLTON

• iris • lily • lotus • morning glory • poppy • orchid

mistletoe • snowdrop • edelweiss • orchid • foxglove • iris • poppy • rose • thistle • ivy

sunflower • lotus • iris

edelweiss • hellebore • tulip

morning glory • poppy • rose • sunflower • vanilla flower • sweet pea • thistle • weeping willow

poppy • edelweiss • camellia • wild oats • hydrangea • hawthorn • chrysanthemum • weeping willow • vanilla flower

PRESTEL
Munich • London • New York

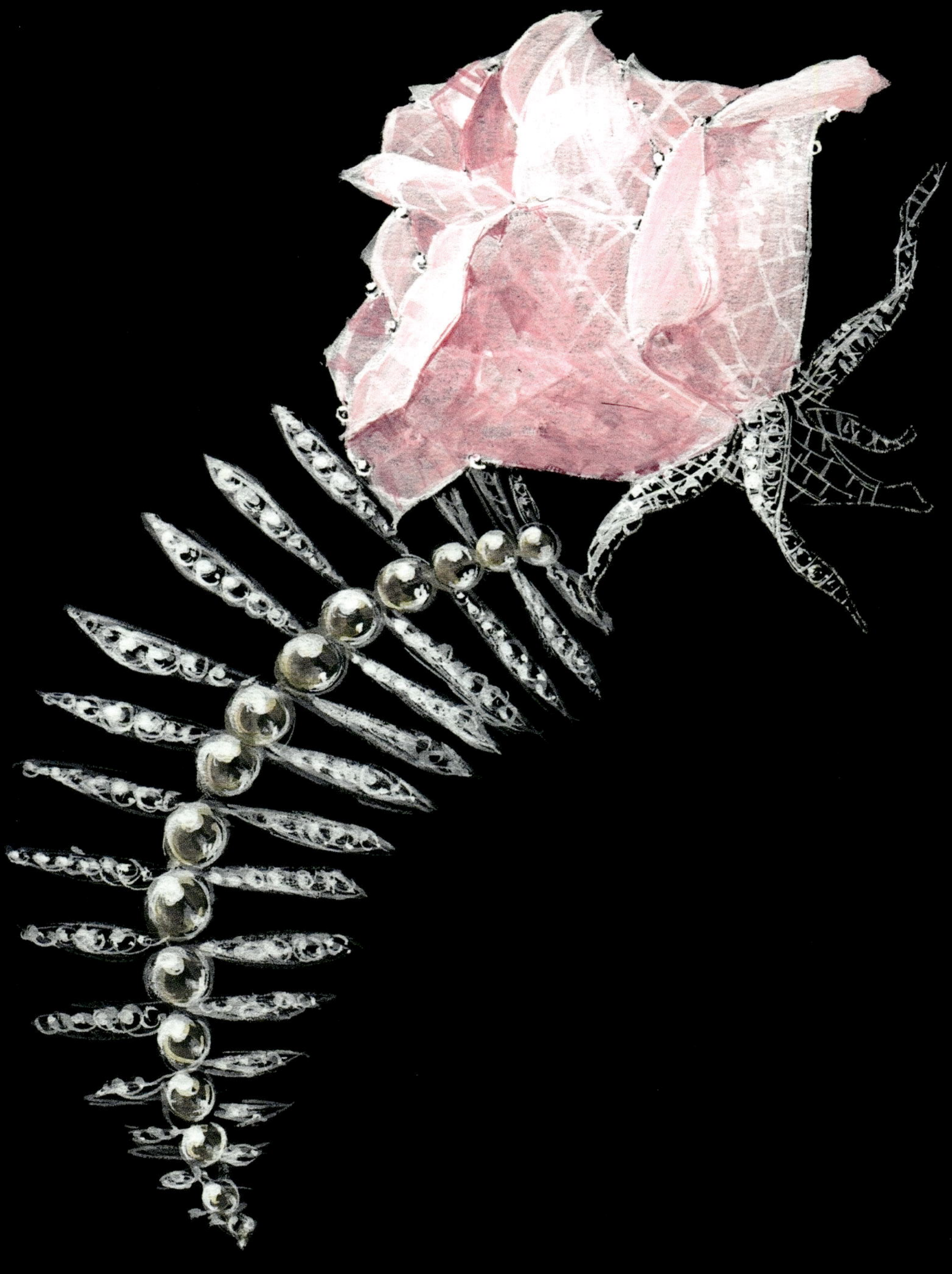

Rose
SABBA Paris
2014

CONTENTS

Making portraits of flowers,
like those of faces,
is inseparable from our nature,
our need to save and remember;
marble, paint, gems,
these are all the same
to memory and the future.

Joel Arthur Rosenthal
10 April 2014

Introduction

The artist is the confidant of inanimate Nature.
Flowers converse with him through the gracious bend
of their stems, the lilting hues of their petals.
Each corolla in the grass is an affectionate word
addressed to him by Nature.

Auguste Rodin

The simple forms of flowers have a powerful beauty that has seized the imagination of artists and jewellers since the ancient civilisations of Egypt and Greece. Women have periodically adorned their hair or dress with 'posies', garlands and wreaths of flowers, a custom that was translated into metal and stones by the jeweller's art. Capturing the perfect colour and blossom has long challenged jewellery designers, who transform the lines of a petal, corolla or flower head into sculptures that have everything of the plant except its scent. Using a combination of botanical drawings and references, rare floral specimens and the coloured stone-tipped brushes of their imagination, jewellers recreate the art of nature herself.

Flowers and jewels are natural phenomena, rooted in the earth, yet have a compelling magic that can produce a heady combination of lust, desire and greed. Throughout various periods in history, 'hunters' have risked their lives and ventured through inhospitable terrain in pursuit of a flawless diamond, nugget of gold or exotic species of orchid. During Holland's 'tulip mania', in the mid-seventeenth century, a humble tulip bulb was as precious and valuable to the owner as a carved Mughal emerald or Burmese ruby. All have been used as adornments since man first caught glimpses of coloured stones gleaming underneath the earth, or the green shoots that pushed through the soil to unfurl into cups that spilled over with rainbow tints. Flowers were painted on the walls of temples at Karnak and carved into hard stones, laurels wreathed the heads of victorious Roman soldiers, and Victorians studied the language of flowers and pondered the meaning of each gemstone.

The fragility of the flower and intense hardness of stones fascinate because neither can be exactly reproduced. We may be able to mimic the chemical composition of a diamond, but the results won't show the innate phosphorescence of the gem, nor its colour or history. To the frustration of many gardeners, the blue rose remains elusive; and the perfect herbaceous border or rural idyll within a garden will always be subject to the vagaries of nature. Our eyes fill with wonder as we look into the mesmerising depths of a three-million-year-old natural stone, or watch the first wild snowdrops drifting like foam on a sea of green, and observe the first heart-stopping violet raising its tremulous purple head each spring. Flowers and jewels appear to be conjured from the earth by a form of primeval magic.

It is colour more than anything that heralds each new season, and there is a comforting reassurance in the repeated patterns and jewel-like shades of the landscape. The lovely lush greens of spring sprout from the earth with an intensity similar to that of a grassy peridot or moss-coloured beryl. The summer landscape in Scotland turns grape-purple: a mauve blaze of heather, peppered with pink or tanzanite blue thistles, tumbles down hills, and inky-black lochs, like jet, shimmer beneath an amethyst veil of violet. The burnt, crisp, leaf-strewn golden colours of autumn like a magnificent sunset fade as the light from the sun slowly dwindles and winter turns the landscape to icy rock crystal, dotted with the white satin pearlised petals of camellias and ruby-red holly berries.

Jewellers are drawn to the challenge of conveying the essence of each season in their work, as well as the complicated curving of the variously shaped petals of individual flowers. Some blooms in particular, such as the rose, peony or orchid, hold a universal appeal for jewellery designers, and are recreated as close as possible to nature, with accurate colours and petal shapes. Other flowers lend themselves to more abstract representation, designers creating a flow of light and colour on these organic sculptural forms.

There is nothing more difficult for a true painter than to paint a rose, because before he can do so he has to first forget all the roses that were ever painted.

Henri Matisse

Jewellers similarly work from their imagination. Some invent new species, or use unusual arrangements of stones, unnatural proportions or particular shapes to create their own unique plants. Others might choose to study the fragility of flowers, depicting one moment in the life of a bloom, either budding, flowering or slowly withering, documenting with hard stones, pearls and enamel that one sublime moment in nature, so that it lasts forever in a jewel.

There are few flowers that are not cultivated by jewellers. They recognise the individual beauty of each. The rose may have its magnificence; but the tiny woodland lily of the valley has an equally beguiling innocence and fragrance; the daisy its simple charm; each lends its own particular loveliness to each season. Flowers are subject to fashion; each generation finds its own flower, so jewellers creating floral jewels document the plant life of their period. The orchid was the flower *du jour* for Victorian hothouses, the thistle was a favourite pinned to the lapels of 1940s fashionistas, whereas now, as the world frets over environmental issues, biodiversity and hedgerow regeneration, a new wave of floral jewels reflects a revived interest in wild flowers and retro-romantic wayside blooms. Humble buttercups and dandelions are the focus, just as they were when René Lalique created jewels around 1900; slender golden branches of hawthorn and blackthorn hold clusters of rose-gold berries, plump and ripe with citrines and black pearls.

Whether traditional garden flowers, the wild beauty of weeds or old-fashioned blossoms, all flowers are remarkable for their fragility and transience. In the hands of jewellery designers, using their keen powers of observation and craftsmanship, flowers are invested with an eternal life of marbled stone-shades of colour that never fade, and precious shapes that do not wither. Jewellery designers are the ultimate conservationists of our floral life.

GEMSTONES FOR EVERY SEASON

As the year is divided into four cycles of spring, summer, autumn and winter, so each season has been attributed its own particular gemstones.

SPRING

Emerald

Amethyst

Green Diamond

Chrysoberyl

Peridot

Watermelon Tourmaline

SUMMER

Ruby

Spinel

Pink Topaz

Fire Opal

Citrine

Rubellite

AUTUMN

Topaz

Sapphire

Azurite

Tourmaline

Cairngorm

WINTER

Diamond

Rock Crystal

White Sapphire

Moonstone

Labradorite

White Opal

BIRTH STONES & BIRTH FLOWERS

January
Garnet & Snowdrop

February
Amethyst & Primrose

March
Jasper Bloodstone & Violet

April
Diamond & Daisy

May
Emerald & Hawthorn

June
Agate & Honeysuckle

July
Turquoise & Water Lily

August
Carnelian & Poppy

September
Chrysolite & Morning Glory

October
Beryl & Hops

November
Topaz & Chrysanthemum

December
Ruby & Holly

lily of the valley • narcissus • pansy • peony • tulip • violet • calla lily • foxglove • heliotrope • iris • lotus • morning glory

anemone • blossom • daisy • dandelion • hydrangea • iris • wild oats • holly • ivy • mistletoe • snowdrop • winter plum • blossom • daisy •

anemone • blossom • daisy • dandelion • lily of the valley • narcissus • pansy • peony • tulip • violet • calla lily • foxglove • heliotrope • poppy • lily • lotus • morning glory • rose

anemone • blossom • daisy • dandelion • hydrangea • iris

camellia • edelweiss • hellebore • holly • ivy • mistletoe • blossom • rose • narcissus • pansy • peony • tulip • violet • calla lily • foxglove • heliotrope • poppy • lily • lotus • morning glory • rose

poppy • rose • sweet pea • thistle • vanilla flower • weeping willow • chrysanthemum • hawthorn • hydrangea • orchid • wild oats • camellia • edelweiss • hellebore • holly • ivy • mistletoe

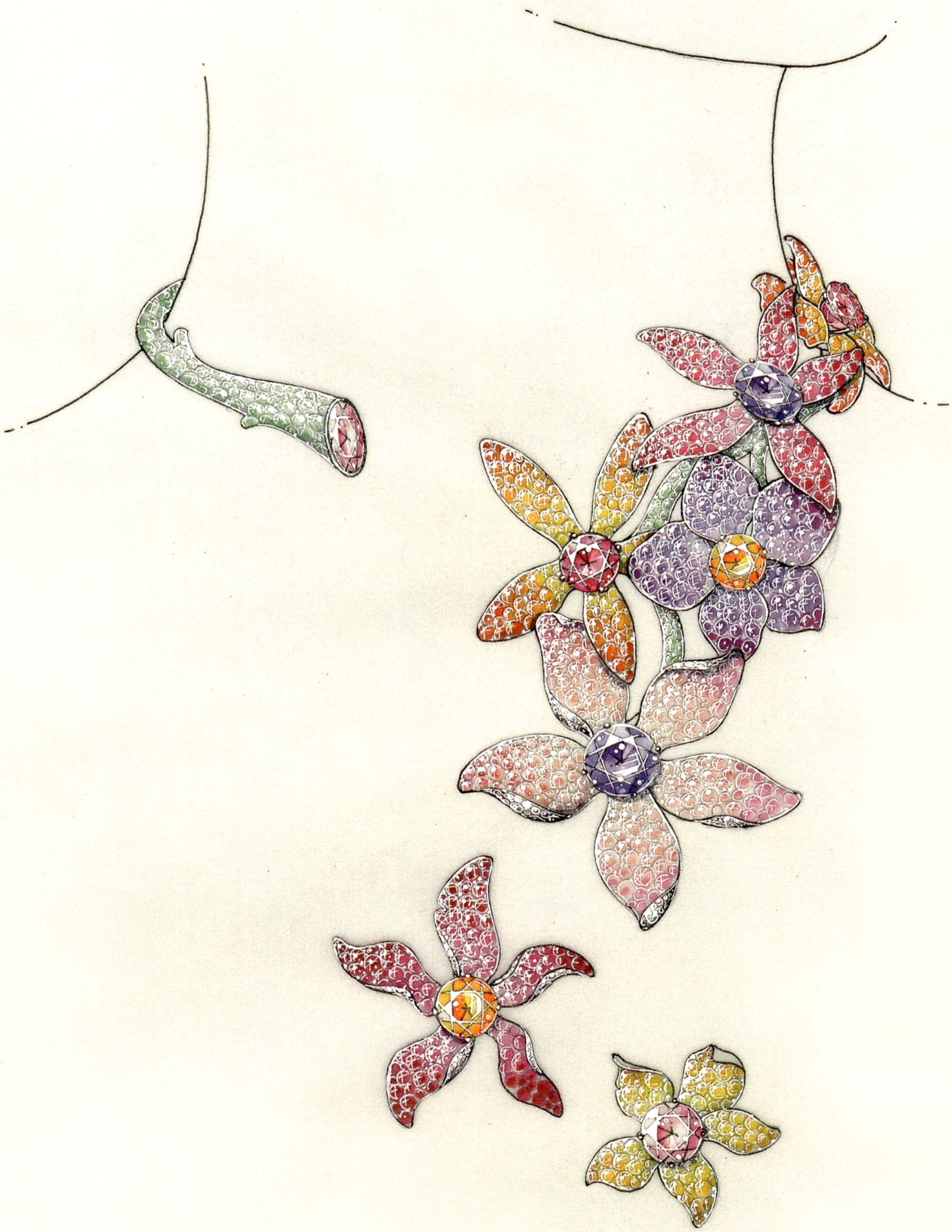

Pansies
Lorenz Bäumer
2008

Spring

In spring time when the leaves are young,
Clear dewdrops gleam like jewels, hung
On boughs the fair birds roost among.

Seasons
Christina Rossetti

When spring's gentle rays warm the soil, bulbs that have lain dormant, hibernating through the dark days of winter, stir beneath the ground, racing to reach the sun before the sunbeam path is obscured by fresh foliage, as trees grow their leaves. The snowdrop leads the way through the frozen earth, striving towards the light: the first delicate wildflower seen for months, a symbol of hope to the winter weary. The landscape gently comes to life as fragile buds and green-tipped tender shoots sprout under the protective boughs of trees. Winter's white pallor is swept away by little colonies of ruby-red and sapphire-blue pansies, turning their dewy-eyed faces to the sun, whilst bright jonquils and daffodils bend and sway, tossing their canary-yellow or diamond-coloured heads in the new air.

Jewel-like garlands sparkle in fields, as festoons of green garnets, tsavorites, moss-coloured peridots and emeralds weave a lush cover for grassy lawns. The precious, myriad greens not only herald spring, but represent life itself.

As sure as what is most sure, sure as that spring primroses
Shall new-dapple next year, sure as tomorrow morning,
Amongst come-back-again things, things with a revival,
things with a recovery
Thy name…

Some Unfinished Poems and Fragments
Gerard Manley Hopkins

The soft shadows of the velvety purple, gold and blue petals of the pansy follow the snowdrops' path through to the sun. The pansy was born from two centuries of crossbreeding the viola tricolour with other wild plants. From nature's tiny weed, their pretty round faces became showpieces in grand Victorian gardens.

The beauteous pansies rise
In purple, gold and blue
With tints of rainbow hue
Mocking the sunset skies

The Angel of the Flowers
Thomas John Ouseley

Delicate sprigs of naturalistic jewellery decorated with recognisable flowers emerged during the early nineteenth century, partly inspired by the new pastime of gardening, which was then in its heady infancy. The idea of gardens as a place to grow plants and flowers for decorative purposes, as opposed to medicinal

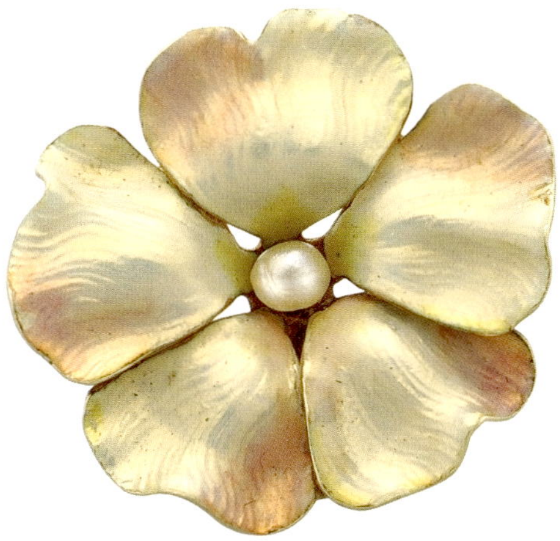

Pansy
Unknown jeweller
c. 1890

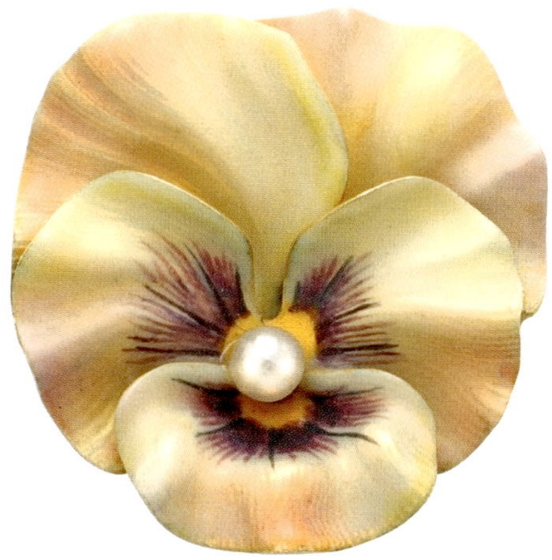

Pansy
Unknown jeweller
c. 1890

properties, was a new phenomenon, which prompted daring plant-hunting expeditions all over the world, to bring new botanical species to England.

This enduring interest in botany, coupled with the development of hothouses to propagate the new varieties, literally kept inspiration alive for jewellers, who used fashionable flowers, such as chrysanthemums, dahlias, fuchsias and the newly bred pansy, as design motifs. Floral postcards, keepsakes and poetry of the time, alongside floral jewels, show that accurate imitations of nature were all the rage.

Since the shape of the pansy's petals resemble a human face, the pious pansy is associated with deep contemplation, humility and loving thoughts – indeed, its name is derived from the French word *pensée*, meaning thought.

There's rosemary, that's for remembrance; pray you,
Love, remember: and there is pansies, that's for thoughts.

Hamlet
William Shakespeare

In literature, references to the pansy, originally called heartsease or love-in-idleness, express a delicacy and tenderness in love, as well as alluding to the whimsical nature of the heart. In Shakespeare's *A Midsummer Night's Dream*, pansy juice is used by Oberon as a love potion:

Yet mark'd I where the bolt of Cupid fell:
It fell upon a little western flower,
Before milk-white, now purple with love's wound,
And maidens call it love-in-idleness.

Fetch me that flower; the herb I shew'd thee once.
The juice of it on sleeping eye-lids laid
Will make or man or woman madly dote
Upon the next live creature that it sees

In 1926, the modernist artist Georgia O'Keefe painted a huge black pansy in such impeccable close-up detail and colour that no one could ignore its beauty. 'When you take a flower in your hand and really look at it,' she explained at the time, 'it's your world for the moment.' A gemstone can offer a compelling visual experience, similar to that of a flower. If you look deeply into a finely cut amethyst stone, it has a mesmerising quality that pulls you down into the depths of its intense purple pool, crystallising your world in that brilliant

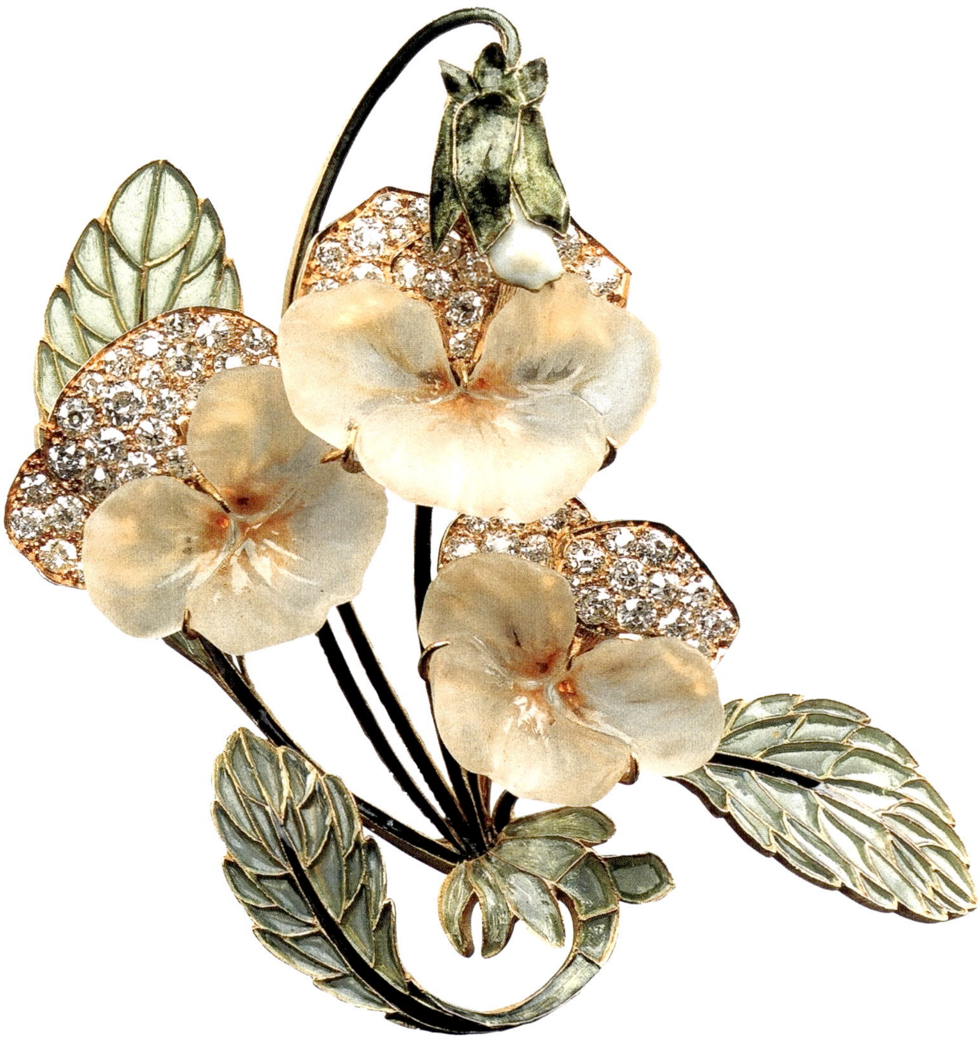

Pansy
Lalique
c. 1903–4

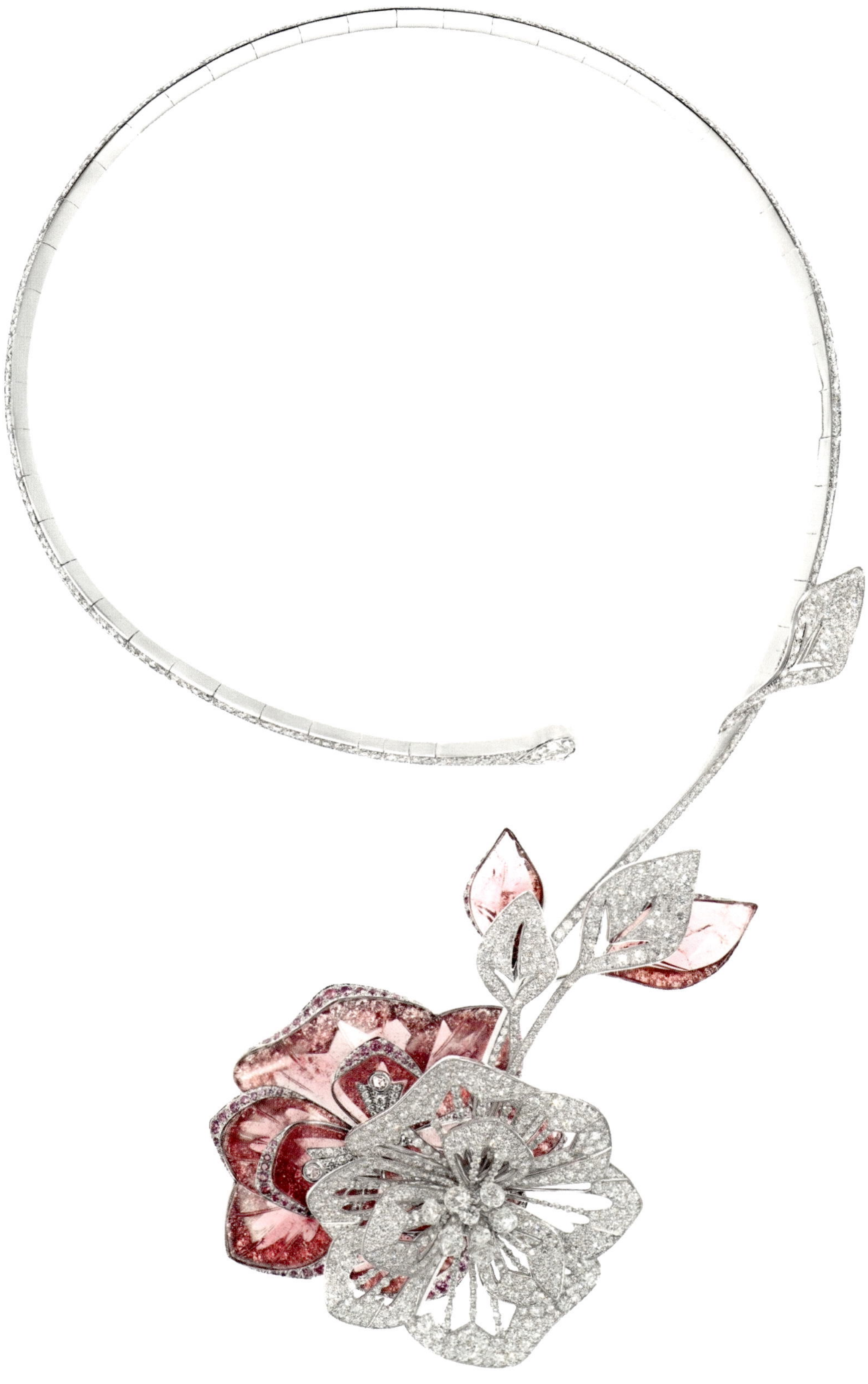

Pansy
Boucheron
2013

moment. Designer Anna Hu recently took inspiration from one of O'Keefe's paintings, creating a bloom with purple titanium petals and rows of briolette-cut diamonds, to draw the eyes deep into the blossom's centre.

The nineteenth-century French jeweller Frédéric Boucheron, aware of the sentiment associated with the flower, would send a bouquet of pansies to his wife Gabrielle before his many journeys abroad, accompanied by a handwritten note saying 'Je pense à toi'. The flower provided inspiration for a magical pansy tiara set with 250 diamonds, the white gold pansy faces made with polished hematite, framed by six snow-set diamond pavé petals with diamonds pistils.

The flower was a favourite of the singer and dancer Caroline ('la Belle') Otéro, who rarely performed without a pansy pendant, and for whom Boucheron created a pansy corsage brooch. In homage to that flower, a modern necklace was created by Boucheron in pink tourmaline and rock crystal, with three-dimensional snow-set diamond petals and blazing diamond gold bead pistils. Beneath it lies another grey mother-of-pearl pansy, like the shadow of the first, to be detached and worn as a 'cocktail' brooch. Victorian and Edwardian pansy brooches were intrinsically pretty and wearable, and, as the nineteenth century progressed, they became more complex and elaborate, their weight supported by the thick brocaded bodices of the time. These heavy flowers wilt on light contemporary fabrics, so jeweller Eliane Fattal, in collaboration with S. J. Phillips, adapts original heavy-set diamond and demantoid green garnet pansies, giving them naturalistic diamond stems, and mechanisms for alternative new stable positions, twisted through hair or around a modern finger.

During the 1940s, Fulco Santostefano della Cerda, Duke of Verdura, fine jeweller and artist, created a pansy with a 43-carat peridot stone, wrapped around tanzanite petals. *Vogue* commented at the time on his narcissus brooches, declaring them to be 'realer than real with emerald stems, diamond petals, centres of canary yellow diamonds'.

Another intense shade of purple that raises its faithful head each spring, from amongst its shelter of bracken, is the delicate and modest violet, an emblem of devotion and loyalty.

The fragrant violet was used to sweeten wine at festivals during the reign of Charles II and was crystallised as a sweetmeat and as a sugar for conserves. Many seventeenth-century recipe books were filled with recipes for 'daynty sirrup of violets'. Empress Josephine grew the modest violet in large numbers in her famous garden at the Château de la Malmaison, and shared her passion for botany with Napoleon. When exiled to Elba, he declared he would return again to Paris with violets, so supporters of the former emperor were to be seen with tiny mauve sprigs in their lapels. On his return from Elba, Napoleon collected violets from Josephine's garden, keeping them in a locket until his death on St Helena.

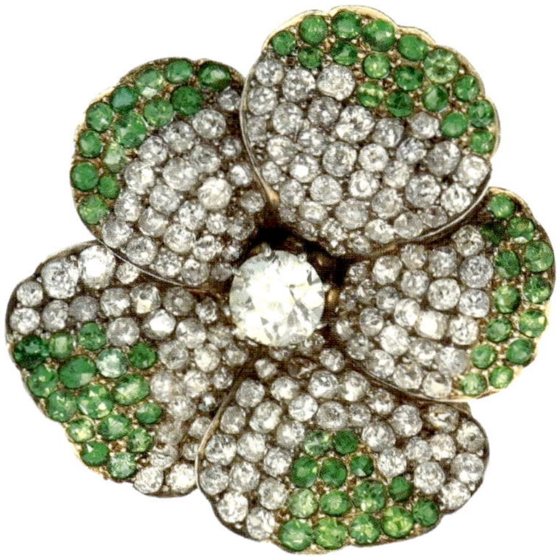

Pansy
Eliane Fattal for S. J. Phillips
2013

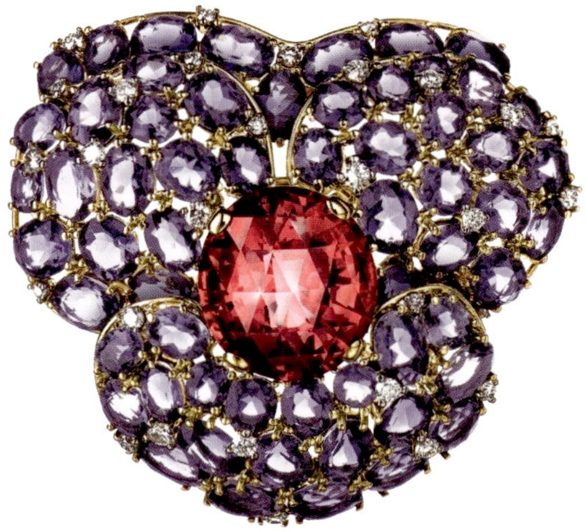

Pansy
Verdura
2004

The drooping position of the violet ensures its shimmery amethyst-coloured petals are shaded by its green flower sepal, acting as a canopy to protect the unripe seeds from dew and rain. It is only when the seeds are mature that the flower rises and stands proud on its stem.

> *At first it seemed that green things would never cease pushing their way through the earth, in the grass, in the beds, even in the crevices of the walls. Then the green things began to show buds and the buds began to unfurl and show colour, every shade of blue, every shade of purple, every tint and hue of crimson. In its happy days flowers had been tucked away into every inch and hole and corner.*
>
> *The Secret Garden*
> Frances Hodgson Burnett

Nineteenth-century 'nosegays' were the subject of a fashion revival during the 1930s and 40s, when fine jewellers, among them Boivin and Verdura, created fresh posies of violets, with amethyst-carved petals and golden stems, tied together with ribbons. Verdura was intrigued by the idea of flowers representing specific sentiments, and interested in traditional nosegays or 'tussie-mussies', which were little bunches of flowers and herbs given to convey a message in small silver filigree containers, attached with a chain to the recipient's dress.

During Verdura's childhood on the island of Sicily, he loved to roam in the lush subtropical gardens surrounding the family's homes: Villa Nicemi, their country estate outside Palermo, and Palazzo Verdura within the city itself. He meandered down paths bordered by cherry trees and quinces, along fragrant avenues of oranges, lemons, succulent figs and peaches, all the while accumulating imagery and colours in his mind, which would give him an instinctive feeling for nature in his later life as an artist and designer. A luscious pomegranate ripening in the Sicilian sun would be replicated in a yellow gold and peridot skin, bursting with ripe cabochon ruby seeds. Yellow diamond golden pineapples, birds pecking at jewelled berries, ears of golden corn and lustrous amethyst aubergines, were all inspired by his island childhood. 'I'm more Sicilian', he would say, 'than a prickly pear'.

A major event on the social calendar during Verdura's childhood was the 'Battle of Flowers', a spectacular pageant during which the aristocracy paraded through Palermo in blossom-bedecked carriages. These were such lavish displays that violets, roses and lilacs had to be shipped from Naples and Florence to satisfy the huge demand. The Verdura carriage left in its fragrant wake a trail of sweet-smelling pale pink carnations and wisteria. When clients came to visit Verdura during his career in New York, he instructed staff to say that he was dead, preferring to stay in his private office making detailed gouache

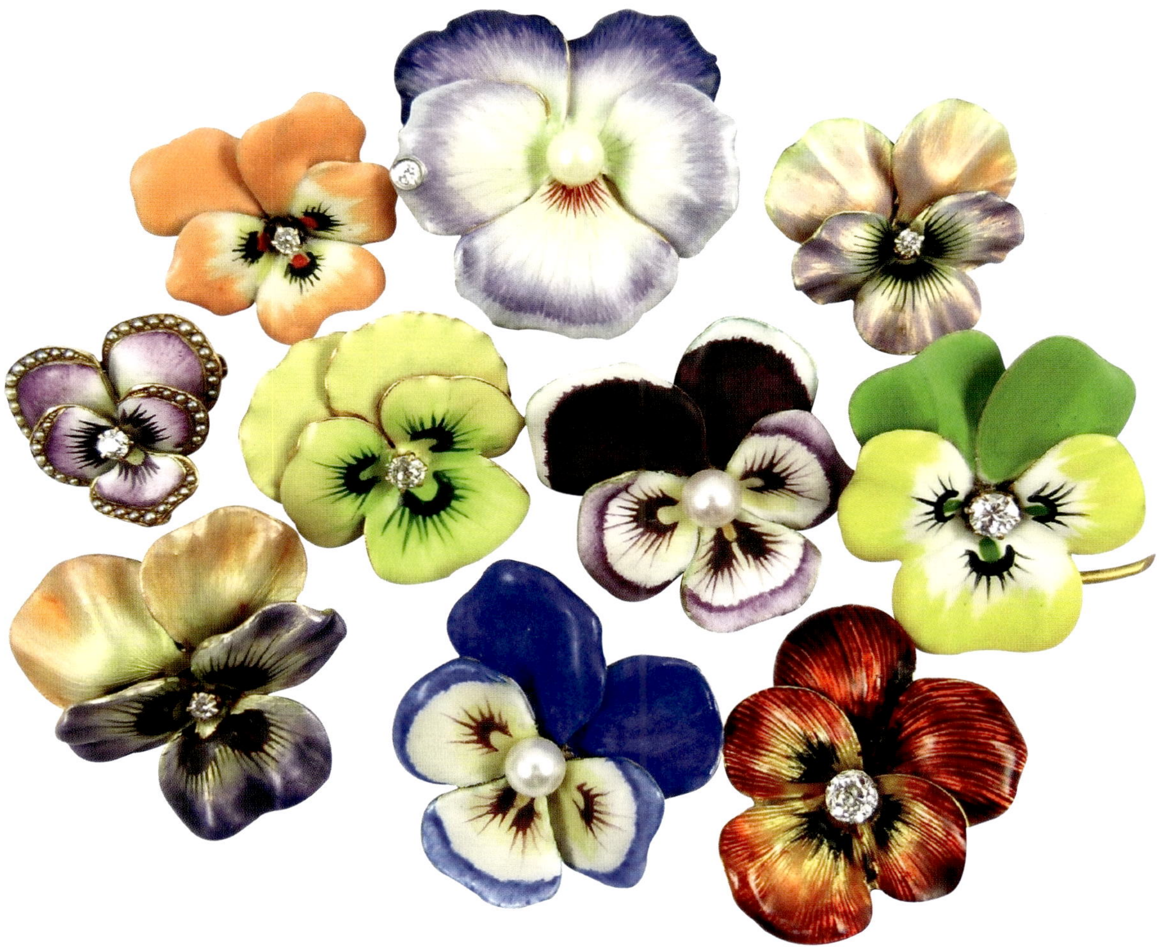

Pansies
Unknown jeweller
c. 1900

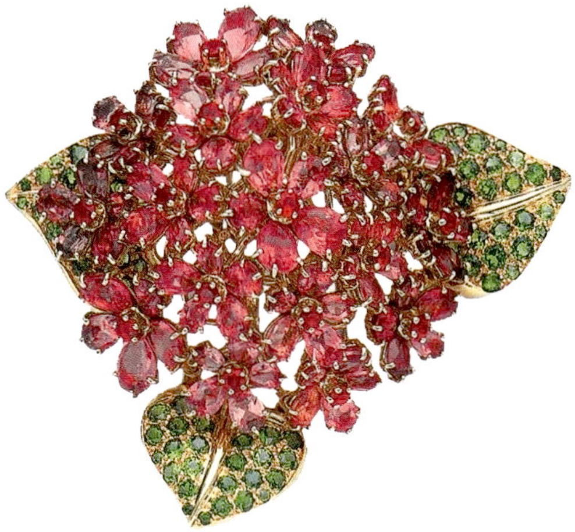

Violet
Boivin
1962

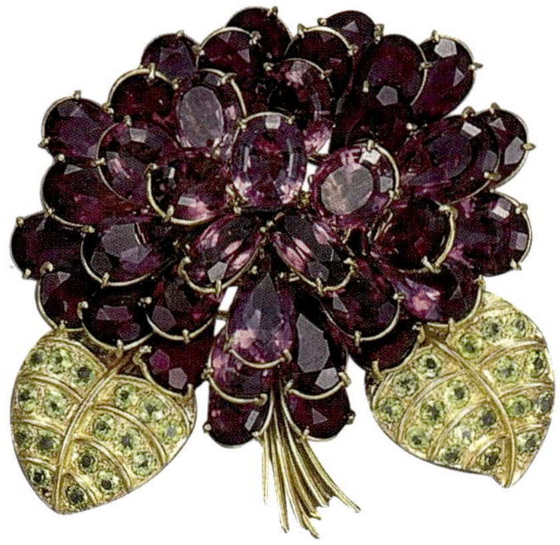

Violet
Boivin
c. 1965

sketches for designs. Many of these were little nosegays and posies of violets, the amethyst shimmering on the page with glistening white diamond dew drops, often accompanied by yellow diamond hearts wreathed in emerald leaves.

The white violet
is scented on its stalk,
the sea-violet
fragile as agate,
lies fronting all the wind
among the torn shells
On the sand-bank.

Sea Violet
H. D. [Hilda Doolittle]

Like her master jeweller husband René, with whom she created the business before his death in 1918, Jeanne Boivin was a great gardener during the weekends she spent at her L'Enclos de l'Abbaye home in Poissy. Despite employing two gardeners, she tended the roses herself, and, as an early environmentalist, cultivated fruit and vegetables. She left a sweet musky scent trail behind her of tiny bouquets of violets. During his lifetime, her husband made detailed descriptions and annotations relating to flower varieties in drawing books and ledgers, which featured thistles, poppies, ivy, roses and violets. These violets came alive in many of Jeanne's jewellery creations, translated into lilac and mauve amethysts, or rubies with pink tourmaline clips, mounted on tsavorite and peridot leaves.

Jeanne wore the colour violet with grey and ivory, a diamond ring, a string of pearls and, on special occasions, a diamond and ruby umbel spray. Carrots, dill and cow parsley all sport short individual flower stalks, which combine

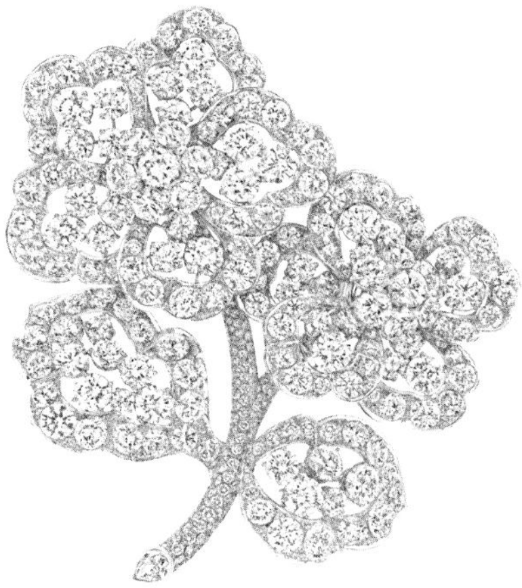

Umbel
Graff Diamonds
2012

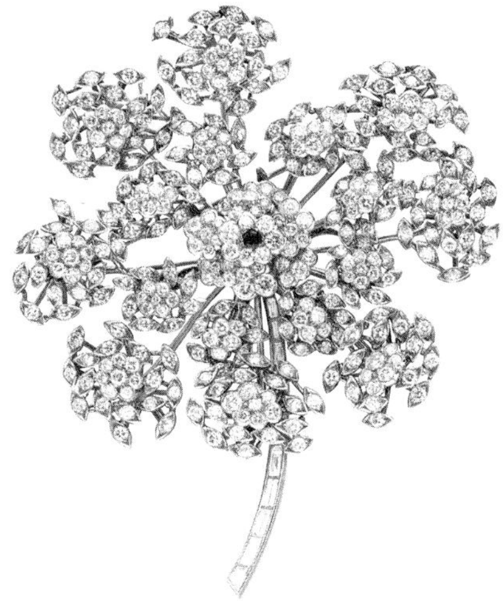

Umbel
Boivin
1938

to create the round flower cluster of the umbel. As the daughter of a cloth merchant and sister of the famous French couturier Paul Poiret, Boivin had a feeling for textures, so it might have been the ethereal quality or the frothy, lacy fabric effect of the delicate umbel that caught her eye, a motif that went on to become one of the jewellery house's most famous designs.

Saluted by *Vogue* during the 1930s as 'the world's most elegant and most talked about woman', Daisy Fellowes commissioned Cartier to make her a daisy brooch with pear-, circular- and emerald-cut diamonds in the centre of her favourite salmon-pink coral.

> *With enchanting murmurs Daisy admired this aspect or that of the feudal silhouette against the sky, admired the gardens, the sparkling odor of jonquils, and the frothy odor of hawthorn and plum blossoms and the pale gold odor of kiss-me-at-the-gate.*
>
> *The Great Gatsby*
> F. Scott Fitzgerald

The name daisy derives from an Old English word meaning 'day's eyes', for the way it opens at dawn and shuts in the evening. The French named the white cluster of petals 'marguerite', derived from the Latin *margarita*, meaning pearl, thinking the white petals resembled a row of opalescent pearls. Van Cleef & Arpels have created chains of ruby, diamond and sapphire daisies in a 'Mystery' setting – a revolutionary technique developed in the 1930s, inspired by Roman mosaics, that fixed precious stones with no mount visible – with tapering petals in swirling forms edged in gold for clients such as Marjorie Merriweather Post and Baron Guy de Rothschild. Another client, Elizabeth Taylor, chose to wear her yellow and white diamond daisies on calibré-cut chyrsophase leaves with a yellow Valentino gown to the 1993 Academy Awards ceremony.

During the seventeenth century, diamond and emerald jewels were highly coveted, but the stones were exceptionally rare. It was this rarity that made jewellers seek out other less expensive but equally beautiful alternatives. In 1734, in Paris, Georges Frédéric Strass created 'paste', using a high content of lead metal powder to produce a hard stone that could be highly polished and cut into any shape. Petals of paste daisies could thus be exaggerated, and often foiled for extra brilliance, shimmering in Georgian candlelight like diamonds. Paste brooches and necklaces were not considered 'faux gems' but exciting precious jewels in their own right. The daisy symbolises sweetness and innocence, its simplicity and lack of pretension being emphasised when formed by gemstone petals and pearls with golden leaves. It highlights the fact that even the simplest of flowers has a significant beauty.

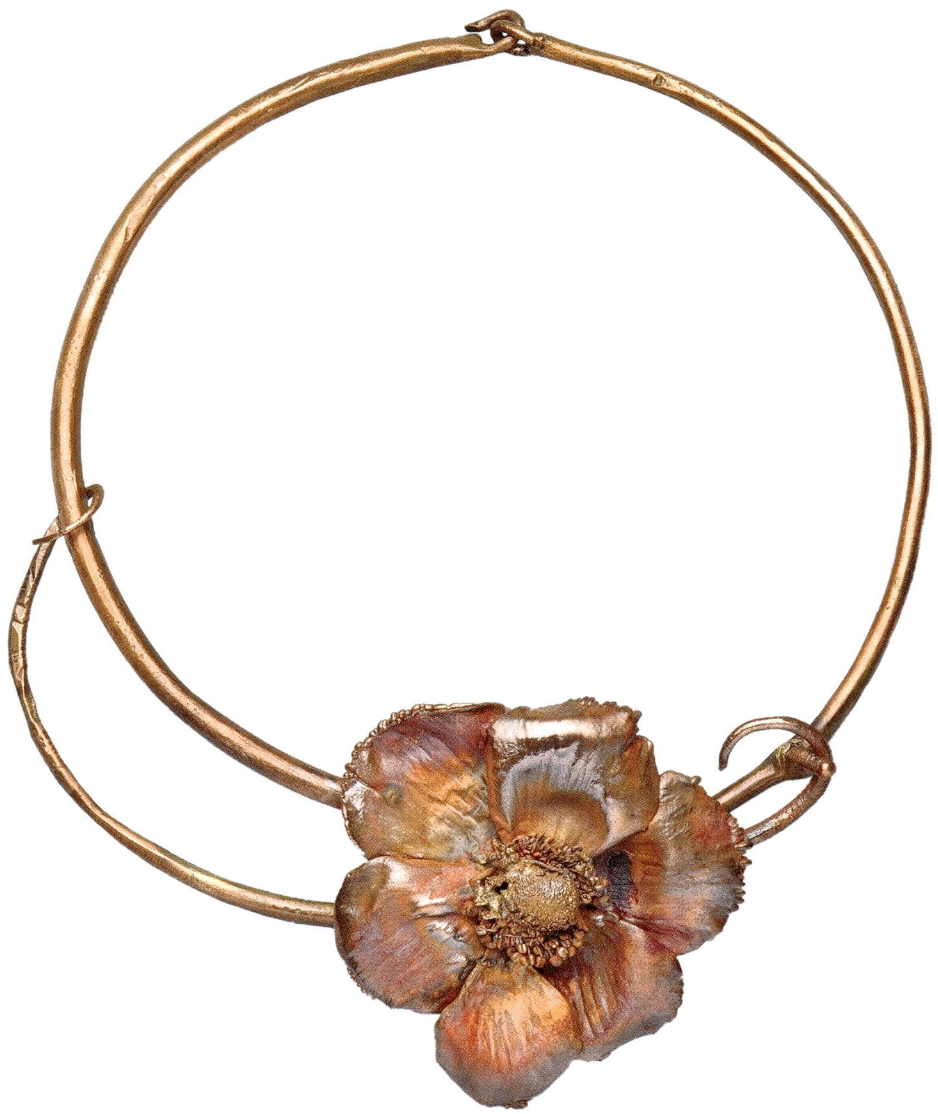

Anemone
Claude Lalanne
2013

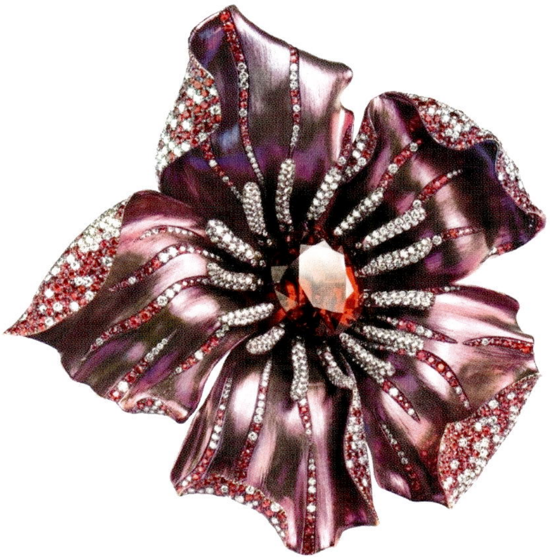

Anemone
Adler
2008

Another flower that grows as thick as daisies in spring meadows and glades is the anemone, or wind flower, whose light seeds are wafted on spring winds to carpet woods with their delicate foliage throughout May. The saucer-shaped cups range in colour from blush shell-pink pearl shades to gleaming purple amethyst and ruby tints.

Youth, like a thin anemone, displays
His silken leaf, and in a morn decays

The Seven Fountains, an Eastern Allegory
Sir William Jones

Jewellers use multi-coloured sapphires to embroider flamboyant petals for the anemone. Pink titanium anemones bud at Adler, embellished with strong pink spinels and diamonds. The artist jeweller Claude Lalanne creates whimsical organic forms from her rural idyll in Ury outside Paris. An anemone is plucked from a nearby open meadow and 'electroplated' by being submerged into a copper bath, thus creating a perfect fossilised form of the flower.

The spring breeze blows dainty blossom petals through town and country in a flurry of pastel-coloured snow drifts. Queen Victoria frequently wore a suite of orange blossom jewellery in frosted gold with white porcelain flowers. She was given the brooch in 1839 by Prince Albert, who added matching pieces throughout the years, one being the wreath for their wedding anniversary in 1846, set with four unripe oranges to symbolise their children.

Blossomed the lovely stars,
the forget-me-nots of the angels

Evangeline
Henry Wadsworth Longfellow

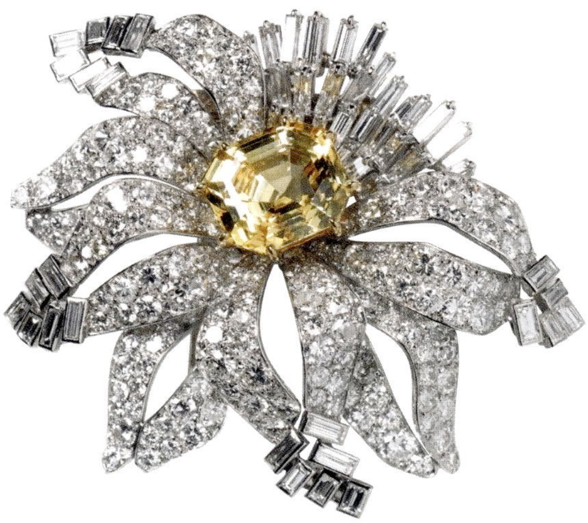

Daisy
Cartier Paris
1962

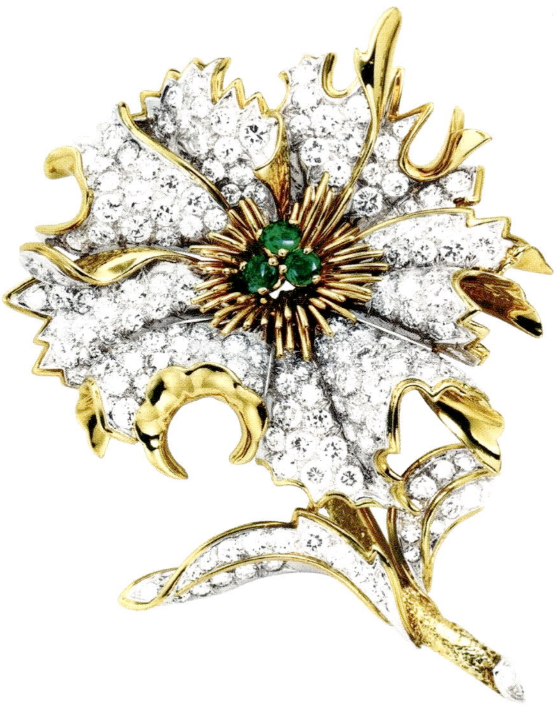

Daisy
Verdura
1962

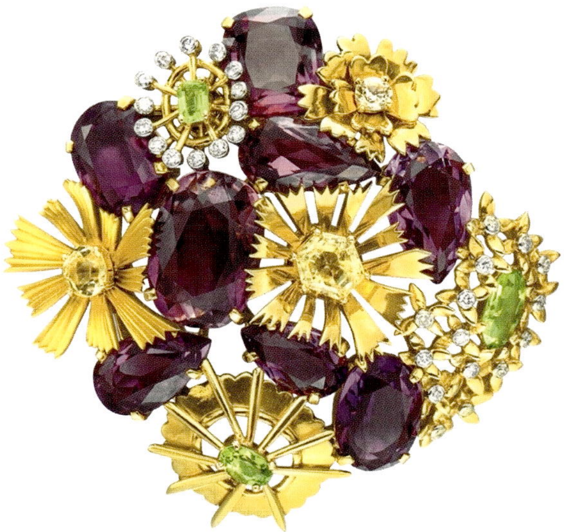

Daisy
Jean Schlumberger
c. 1950

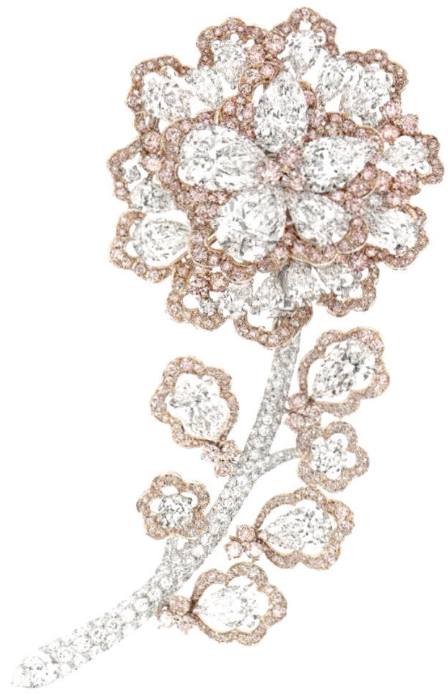

Daisy
Graff Diamonds
2012

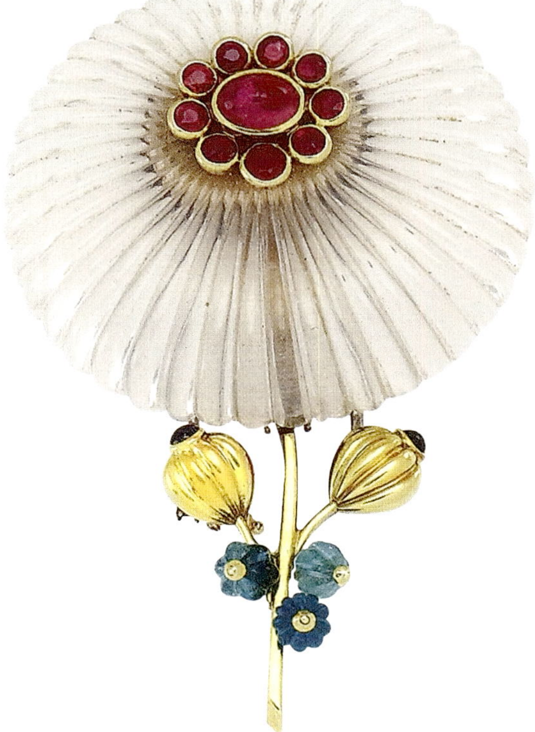

Daisy
Suzanne Belperron
1950s

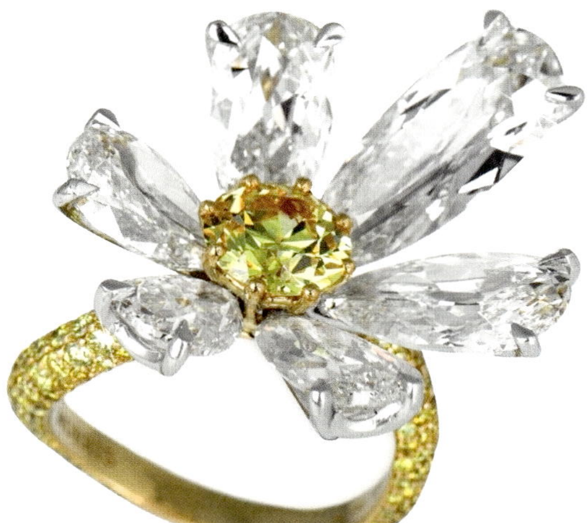

Daisy
David Morris
2014

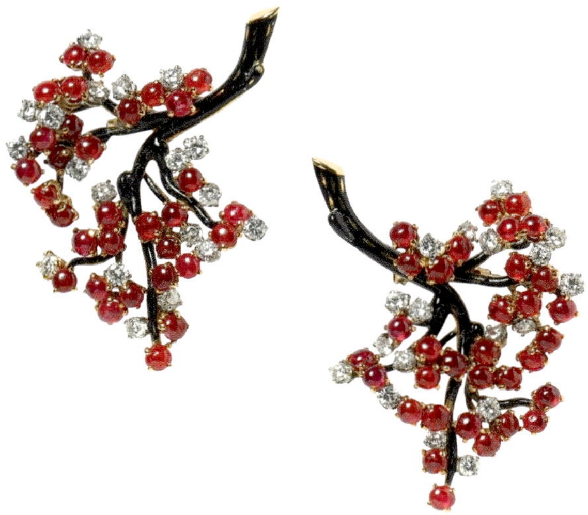

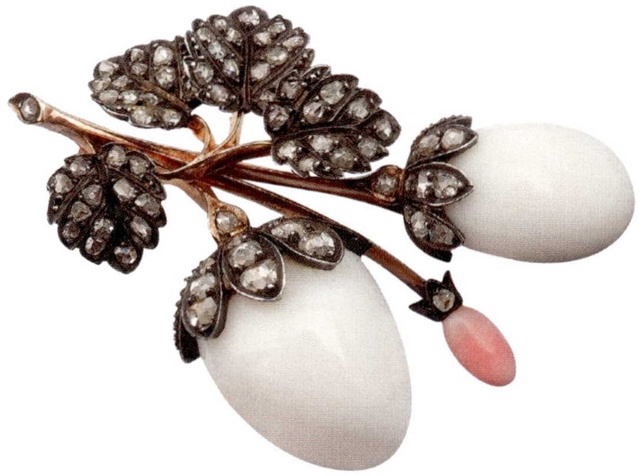

Cherry Blossom
Boucheron
c. 1920

Cherry Blossom
English, unknown jeweller
c. 1880

The cherry blossom season in Japan is the largest floral event in the world. Vast numbers of people engage in the ritual of *hunami*, gathering under the magnificence of the blossoms for festivities involving food and wine. Cherry blossom is strongly associated with *mono no aware*, the awareness of the impermanence and transience of things, symbolic of the brief life of a samurai. In Renaissance Italy, blossoms as ornaments were considered bad omens for women, because their brief life span was reminiscent of death and decay.

And the day came when the risk to remain tight in a bud was more painful than the risk it took to blossom.
Anaïs Nin

'Flowers are in bloom for a very short time, and at the peak of their beauty, with virility, they fall to the ground in no time, all at once', says Karou Kay Akihara, art director of Gimel, describing the scene during cherry blossom season from her atelier overlooking the Seto Inland Sea in the Rokko Mountains. Her blossom jewels are delicate graduations, capturing each stage of the blossom's life, depicting a bud about to burst into a flower, a full bloom, and the petals as they fall gracefully to the ground in a melee of pink diamonds, with a tiny caterpillar creeping over the underside of the flower. In Hong Kong, Michelle Ong captures the delicate fragility of cascading petals with tiny fragments of diamonds.

The sides of those hills were adorned with crystal cliffs so clear a quality. Bright woods lay about them, with trunks as blue as indigo; the leaves, which quivered in profusion on every branch, slid over each other like burnished silver. When the gleams from clear patches of sky glided over them, they shone most brightly with a lovely shimmering. The gravel that crunched on the ground was precious orient pearl: the beams of the sun seemed dark and dim by comparison with that splendour.

Pearl
Anonymous late fourteenth-century author

Another spring flower, which, like blossom, became a symbol of life's transience and *vanitas*, is the tulip. The flower was prized as an emblem of nobility and abundance, and was often depicted alongside skulls in paintings by seventeenth-century Dutch masters. These beautiful, bright, star-shaped blooms, with soft orange and purple flames on the outer petals and hints of green, face the light, closing their petals at dusk.

The tulip was originally valued for its flamboyant colour palette and the way the shades could, in the words of the English botanist John Rea, alter 'into several glorious colours, variously mixed, edged, striped, feathered, flaked or speckled, even to admiration'. These colour changes were unpredictable, as tulips grown from seeds wouldn't necessarily imitate their parents; a plain tulip might suddenly 'break', returning the following year a different colour entirely, or with ruffles or stripes, bewitching gardeners in the process.

Mid the sharp short emerald wheat, scarce risen three fingers well,
The wild tulip, at the end of its tube, blows out its great red bell
Like a thin clear bubble of blood, for the children to pick and sell.

Up at a Villa – Down in the City
Robert Browning

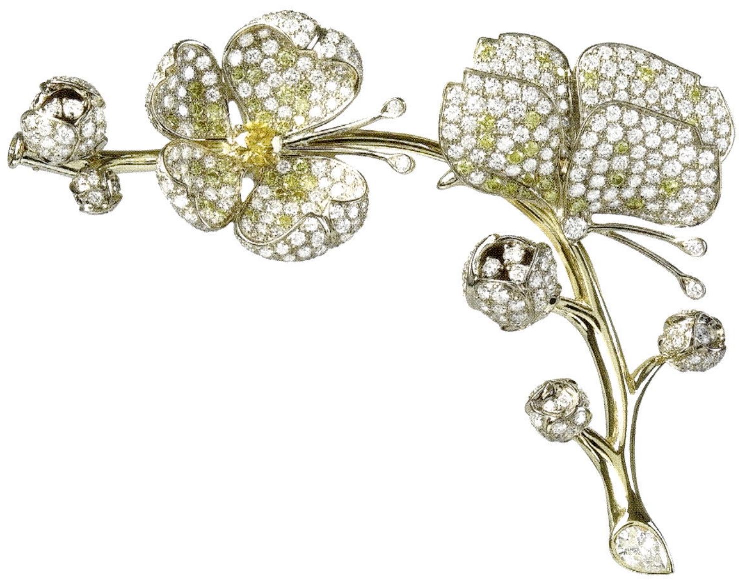

Cherry Blossom
Van Cleef & Arpels
2009

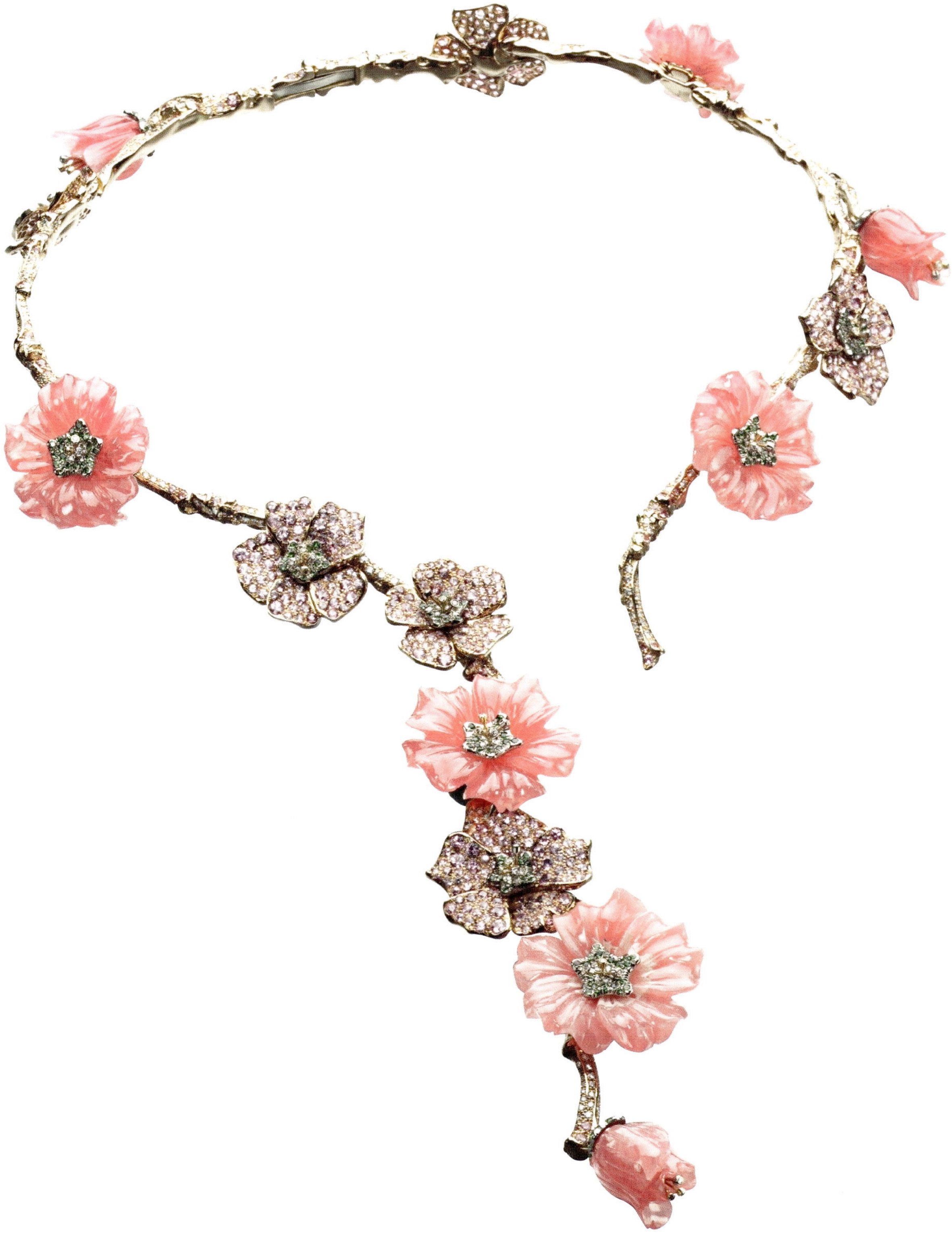

Cherry Blossom
Suzanne Syz
2007

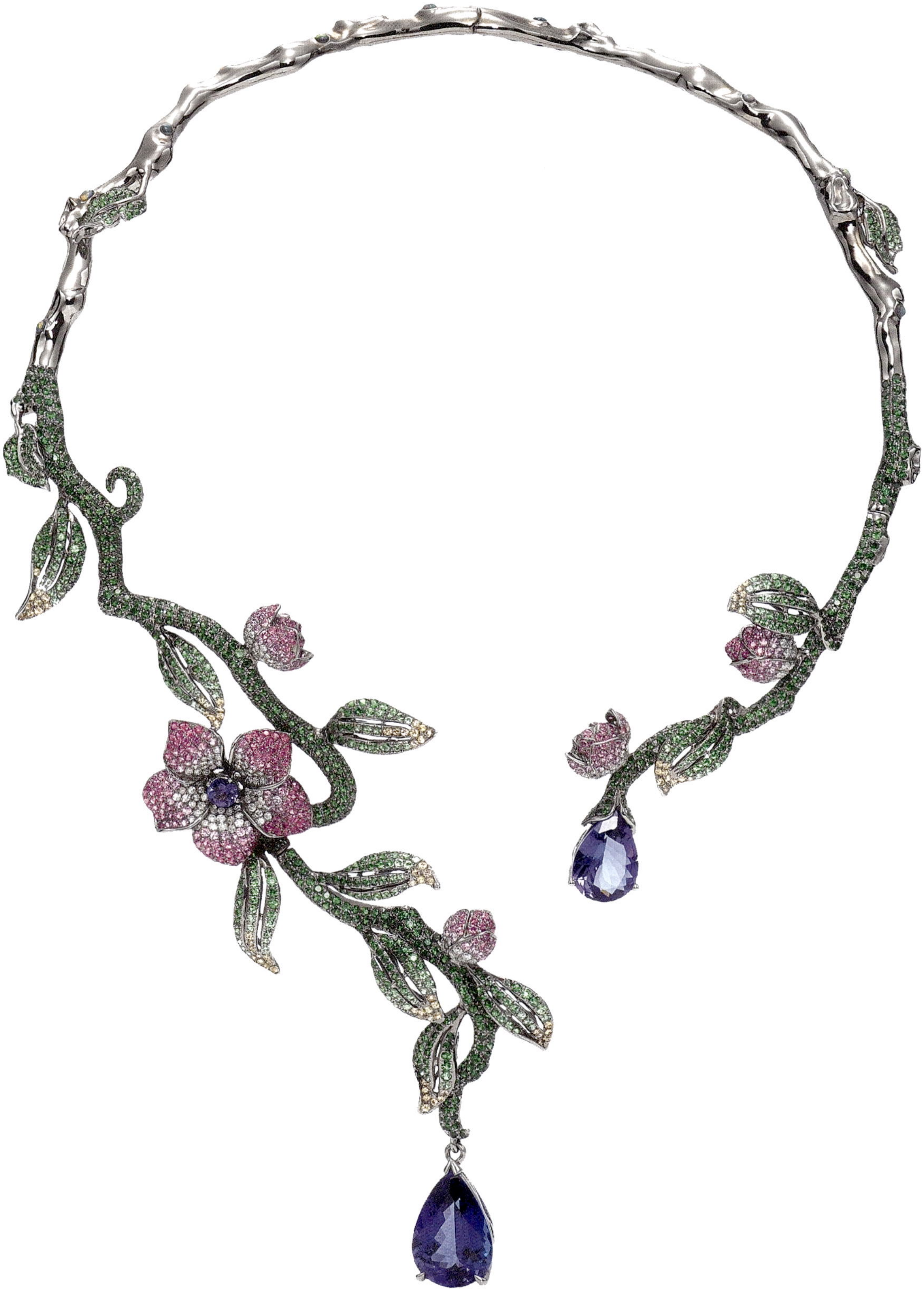

Apple Blossom
Wendy Yue
2013

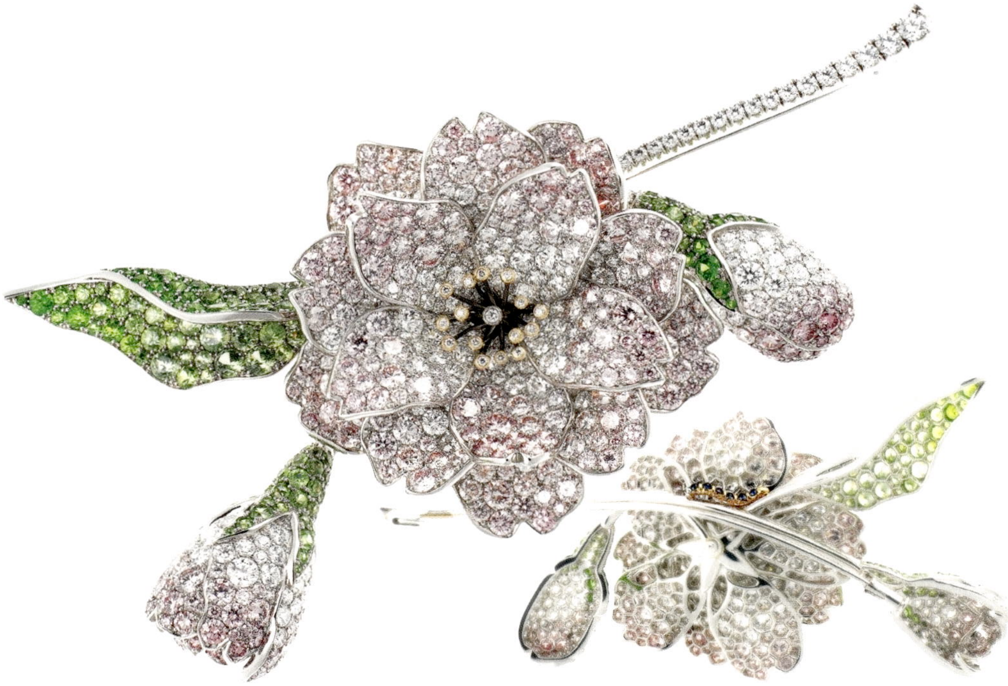

Cherry Blossom

Gimel
2005

In *The Curious Gardner,* Anna Pavord described the tulip as wild, irrepressible, unpredictable, strange, subtle and elegant. 'Best of all are the crazy parrot tulips such as "Rococo" with red and pink petals feathered and flamed in crinkly lime-green', she wrote. The history of the tulip is tumultuous. It has provoked desire, greed, devotion and anguish, as well as cultural interest like no other flower, having been at the centre of political upheavals and economic booms and busts.

> *Against another wall were white apple blossoms on branches cut into sharp crucifixes and forced to lie flat against the stone. Below, the huge frilled lips of giant tulips in shades of white and cream nodded in their beds. They were almost finished now, spread open too far, splayed, exposing obscene black centres. I've never had my own garden but I suddenly recognized something in the tangle of this one that wasn't beauty. Passion maybe. And something else. Rage.*
>
> *How I Live Now*
> Meg Rosoff

Tulips originated in Persia, where they were used as a declaration of love, the vibrant red colour of the petals announcing ardour, whilst the coal black centre was symbolic of a heart burnt by passion. Tall tulips were favoured, with dagger-shaped petals and narrow pointed tips, and given fanciful names such as 'Elixir of love' or 'Those that burnt the heart'. Such was their importance in the cultural and artistic life of the Ottoman Empire that tulip festivals were held in the sultan's gardens, and the reign of Sultan Ahmed III in the early eighteenth century – during which time art, architecture and culture flourished – was known as the 'tulip era'. The tulip owes its name to the fact it was worn in the Turkish tradition in turbans, the Latin translation of turban being *tulipa*; when the flower made its way to Vienna it was compared to red turbans for its colour and shape.

The first Dutch tulip was planted in 1594 at Leiden University's botanic garden, provoking a tulip fever for a time amongst the nobility; if you were wealthy and had no tulip collection you were considered a philistine. The fashion spread rapidly to the merchant and middle classes, and to shopkeepers who all vied with one another, prepared to pay preposterous prices to trade in tulip bulbs. These speculators spent all day in Haarlem taverns haggling and buying bulbs they had never seen, gambling on new varieties and banking on the fact that prices would continue to rise.

> *There is a purity about our love of flowers; it is an act of homage untempered by greed. Tulips are the exception to this; when I think of them a lust rises within me, a shameful wave of heat... Yet they are more valuable than jewels, than paintings, than gold.*
>
> *Tulip Fever*
> Debborah Moggach

In February 1637, ninety-nine tulips sold for 90,000 guilders, which is equivalent to £1.7 million today, and one viceroy bulb could cost three times the amount of a painting of it by a contemporary Dutch master. When the market crashed, the Dutch government intervened and thousands were made destitute due to their passion for the tulip.

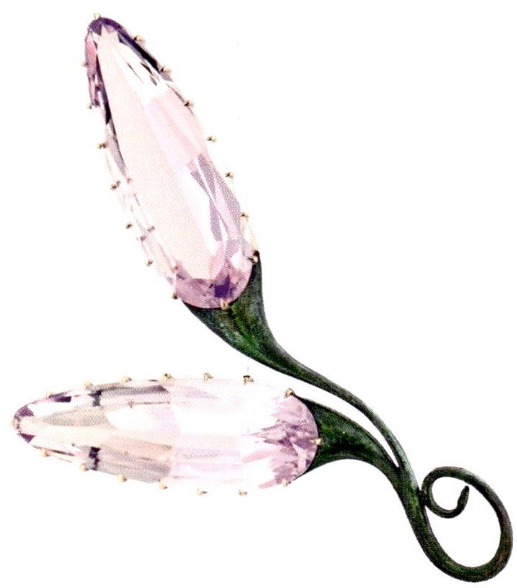

Tulip
James de Givenchy for Taffin
2013

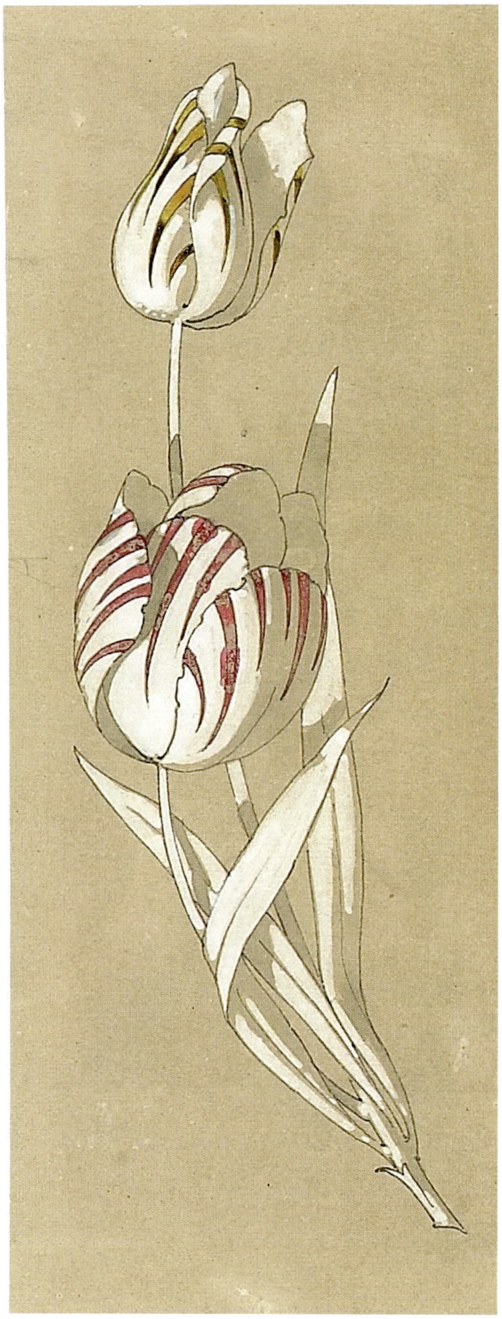

Tulip
Chaumet
c. 1890–1900

It is ironic that the 'breaking' of the tulip is now known to be caused by a virus in the plant, so the colouring and feathering so admired as a sign of beauty was in reality a symptom of their decay.

During the 1950s, Jean Schlumberger worked for Tiffany & Co., creating exuberant and voluptuous tulips. Observing nature with an artist's eye, rather than a botanist's, and influenced by his coterie of friends, such as Salvador Dalí and Elsa Schiaparelli, he designed fanciful surrealist interpretations of flowers. For Mrs William 'Babe' Paley, considered the most elegant woman of her generation, he created a necklace with insects crawling towards the precious drooping diamond tulips. Another style leader, Daisy Fellowes, fastened one of his diamond flower brooches on her shoulder, alongside a real flower. He often designed butterflies or pretty insects to hover by a bud, attracted by the colours of a sapphire and tourmaline spray brooch or double daisy brooch, which were the chic jewelled accessories to be clipped onto the lapels of New Look suits.

'I saw nature and found verve', Schlumberger said. Jade pea pods and succulent diamond strawberries, studded with tiny golden seeds, were all arranged in his fantasy garden, overgrown with tangles of flowers and foliage, forged around precious rockeries of coloured stones and enamel. 'Clear, transparent sun yellows. Wonderful lacquer reds. Acid spring greens. The clear blue of the Southern sky', wrote *Vogue* editor Diana Vreeland when describing the floral colours of a Schlumberger piece.

During the tulip era in Constantinople, Lady Mary Wortley Montagu was the wife of the English ambassador to Turkey, where she closely observed the traditions of flowers in the sultan's court. Her *Turkish Embassy Letters*, published in 1763, sparked a trend for the language of flowers, as she revealed the secrets practised by ladies in the harems. A billet-doux in nosegay form would be delivered by a servant, keeping thoughts unspoken, but conveying a coded message to the person receiving it.

An exquisite invention this,
Worthy of Love's most honeyed kiss
This art of writing billet-doux
In buds, and odours, and bright hues!
In saying all one feels and thinks
In clever daffodils and pinks;
In puns of tulips; and in phrases,
Charming for their truth, of daisies.

Love-Letters Made of Flowers
James Henry Leigh Hunt

During the early nineteenth century, 'acrostic' jewellery was popular, which would spell out a message via the first letters of the various gemstones in a jewel. An admirer might send a bracelet set with ruby-emerald-garnet-amethyst-ruby-diamond, spelling out the word 'regard'. Overcoming the strict social etiquette of the time, Victorians began expressing their innermost feelings with symbolism, using carefully chosen combinations of flowers and precious stones.

Acorn — fecundity
Daisy — innocence
Forget-me-not — true love
Ivy — fidelity and marriage
Laurel — triumph of love
Mistletoe — a kiss
Lily of the valley — a return to happiness
Oak — invincibility and strength
Rose — every aspect of love
Thistle flower — the pleasure and pain of love
Pansy — think of the giver

The message of a flower could also be heightened by the choice of stone. Many diamond tiaras were created at the time, heralding their sparkling messages of love in rambling wild roses, carnations or ivy, trailing around a newly married woman's coiffure. The popularity of messages in flowers coincided with mid-century books about gem lore and lapidary, listing their history, geography and chemistry, one example being Madame de Barrera's *Gems and Jewels*.

Probably the first objects chosen from nature's jewelled casket for personal adornment were shells, seeds and softer organic stones, which could be easily strung together, followed by harder stones, when simple tools were available. A stone wasn't only admired for its beauty: each gem was thought to possess zodiacal concordance with the seasons of the year and certain affinities with various virtues. Early on power was attributed to them, with a belief that if a talisman was worn with the appropriate zodiacal gemstone it would offer protection. It was thought that if the wearer believed in the benefits they would manifest themselves just as strongly as vibrations from the body of the stone itself.

Amethyst — devotion
Diamond — eternity
Emerald — hope
Moonstone — innocence
Pearl — love
Ruby — passion
Turquoise — remembrance and true love

The Pre-Raphaelite artist Sir Edward Burne-Jones was fascinated by the lore of gemstones, writing about their meanings to his friend Frances Graham, following her marriage to Sir John Horner in 1883:

Sapphire is truth, and I am never without it. Ruby is passion, and I need it not. Emerald is hope, and I need it; but cut emeralds are like glass and not better, and a fat round one is hopeless to get;

and a diamond is strength, and it sparkles and fidgets and is of this world – and amethyst, or as the little stone man I know called it 'Hammersmith', is devotion – I have it – and topaz is jealousy, and is right nasty. Sapphires I make my totem of!

According to the Victorian language of flowers, the peony meant bashfulness, the slow almost reluctant opening of its magnificent abundant petals coming to symbolise female purity. Legend has it that the name peony came from Paeon, a pupil of Asclepius, the god of medicine. Fearing his power might be eclipsed by the knowledge of his student, Asclepius plotted against him. Zeus intervened, turning Paeon into a peony, hence the belief in the flower's healing powers.

Guillaume de Salluste advised that peony seeds could prevent nightmares: 'About an infant's necklace hang peonie. It cures Alcyeds Cruell maladie. This plant also prevents the mocking delusions that the Fauns bring on us in our sleep.'

In China, the voluminous peony was named *fuguihua*, 'flower of riches and honour', symbolising nobility and honour. Peony motifs decorated imperial palaces and were a constant feature in Chinese art; by 1903, the Qing Dynasty had declared it to be the floral emblem of China. The flower was also used medicinally, the fallen petals being parboiled and sweetened as a tea-time delicacy.

Being perfect artists and ingenuous poets, the Chinese have piously preserved the love and holy cult of flowers; one of the very rare and most ancient traditions which has survived their decadence. And since flowers had to be distinguished from each other, they have attributed graceful analogies to them, dreamy images, pure and passionate names which perpetuate and harmonise in our minds the sensations of gentle charm and violent intoxication with which they inspire us. So it is that certain peonies, their favourite flower, are saluted by the Chinese, according to their form or colour, by these delicious names, each an entire poem and an entire novel: The Young Girl Who Offers Her Breasts, or: The Water That Sleeps Between the Moon, or: The Sunlight in the Forest, or: The First Desire of the Reclining Virgin...

The Torture Garden
Octave Mirbeau

When Europe fell in love with chinoiserie during the eighteenth century, the exotic Eastern bloom brought style and balance to English gardens. Their multiple layers of crumpled petals contained a sense of lush abundance, as well as a romantic nostalgia, as their heads drooped under the weight of their exploding underskirts of pastel petticoat petals. A fan of their voluptuous beauty, the French actress Sarah Bernhardt always had a bowl of pale pink Japanese-style puffball peonies around her.

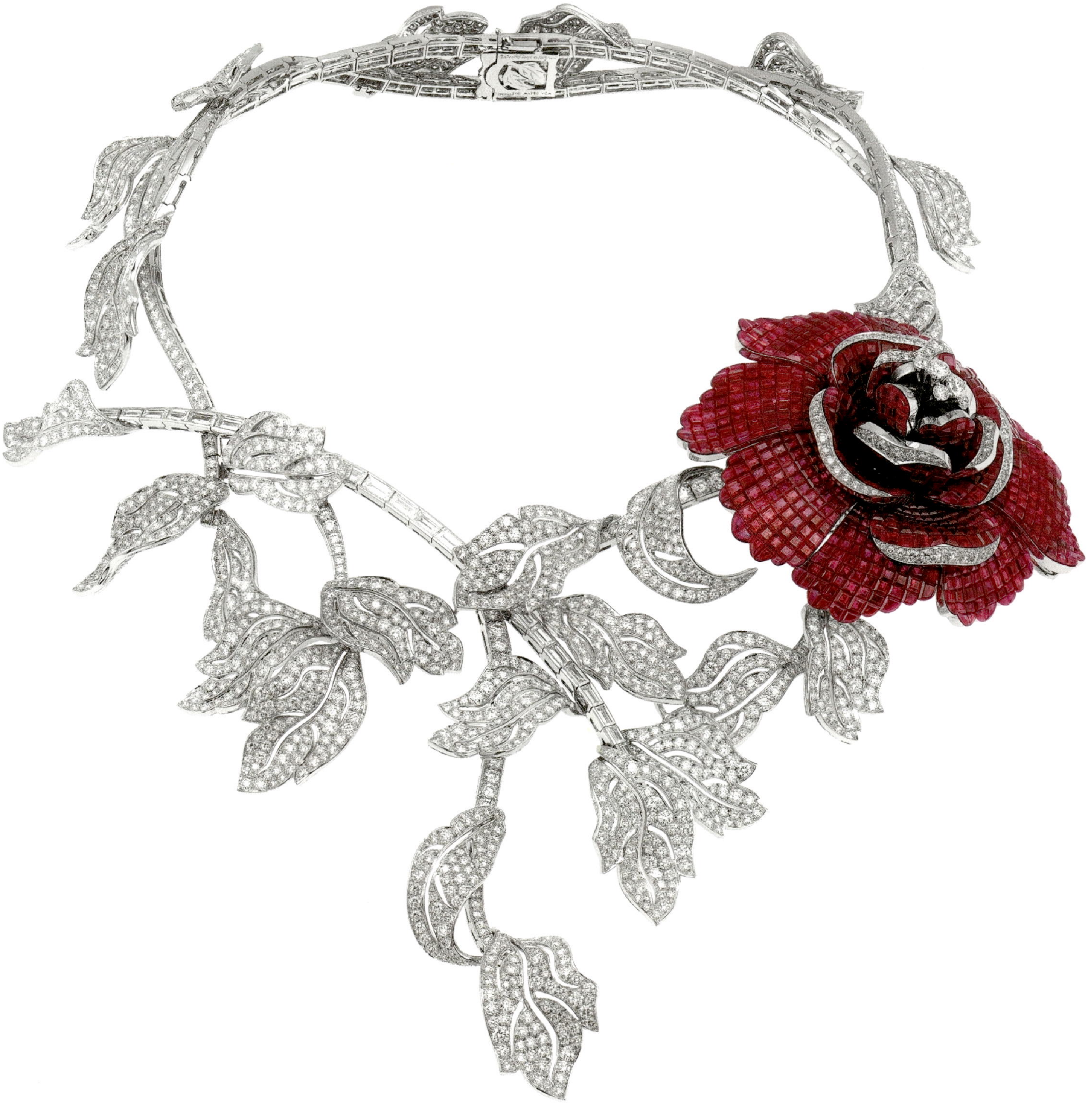

Peony
Van Cleef & Arpels
2014

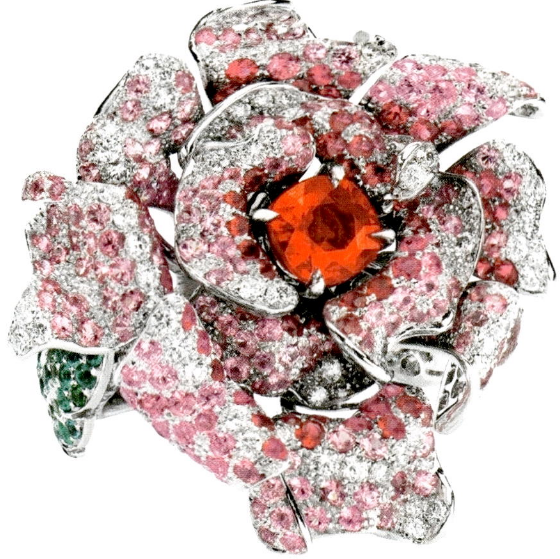

Lady Peony
Anna Hu
2010

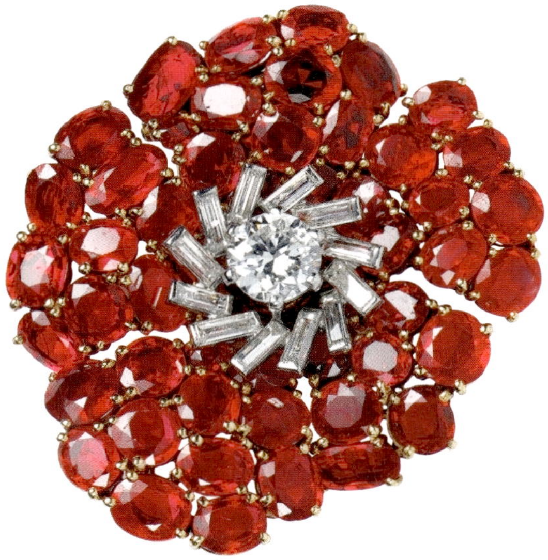

Peony
Cartier
1938

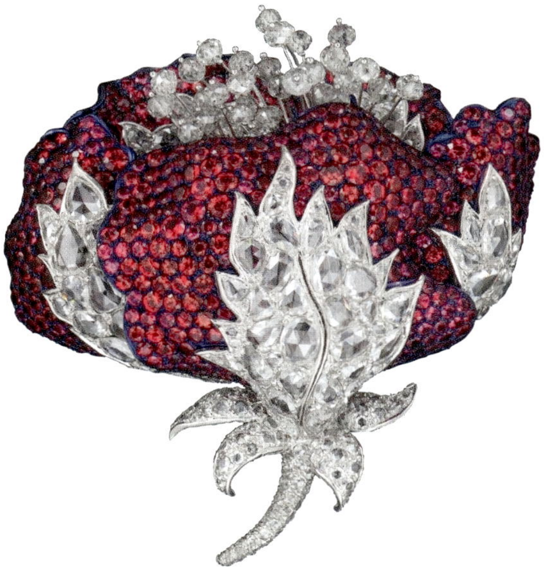

Peony
Michelle Ong
2002

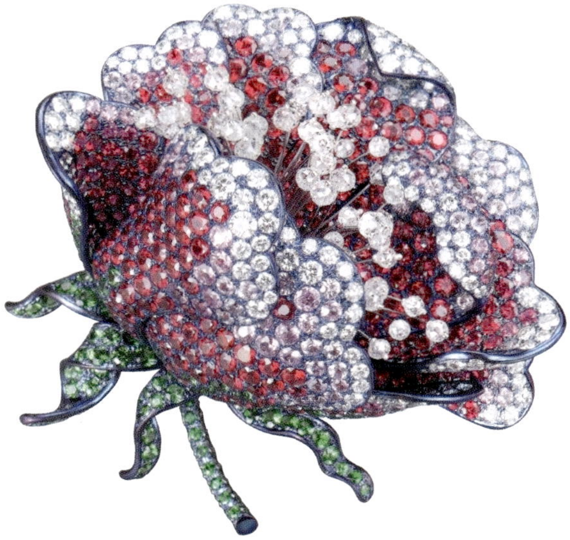

Graceful Peony
Michelle Ong
2008

Van Cleef & Arpels drench their full-flowering peony petals in colour using red rubies Mystery-set into red gold on a rambling stem of round- and baguette-cut diamonds. Each ruby is perfectly matched and individually cut to imitate the petals furling over with yellow diamond centres and veins shimmering in diamond-set leaves. The peony's complex shapes are given volume, they are never *trompe l'oeil* flowers.

'The peony carries a great deal of symbolism for positive energy, love and luck', says jeweller Michelle Ong of Carnet. Ong takes inspiration for her floral designs from walking through the Botanical Gardens near her home on Hong Kong Island, as well as from her childhood rose garden which she remembers bursting with vivid yellow, red and pink buds and blossoms. She visits the flower market on the Kowloon side, walking through the bustling stalls that offer brilliantly coloured orchids, lotus flowers and the white national flower bauhinia. There is always a vase of cut white, pinky purple peonies in her office, and she uses the soft, round, blousy petals that she loves as inspiration for visual ideas. The petals are formed by layers of stones, such as rose-cut diamonds, set tightly together so they are almost transparent, allowing more light into the pieces. As she works, she refers to the blooms from the flower market, closely observing their different stages; catching them at the ideal moment when the petals are starting to gradually unfold, she then adds to her pieces what she describes as 'frosting' – the adding of gemstones.

Ong's Graceful Peony brooch shows the mythical beauty of the flower, by including every aspect of it in a graduation of feminine pink and brilliant white stones in a realistic bejewelled bloom. 'Other times I may wish to capture the qualities more abstractly – taking artistic licence, manipulating the form, making something new', she says, 'perhaps playing with the juxtaposition of the flower's form and precious gems. I incorporate stones depending on which angle I look at the flower.' A Lady Peony ring by Anna Hu resembles a small sculpture, replicating the flower with a realistic appearance, as if the actual flower has been dipped in gemstones.

The Naiad-like lily of the vale,
Whom youth makes so fair and passion so pale,
That the light of its tremulous bells is seen
Through their pavilions of tender green

The Sensitive Plant
Shelley

Naturalistic sculptured scallop-edged 'bells' have been a hardy perennial in the jeweller's art. Among them are the bluebell, snowdrop, and the sweet-scented lily of the valley (May lily or May bells), whose delicate green sprigs shoot up in early spring, with tiny drops of iridescent pearl-like caps. The flower symbolises a return to happiness, as illustrated in the fable that the nightingale only returns to the wood when the lily of the valley blooms in May. The legend that the lily

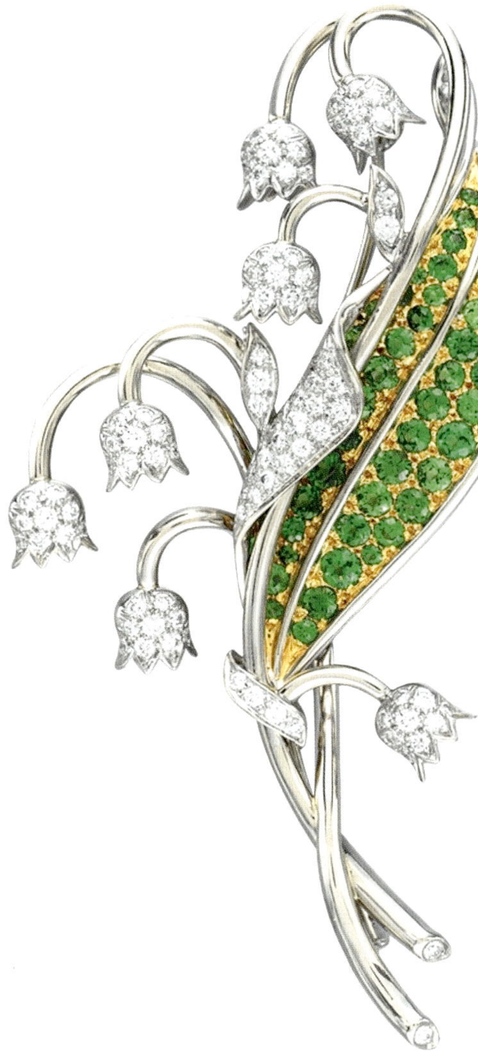

Lily of the Valley
Tiffany & Co.
Early 20th century

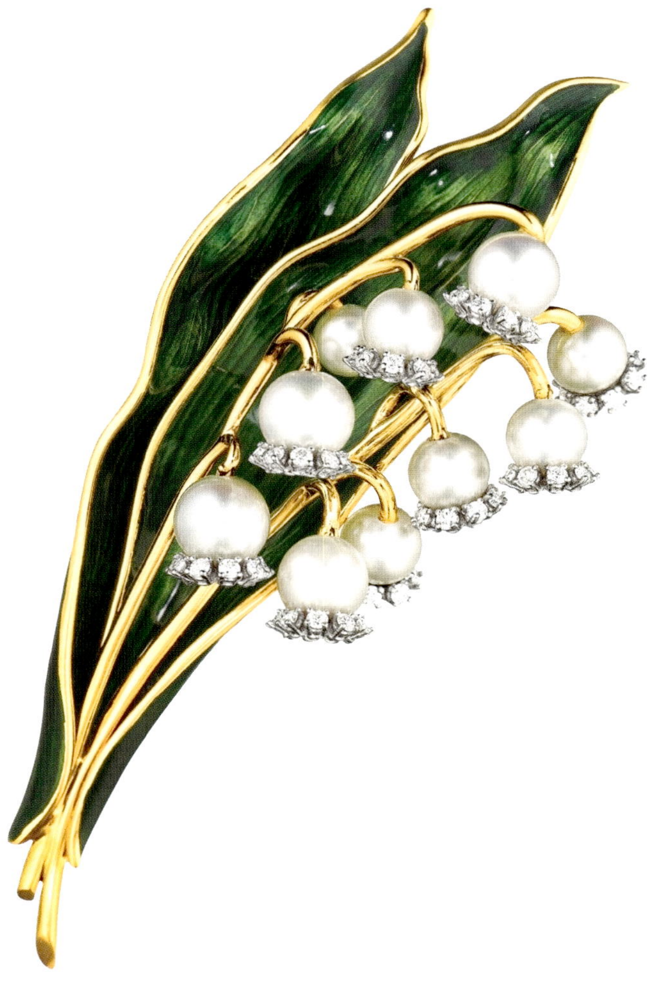

Lily of the Valley
Verdura
1965

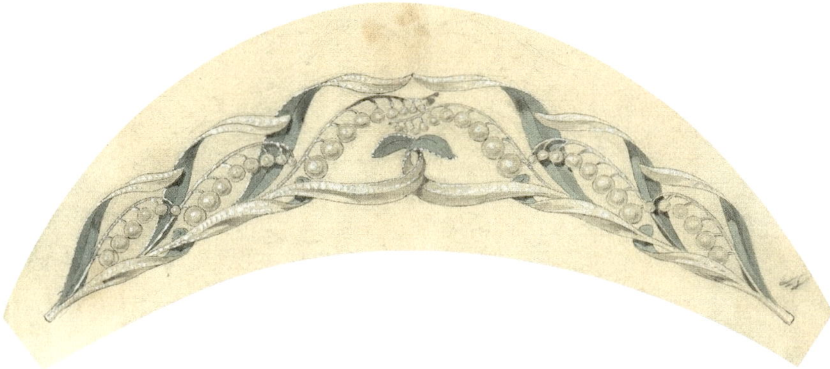

Lily of the Valley
Chaumet
1901

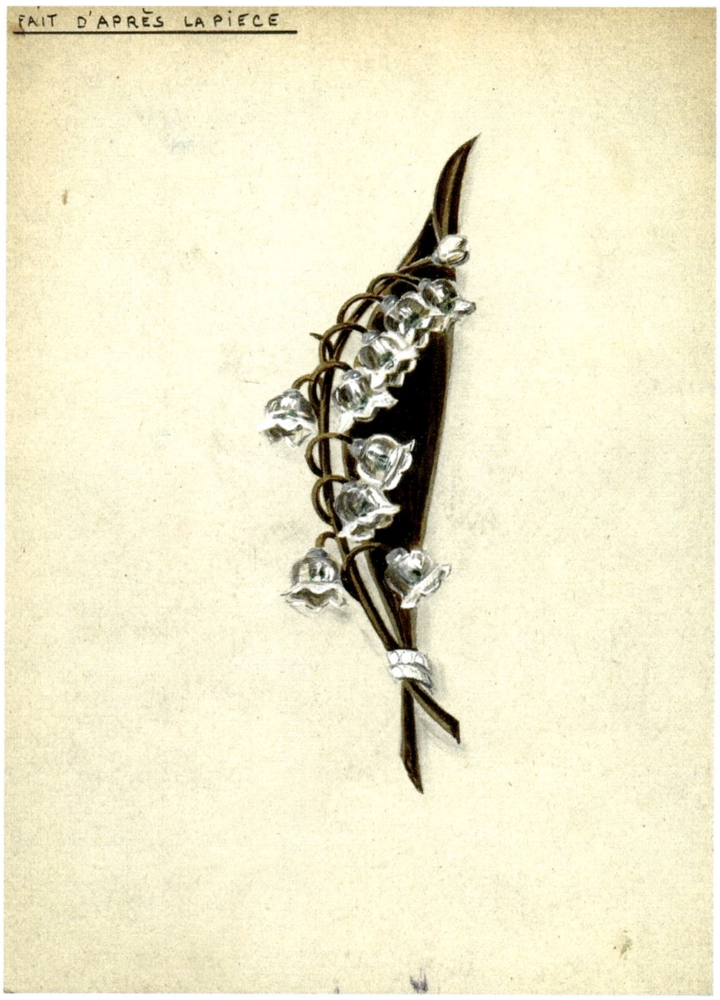

Lily of the Valley
Van Cleef & Arpels
1939

of the valley sprang from the tears wept by the Virgin Mary during the crucifixion of Jesus explains their alternative common name, 'Our Lady's tears', and their use as a symbol of humility in Christian painting.

On 1 May 1561, King Charles IX of France was presented with a bunch of lily-of-the-valley flowers (*muguets* in French) to bring him luck and prosperity. He was so touched by the gesture that each year he gave sweet-smelling blossoms to the ladies of the court, beginning the tradition of the Fête du Muguet when gifts of lily of the valley are given as a *porte-bonheur*. The tiny fragrant flower holds a place of particular importance in French *haute couture* and *joaillerie*, inspiring designers to replicate the white bell shapes in fabric and stones. One of the first diamond arrangements used by Cartier in the late nineteenth century was named Muguet, with smaller stones being set around a larger stone, creating a bell-like shape.

The small, velvet-lined salon of Joel Arthur Rosenthal (JAR), near the Place Vendôme in Paris, is the precious garden nursery where the most beautiful jewelled flowers are nurtured into blossoms over years of painstaking design and crafting cultivation. Rosenthal works directly from nature, but his spring flowers, never exotic varieties but well-documented everyday blooms, command attention for their spectacular beauty. Fresh, dewy, budding and blooming flowers and gently wilting fallen petals have a realism that is not tempered by the unattractive side of nature. They are mounted in 'tweed settings' of tonal washes of gemstones, chosen for the painterly effect of their colours. Bouquets of lily-of-the-valley flower heads quiver delicately on diamond pins, and the heart-stopping moment a gleaming white fragile bell head drops its weight onto a diamond stem is realised by a tear-drop Oriental pearl. Reviewing the 2013 *Jewels by JAR* exhibition at the Metropolitan Museum of Art in *Vogue*, I wrote:

> *His life-size geranium brooch will dazzle a new generation; others will be pulled towards the realism of a gently petalled garnet lilac sprig, so convinced of its naturalism they might think they can smell its sweet fragrance.*

Violets with blush-pink diamond centres, woven stone carpets of red and purple stone pansies, three-dimensional gardenias carved in white agate with diamond-studded stems, sapphire wisteria, copper and diamond freesias, and boldly executed blousy green garnet, ruby, pink sapphire and enamel parrot tulip petals come to life in Rosenthal's imagination. Surrounded by botanical journals and drawings, gardening books and horticultural magazines on tables next to vases full of faded velvet-coloured roses and tall-stemmed flowers, Rosenthal visualises his pieces quickly, but executes them painstakingly slowly.

Unlike most other designers, Rosenthal's creation is descriptive; it begins with words not drawings, which are transcribed and refined in thousands of hours of work by a handful of artisans. Rosenthal might only work on a piece when the particular flower is in bloom, requiring years of observation: wire and paper mock-ups are made, followed by the setting of pearls and stones into clay models as experiments for the final mounting. In a reversal of the childhood game, 'He loves me; He loves me not', in which each petal of a daisy is pulled away to reach the corolla of the flower, each section of a Rosenthal jewelled flower is made separately, the entire head being formed petal by petal. A lilac brooch is moulded from hundreds of aluminium sculpted floral shapes, before being mounted with 21,000 violet sapphires, garnets and diamonds.

Each facet of a flower comes to life in Rosenthal's hands. Deep within the bloom there is a lavish display of colour, as there would be in the natural world. Texture is recreated through the use of reverse-mounted diamonds or unusual metals, such as pewter, copper and aluminium, used to give accurate natural colour depictions, like the bronzed silver of an olive branch. Rosenthal even manages to evoke the 'temperament' of a flower. A wild-looking iris, with openwork diamond and white sapphire undulating petals and clusters of dense woven stones, shows the inherently unpredictable and chaotic nature of the plant.

White bud, that in meek beauty dost lean
Thy cloister'd cheek as pale as moonlight snow,
Thou seems't beneath thy huge, high leaf of green,
An Eremite beneath his mountain's brow.

Lily of the Valley
George Croly

Elizabeth Taylor sported a precious *porte-bonheur*, given to her by the actor Rex Harrison during their filming of *A Little Night Music* in Vienna, as a gift for her wedding to the senator John Warner. The lily-of-the-valley sprig was made of carved and frosted rock crystal, with diamond and nephrite leaves, gathered by a circular-cut diamond ribbon. 'Designed as a simple bouquet of my favourite flowers', she said. The flowers were a birthday emblem for Queen Victoria, but also a symbol of grief, as she sent a bouquet of them in 1870 for the funeral of her private secretary General Grey, writing to his daughter, 'As they were his favourite flowers so they are mine. He sent them to me on my poor old birthday from his garden and I therefore wish that this small tribute of affection and friendship should be placed on his last resting place.'

Another enthusiast of the delicate flower was the couturier Christian Dior, who wore a lily-of-the-valley buttonhole for his first runway show in 1947. Being superstitious, he viewed the flower from that moment as his lucky charm, so nodding sprigs of it followed him for the rest of his life, sewn into the linings and pockets of his haute couture dresses just before a show. 'Colour is what gives jewels their worth, they light up and enhance the face',

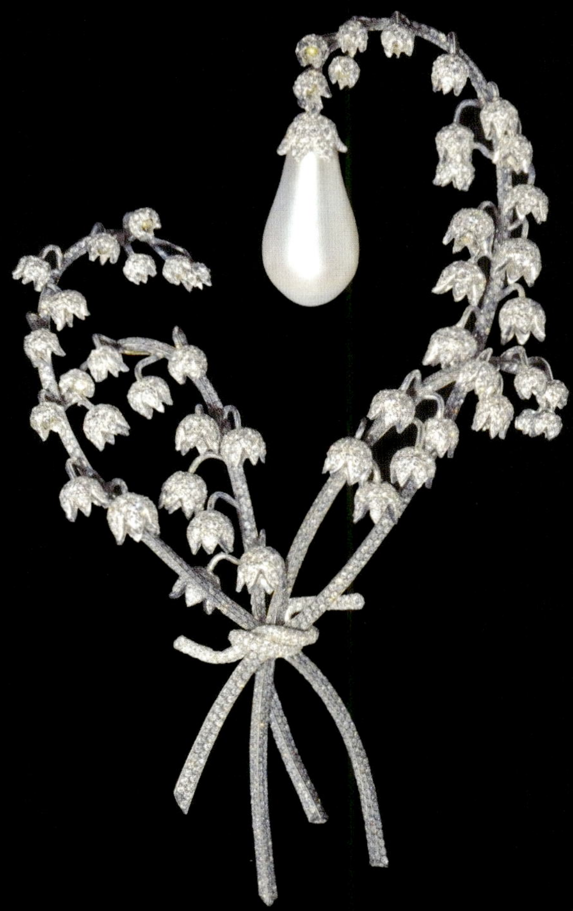

Lily of the Valley
JAR
1991

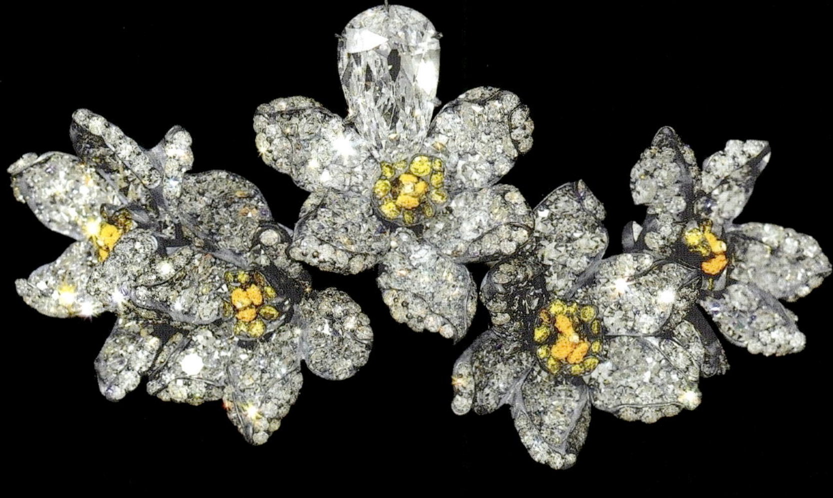

Narcissus
JAR
2013

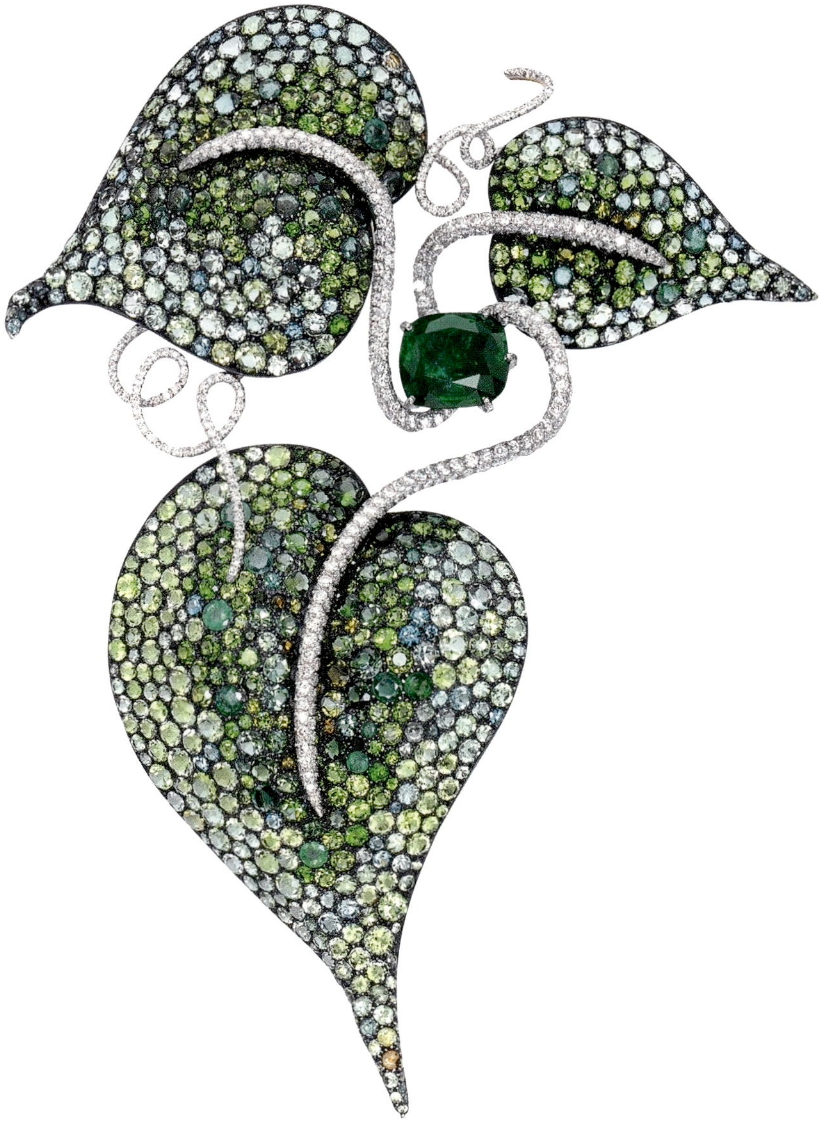

Green Spring Leaf
JAR
1989

Dior said. Victoire de Castellane, creative director at Dior Joaillerie, combined Christian Dior's love for colour with his beloved lily of the valley, creating an exuberant necklace in one vibrant sprig of emerald leaves, laden with white pearl and diamond floral flourishes.

A passion for flowers inherited from my mother meant that I was at my happiest among plants and flower-beds… my chief delight was to learn by heart the names and descriptions of flowers in coloured catalogues of the firm of Vilmorin and Andrieu.

Christian Dior

Dior inherited a passion for flowers from his mother, picking up gardening tips and ideas on shapes, scents and colours while watching her garden in his childhood home in Normandy. Dior would walk into his Avenue Montaigne showroom every Monday morning with fresh flowers from his Milly-la-Forêt mill-house garden; these would sit on his desk while he designed gowns that would give Parisian women flower-like shapes. 'I drew women-flowers with soft shoulders, full busts, waists as slender as lianas and wide skirts like corollas', he wrote in his memoirs. On other days of the week, fresh flowers would arrive from the famous florist Lachaume on the Rue Royale, and homes in Paris were sought that had space for a wrought-iron conservatory in which he could grow his plants.

'The New Look profiled a supple silhouette with skirts as full as corollas or as slender as flower stems', wrote Florence Muller, curator of the 2013 *Dior Impressions* exhibition. Dior loved botany, but observed nature with the eye of a couturier rather than a horticulturist. He named pieces in his New Look collection after the delicate whorls of petals at the centre of a flower. He used the colours of the Impressionists for his couture gowns, imbuing his designs with a nostalgic femininity, and botanical references were apparent in their silhouettes, including the tulip in 1953, which was followed by the lily of the valley.

'Volume of the hat, volume of the bust, volume of the skirt, three softened rectangles that envelop the face evoke a cluster of lilies of the valley flowers', Dior explained in the press memo for the spring/summer 1954 collection. He also used details of the lily of the valley in his embroideries, explaining that the quivering of the flower was more important than the bellflower itself. He created special cotton thread to give the desired suppleness and spring, enabling the fabric flowers to move and sway with the model's movements as she walked on the runway.

Jeweller to the Russian royal family, Peter Carl Fabergé also loved to create movement in his designs, sculpting hardstone and enamel flowers, originally as hair ornaments or brooches, mounted on springs, *en tremblant*, to mimic the swaying of real flowers in a spring breeze. Later, these flowers were displayed as though real flowers, mounted in rock crystal vases, simulating water to make the blooms as realistic as possible. The grand duchess Maria Pavlovna had a great passion for Fabergé's floral creations, her collection containing cornflowers, forget-me-nots, cacti and dandelions set with large Siberian sapphires, amethysts and aquamarines. Queen Helen of Romania had a pearl lily of the valley with rings of rose diamonds, like halos shining from the bell-shaped petals; as the refractive index of rock crystal and water are very close, the stalk appears to break as it enters the water.

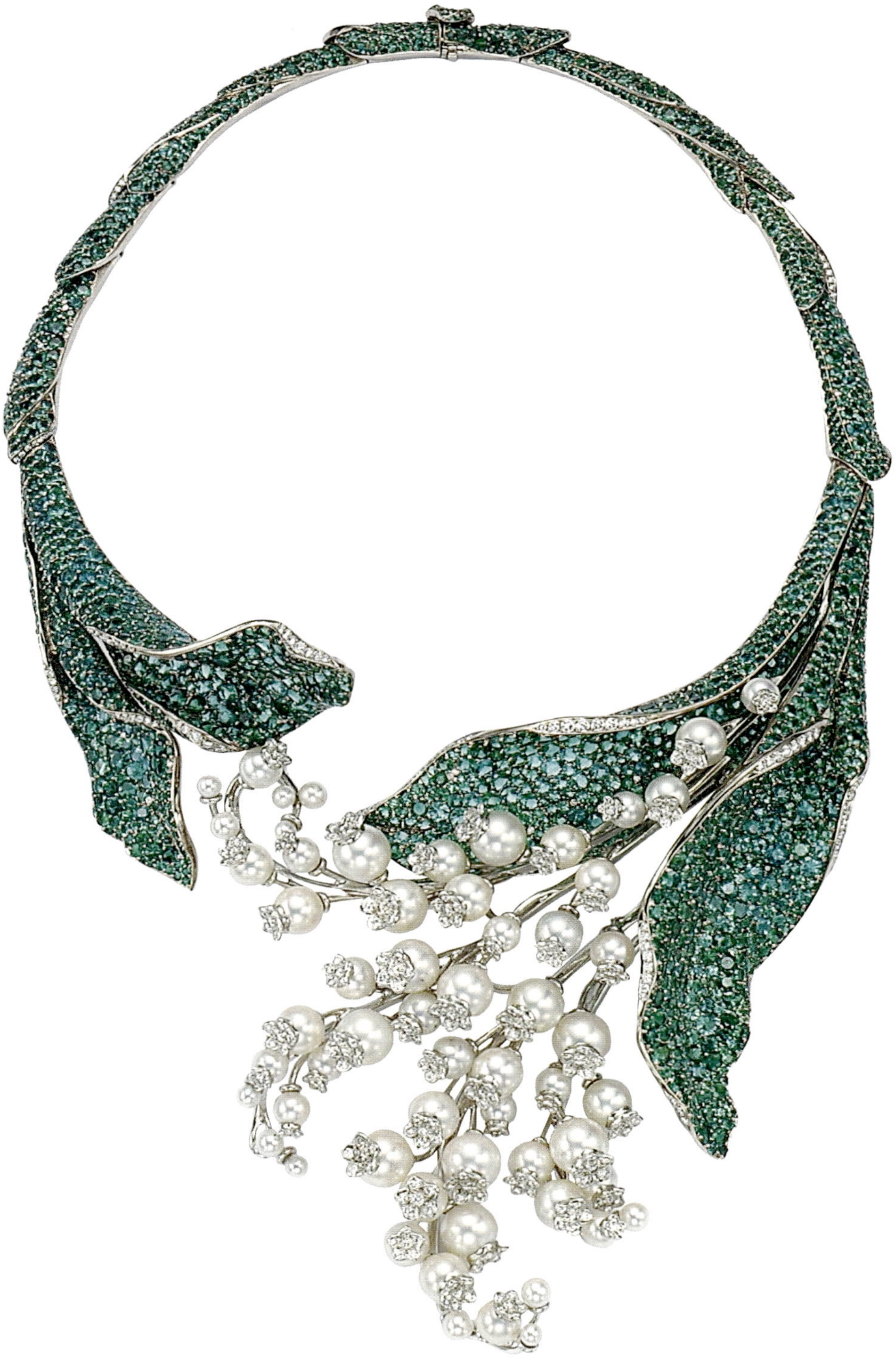

Lily of the Valley
Victoire de Castellane,
Dior High Jewellery
1999

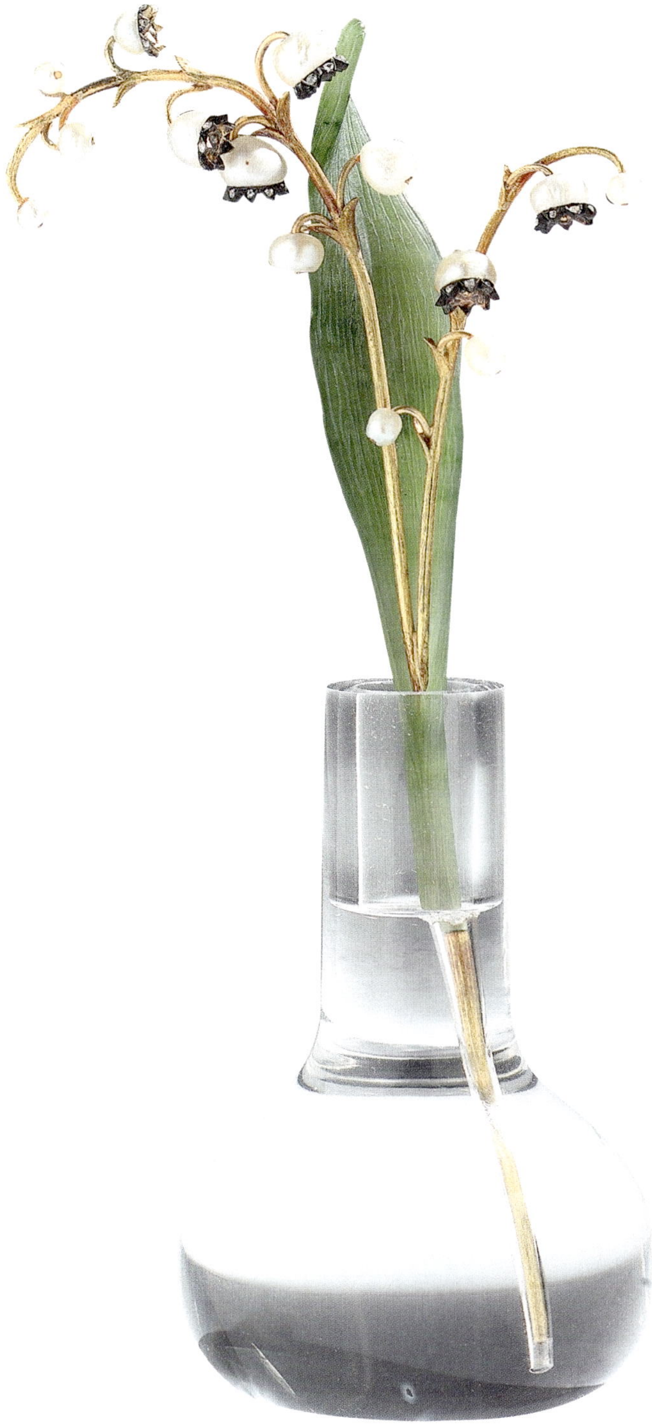

Lily of the Valley
Fabergé
c. 1900

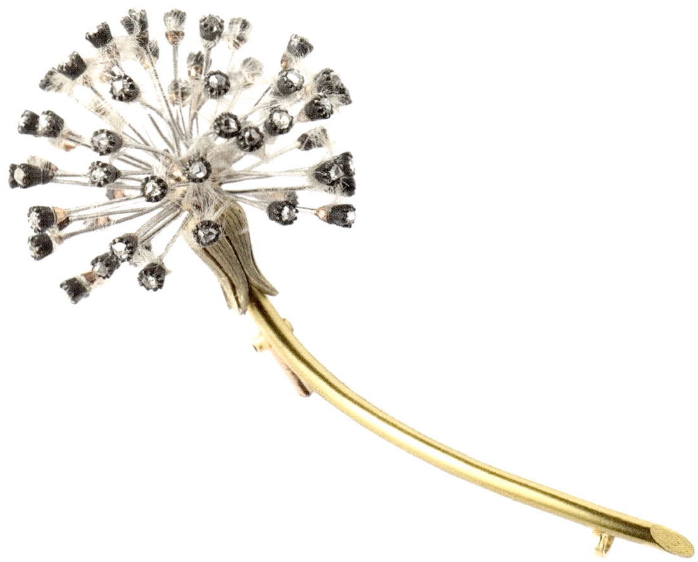

Dandelion
Fabergé
c. 1900

In 1899, Tsarina Alexandra Feodorovna bought from Fabergé a delicate, gold-stemmed, bell-shaped flower, with pearl edges and rose diamonds, and Siberian nephrite leaves in rock crystal, lily of the valley being her favourite flower.
At that time, the imperial family had flowers imported from the South of France, which were kept on ice to preserve their freshness. During the flowers' long train journey to Russia, Fabergé was able to travel with them, studying them in great detail before transforming them into enamel and gemstone flowers that would never fade. As the imperial family looked out from the Alexander Palace onto the snow-clad pines around Tsarskoe Selo during long harsh winters, these decorative floral *objets* acted as a reminder that spring would eventually come.

During 1900, Fabergé was producing what was the most refined enamel work of the day, using a *guilloché*, or engine-turned technique designed in the Louis XVI style of the late 1780s. This involved applying five or six layers of enamel, from his vast range of 144 shades, to engraved silver or gold, resulting in translucent, enamel-like rippling silken fabric, to replicate delicate soft petals.

The British royal family also collected the work of Fabergé. There is a reference in Queen Victoria's ledger of 1895 to a payment to K. Fabergé of £20 9s 6d for a 'sapphire and rose pin'. Queen Alexandra owned twenty-two jewelled flower *objets* in precious stone vases. One cherry blossom included two separate golden stems, one supporting the blossom and the other ripe red cherries; another featured an enamel pansy, raspberry plant and a large weighty chrysanthemum bloom, which was so heavy it was set onto steel-strengthened gold stems, bought in 1908 for £117.

As these *objets* found their way to Europe, Parisian craftsmen had the idea of reviving their own eighteenth-century style, and jewelled flowers found fertile ground in the Cartier design studio. Cartier flower vases were housed in glass cases with ivory bases, arranged inside their own glass 'greenhouse' in a stylised manner, sometimes with an insect or grasshopper widening the visual range, so the flower became a still life. In 1925, a veritable garden of flowers was created that included magnolia, lily of the valley, iris, hyacinth and tulip, alongside stained ivory apple-blossom branches, with enamel and moonstone, designed with a Japanese aesthetic. The materials used were as varied as the subjects: carved agate, aventurine and jade were chosen in colours to match the flower with vases and urns created from hardstones, based on eighteenth- and nineteenth-century models displayed in the Louvre. The Cartier archives show that thirty-seven naturalistic floral arrangements were transported in their glass cases around the world in 1907, to patrons such as Lady de Grey in London and John Pierpont Morgan in New York.

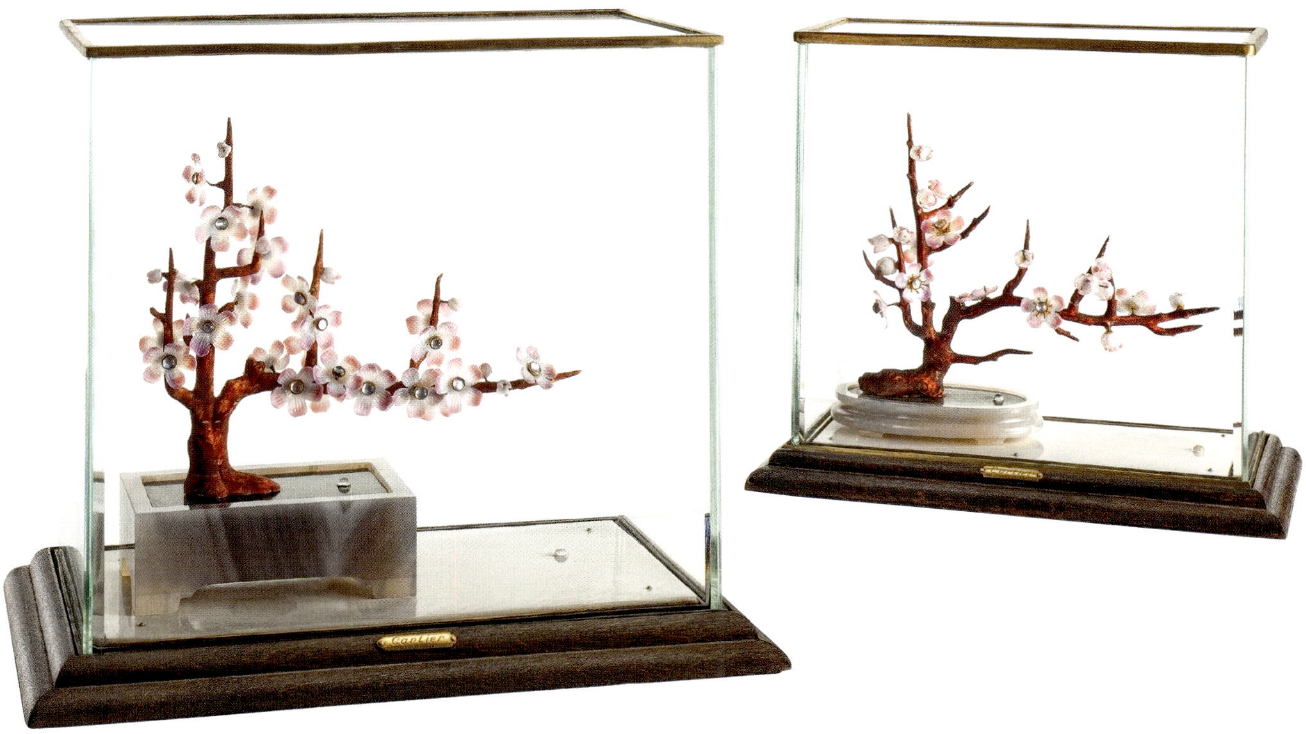

Blossom
Cartier
1926

hawthorn • hydrangea • orchid • wild oats • camellia • edelweiss • hellebore • mistletoe • snowdrop • winter plum

anemone • blossom • daisy • dandelion • lily of the valley • narcissus • pansy • peony • tulip • violet • foxglove • heliotrope • calla lily

heliotrope • iris • lily • lotus • morning glory • rose • lily • sunflower • sweet pea • thistle • vanilla flower • foxglove • wild oats • chrysanthemum • hawthorn • hydrangea • poppy

heliotrope • iris • lily • lotus • morning glory • rose •
lily • sunflower • sweet pea • thistle •
vanilla flower • foxglove • wild oats •
chrysanthemum • hawthorn • hydrangea • poppy

anemone • pansy • daisy • chrysanthemum • narcissus
• hawthorn • hydrangea • orchid
• vanilla flower • foxglove
• wild oats • camellia • heliotrope

heliotrope • iris • lily • lotus • morning glory • edelweiss •
hellebore • holly • ivy • mistletoe • snowdrop • winter plum • anemone
• blossom • daisy • dandelion • narcissus

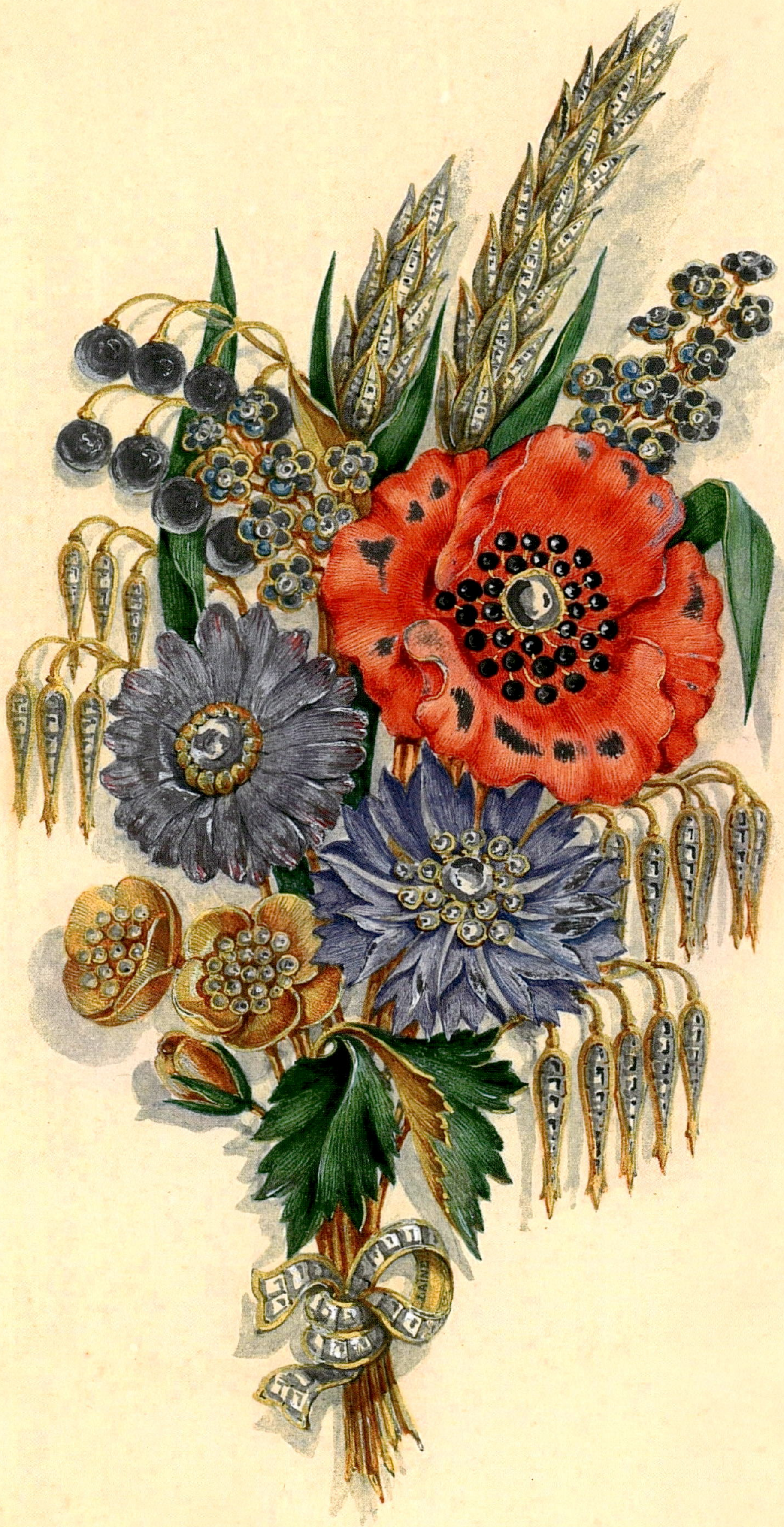

Poppy
Mellerio dits Meller
1855

Summer

Our mother too was distracted from duty, seduced by the rich wilderness of the garden so long abandoned. All day she trotted to and fro, flushed and garrulous, pouring flowers into every pot and jug she could find on the kitchen floor. Flowers from the garden, daisies from the bank, cow-parsley, grasses, ferns, and leaves – they flowed in armfuls through the cottage door until its dim interior seemed entirely possessed by the world outside – a still green pool flooding with honeyed tides of summer.

Cider with Rosie
Laurie Lee

Summer glows with the tranquil hazy lustre of burnished gold, as a muddled clash of wallflowers and dahlias bake in the sun, against stone walls that turn the colour of coral, fire-opal and pink sapphire. Sultry long days made soporific by poppy dust wafting on the hot air as dappled amber beams of light beat down on meadow fields. Dark green leafy bushes are full of bloom, with patches of precious stone colours catching their breath under cooling trees that line the banks of clear meandering beryl-pebbled streams. Tall starry-tipped grassy gardens sway with long-stemmed golden and pastel pink roses, purple foxgloves, Queen Anne's lace and sweet lilac, attracting bees, brilliant hummingbirds and butterflies so the flower-strewn earth moves like a rainbow of breeze-blown colour.

The iridescent colours of the iris in June, deep indigo, orange and blue, winding out of blade-like stems, could be the reason the flower was named after the Greek messenger of the gods, who travelled to earth on rainbows, delivering her messages. Irises create chaotic batches of colour as large outer 'falls' and inner lower petals curl back the vibrant beards and crested combs appearing to bob and turn in every direction.

Green was the silence, wet was the light,
the month of June trembled like a butterfly

100 Love Sonnets
Pablo Neruda

Iris flowers were depicted on the walls of Egyptian palaces, and in ancient Greece these purple blooms, being symbolic of life, were planted on the graves of women to summon the goddess Iris to guide them on their journey to the afterlife. Since the Middle Ages, the soft petals of the iris that unfurl into the shape of a loose cross have been the basis of the fleur-de-lys, adopted by Louis VII in the twelfth century as a symbol of France.

As the white iris grew within the walls of the city of Florence, the fleur-de-lys was chosen as its emblem during the Renaissance, used as a heraldic symbol

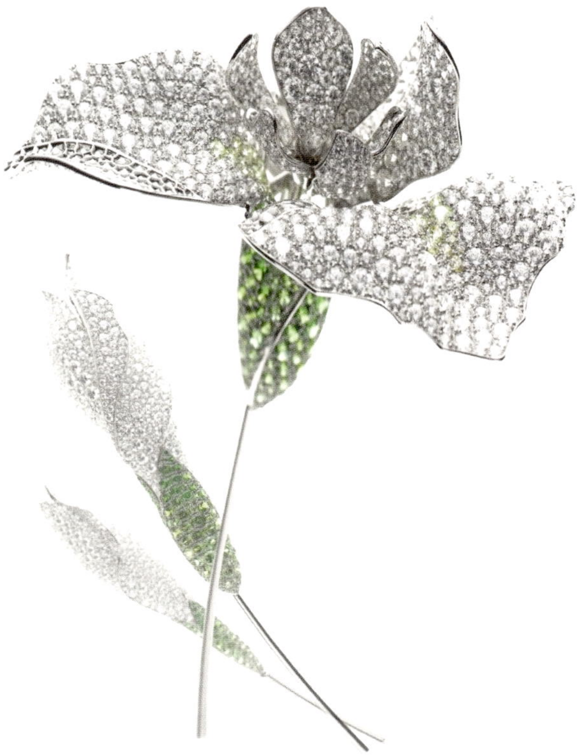

Iris
Gimel
2006

on a red background on the new wealthy city's coat of arms. The Medici family reversed the colours, so that the red iris decorated a white background, setting in motion centuries of breeding that attempted to cultivate a true red-coloured iris.

> *The flowers themselves are a mesmerising synthesis of strength and delicacy, the complexity of petals held high and proud on that unyielding stem.*
>
> *Harper's Bazaar*, May 2013
> Maggie O'Farrell

During the Edo Period in Japan (1603–1868), the cultivation of the Japanese iris reached its peak, drawn by artists with a dignified stance and a glimmering lustre during the rainy season. Golden Japanese irises were engraved with plum blossom in designs by Edward C. Moore at Tiffany & Co. on Japanesque ornamental silver. At the 1900 world's fair in Paris, G. Paulding Farnham, the most able botanical artist working with Moore, showed a breathtaking nine-inch corsage iris using Montana sapphires and green demantoid garnets, to win Tiffany the gold medal for jewellery.

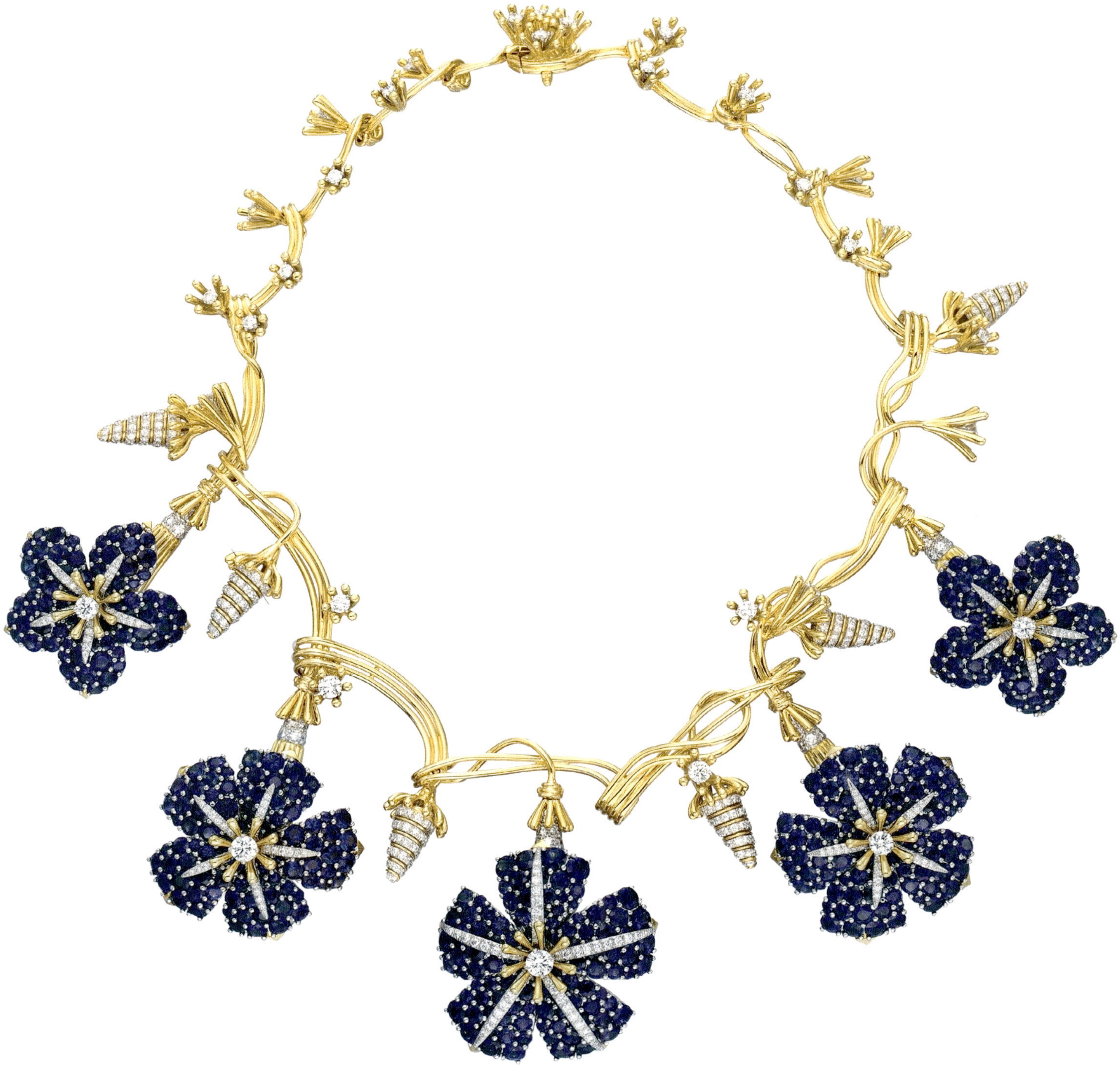

Morning Glory
Jean Schlumberger, Tiffany & Co.
c. 1963

Kaoru Kay Akihara of Gimel is well versed in the ceremonies of tea and flower arranging, making her pieces resonate with Japanese soul and spirit. During the tea ceremony there is a saying, 'ichigo ichie', meaning 'an encounter happens once in a lifetime and never again'. Akihara likens this concept to her jewellery designs, as she expresses the beauty of an iris or spray of morning glory in one arresting moment of nature. In the centre of her iris is a fan of yellow diamonds, giving depth and shade to the petals; the diamonds are held in a honeycomb structure, enabling soft light to be filtered through to the flowering buds. Her morning glory brooches are set with pink diamonds and sapphires with demantoid garnet leaves that depict the flower's freshness at daybreak before the summer temperature rises, heating the plant.

In 1949, the famous writer and creator of Sissinghurst's gardens, Vita Sackville West, described finding companions for roses:

> *Everyone knows, and grows, the lupins; not everyone,*
> *I think, has yet realized the extreme beauty of the irises.*
> *So as June is just the moment to see them in flower I thought*
> *I would remind you of their beauty and their many advantages.*
> *Their beauty is beyond dispute. No velvet can rival the richness*
> *of their falls; or let us say, it is to velvet only that we may*
> *compare them. That is surely enough to claim for any flower?*
> *They suggest velvet, pansies, wine – anything you like,*
> *that possesses texture as well as colour.*

Another gardener who compares the petals of the iris to a tactile fabric is Carolyne Roehm, who notes in her book *Flower* that the 'Iris Germanica is always exquisitely dressed and in the most delicate of pastel coloured taffetas'.

Depicting the texture and colour of iris petals poses a challenge to artists. Claude Monet was famously captivated by the irises that grew outside the windows of his Provençal house. He used vivid brushstrokes to capture the colour of their blooms and the mood of their chaotic emerald whiplash stems, which blow in all directions in his painting *Iris Bed*. 'More than anything I must have flowers, always always', Monet said on his inspiration for *Iris Bed*, 'I perhaps owe becoming a painter to flowers.'

Vincent van Gogh was also captivated by the irises that grew in the fields around the town of Saint-Rémy, where he painted his famous study in 1890, the year before his death in an asylum in Provence. He used intense colours and brushstrokes to mimic the textures of the petals, capturing the effects of sunlight and weather on the contrasting colours and shapes of the flowers. The lone white iris is thought to be self-referential, showing the artist isolated and detached amongst the happy throng of purple flowers with curving silhouettes, bound by twisting lines and black contours. 'The irises violently slash into long strips, their violet petals on sword-like leaves', wrote art critic Félix Fénéon of the work when it was shown in 1889 at the Salon des Indépendants.

As flowers inspire art, so art inspires jewellery design. Anna Hu took Vincent van Gogh's irises as inspiration for a bracelet arranged with lavish blue and purple sapphires, mandarin garnets, demantoid garnets, emeralds and yellow diamonds, with brilliant diamonds marking the single white iris blossom.

Another bright summer flower, whose petals crumple like crimson silk, is the poppy, which spreads like a red raging bonfire through green fields during the late summer months.

The poppies hung
Dew-dabbed on their stalks

Endymion
John Keats

The slumberous position of the poppy's head, drooping forward as if eternally resting, combined with its blood-red colour and opiate qualities, meant it was associated in ancient Greece and Rome with sleep, peace and death. The vivid petals form a dramatic contrast against the black whorls at the centre of the flowers, which contain edible seeds of opium used since Egyptian times as an analgesic.

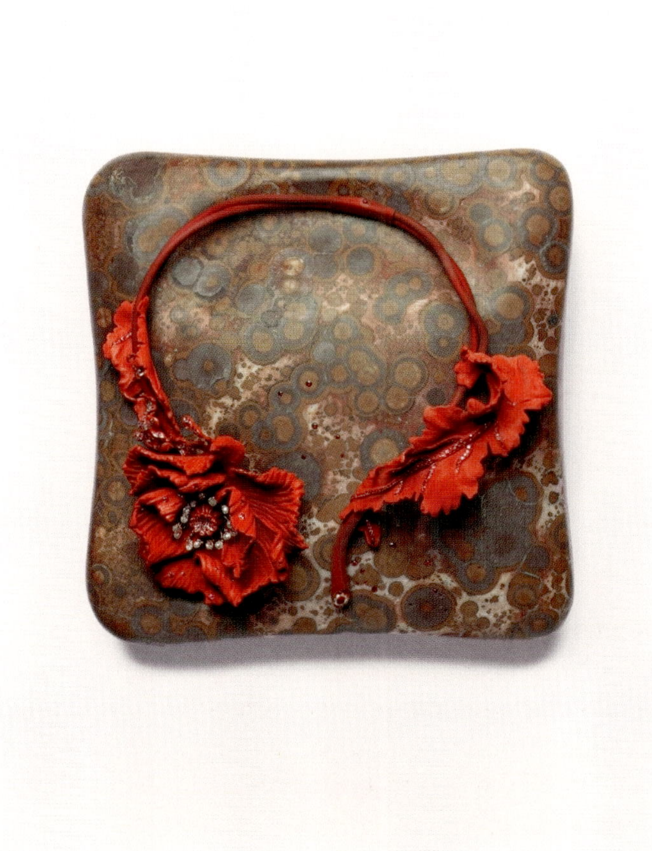

Opiom Velourosa Purpra
Victoire de Castellane
2010

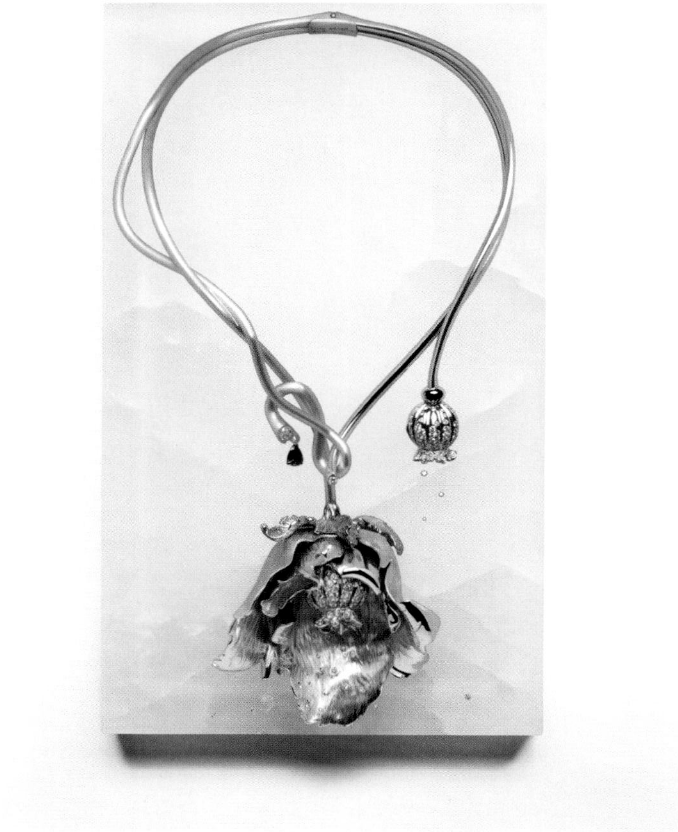

Heroïna Romanticam Dolorosa

Victoire de Castellane
2010

O gentle sleep!
Scatter thy drowsiest poppies from above;
And in new dreams, not soon to vanish, bless
My senses with the sight of her I love

Poppies and Sleep
Horace Smith

In 1804, a German pharmacist isolated a crystalline salt from opium that he named morphine, after the Roman god of dreams Morpheus. At the beginning of the eighteenth century, opiates were freely available to Victorians even as soothing tinctures for children, with comforting names such as Mother Bailey's Quietening Liquid.

Using faux Latin names, Victoire de Castellane has designed poppies to personify an opiate 'swoon', brought on by its hallucinatory effects, as well as the bittersweet promises of escape, offered by mind-altering drugs. The Heroïna Romanticam Dolorosa poppy is a lacquered silver and gold bud, with diamonds, rubies, jonquil diamonds and rock crystal, redolent of Ophelia floating between water and air, illustrating a romanticism in death. In contrast, the Opiom Velourosa Purpra represents a woman full of life. 'A voluptuous woman stretched out in her boudoir, vivid, decadent, flushed', explains de Castellane. The striking, blowsy, fully opened flower, with its intoxicating crimson powder-lacquered silver petals is set with rubies, diamonds and rhyolite. Her creations blur distinctions between the real and artificial, appearing romantic as well as dangerous, chiming with the poppy's associations with both good and evil.

Here are cool mosses deep,
And thro' the moss the ivies creep,
And in the stream the long-leaved flowers weep,
And from the craggy ledge the poppy hangs in sleep.

The Lotos-Eaters
Alfred Lord Tennyson

Following the trench warfare in the poppy fields of Flanders during the First World War, the flower has become a symbol of remembrance, being worn on lapels around Armistice Day each year.

In Flanders fields the poppies blow
Between the crosses, row on row
That mark our place; and in the sky
The larks, still bravely singing, fly
Scarce heard amidst the guns below.

In Flanders Fields
John McCrae

New York-based jeweller James de Givenchy, founder of Taffin, grew up in the countryside outside Paris, surrounded by poppy fields, and his favourite time of year was when the meadows turned crimson red as the flowers opened. He uses recycled Second World War steel gunmetal as the branches on which green and yellow sapphire flowers bud optimistically, symbolic of rebirth.

Poppy clips have flourished at Van Cleef & Arpels in silken, blood-red ruby Mystery settings with stems of baguette-cut diamonds. One such is the Garance clip, with diamond-edged ruby petals and a central grey pearl, surrounded by anthers adorned with tiny sapphire balls representing the dark centre of the flower. One posy contains three poppies: each flower is of a different height, showing a corolla of five petals, set with rubies around a grey pearl heart and dark sapphire beads with loosely tied emerald stems.

The poppy is painted glass; it never glows so brightly as
when the sun shines through it. Whenever it is seen –
against or with the light – always, it is a flame,
and warms the wind like a blown ruby...

Proserpina, Volume 1: Studies of Wayside Flowers
John Ruskin

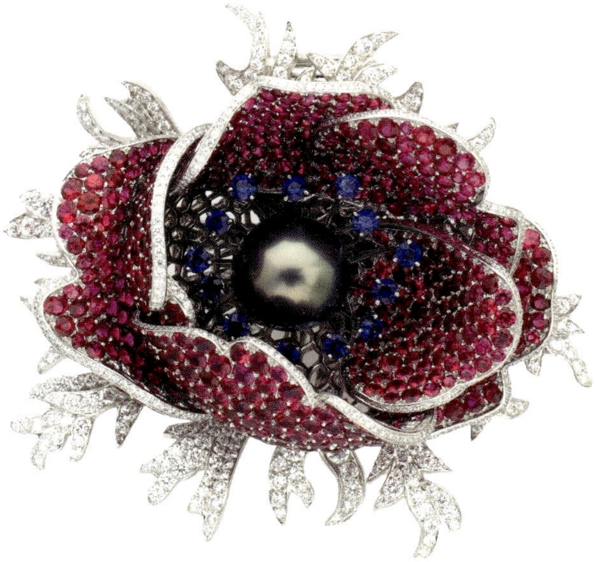

Poppy
Van Cleef & Arpels
2008

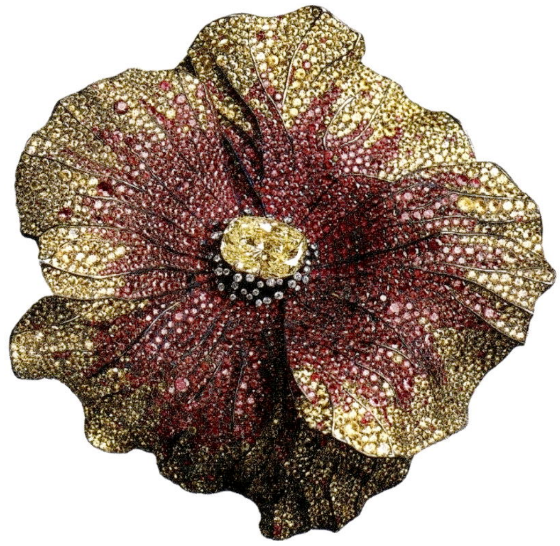

Poppy
Moussaieff
2005

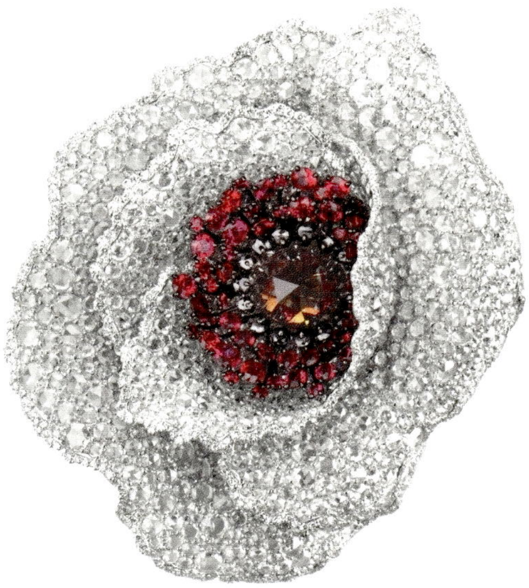

Poppy
Michelle Ong
2009

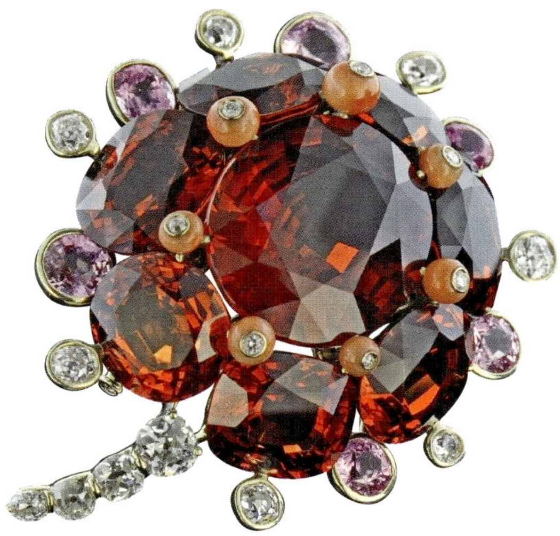

Poppy
James de Givenchy, Taffin
2006

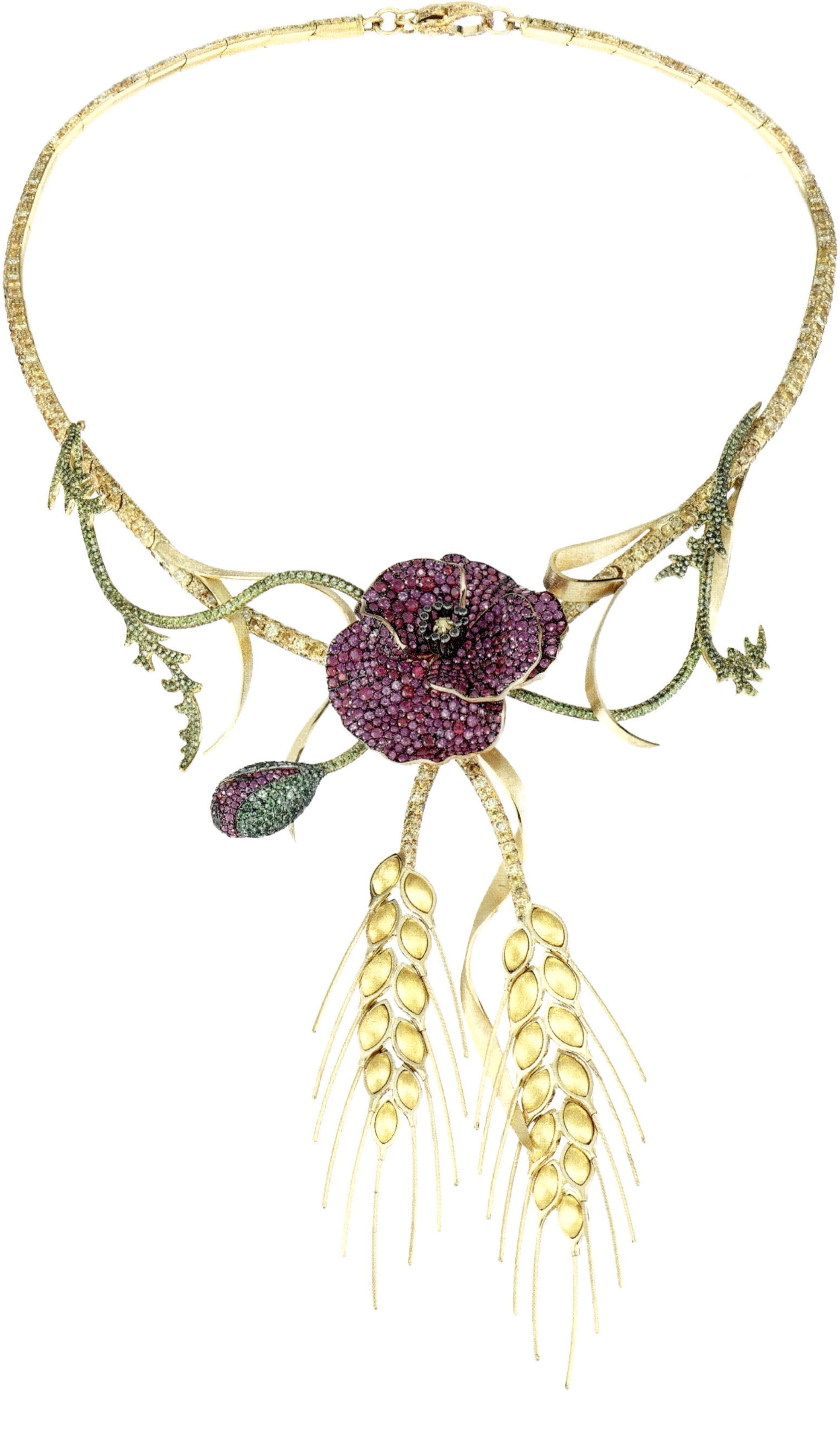

Poppy
Chopard
2013

In 1897, Lalique created a *plique-à-jour* enamel poppy, concentrating on capturing the papery fragility of the petal; by contrast, many contemporary poppies recreate more exactly the poppy's physical appearance. The customary red colour of the poppy is often interpreted by jewellers using pink-hued gemstones. Two pink and green tourmaline poppy flower heads by JAR are linked by a green scrolling stem, which is wrapped around a 37.23 carat pear-shaped diamond. A pink sapphire poppy bobs its head in an abundant summer meadow in a necklace by Chopard, made of curling green tsavorite stalks of grass and golden ears of corn. Whereas the poppy red colour of Michelle Ong's flowers blaze from ruby and fire-opal centres of rose-diamond petals.

During the late eighteenth century in Paris, vast floral summer bouquets were the fashion, chiming with the magnificent diamond bodice ornaments, up to eight inches long in some cases, composed of asymmetrical arrangements of flowers, with stems tied in a loose ribbon bow. The stems and foliage of floral bodice ornaments were often green enamel, or set with emeralds, berries in coral or chalcedony with diamond flower heads made up of a mixture of roses, fuchsia, carnations and chrysanthemum *en tremblant* (i.e. on a spring), shimmering as the wearer moved. Floral-style rings called *giardinetti* (miniature gardens) were also popular, with tiny stone-foiled and colourful gemstone blossoms in baskets and vases.

The French empress Eugénie, wife of Napoleon III, wore naturalistic jewellery in the form of parures of currant leaves and berries. A new fashion was sparked when she was painted by her favourite portraitist Franz Xaver Winterhalter with diamond vines threaded through her hair. She revitalised the style for jewelled swags of flowers and fruits when she had the French crown jewels restyled using the Versailles code of motifs used in Marie-Antoinette's jewels.

The interest in naturalism during the Renaissance resulted in herbals and flowers being drawn from life, and even non-botanical artists such as Leonardo da Vinci and Albrecht Dürer produced extraordinary drawings and paintings of plants. During the nineteenth century, botanical illustrators travelled to remote areas to document native species in the wild, making for greater accuracy. Fine jewellery houses keep collections of botanical drawings, gouaches and watercolours in their archives: sometimes these are drawn from nature, other times nature has planted a seed that germinates when imagination is added.

As well as drawing real specimens, Tiffany & Co. used photographs of oriental poppies, roses, carnations and lilacs as reference material. These photographs came from an archive presented by Charles Aubry to Eugène, son of Napoleon III of France, which found its way into Tiffany's design library when the company purchased a large number of the French crown jewels in 1887. Cartier designers worked from accurate early photographic reference books such as P. Plauszewski's *Encyclopédie Florale* when seeking ideas for their floral jewels. As well as using reference books, Louis Cartier sent his young jewellers out

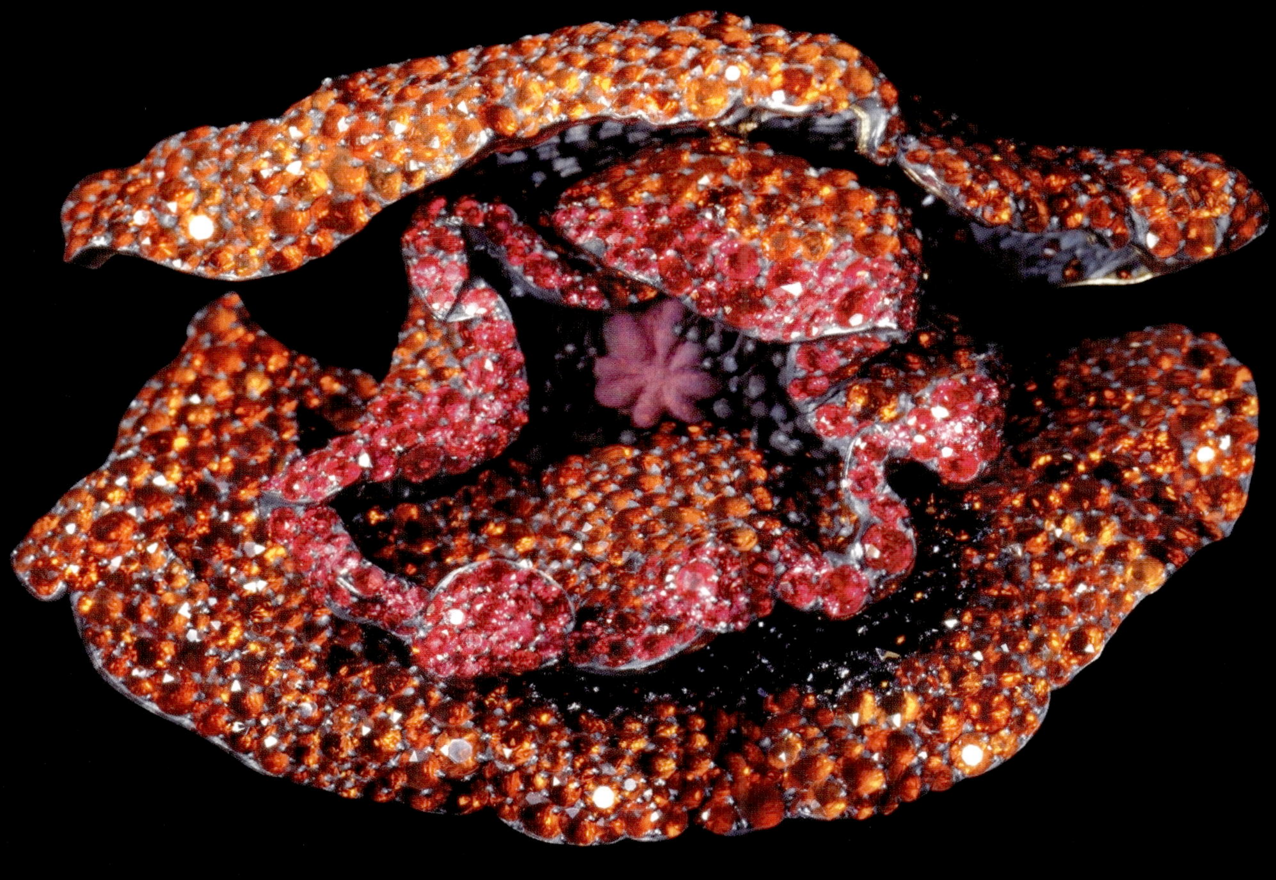

Poppy
JAR
1998

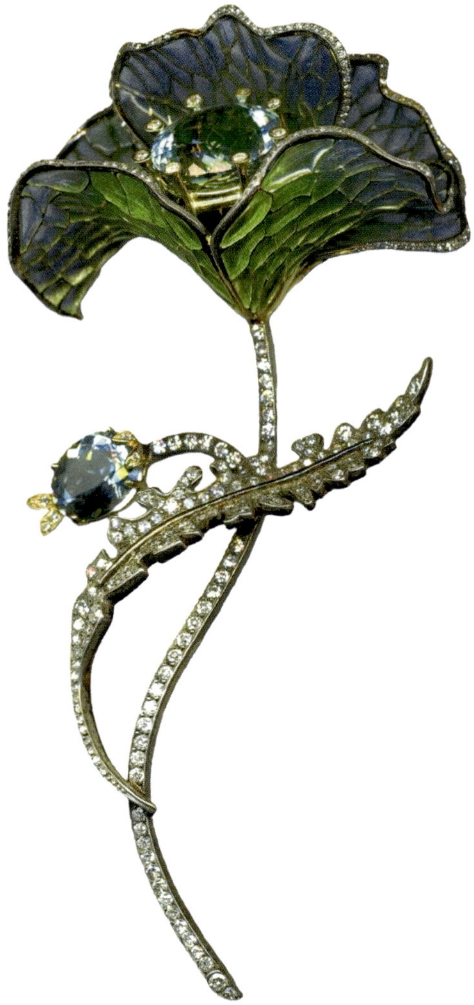

Poppy
Moira
1998

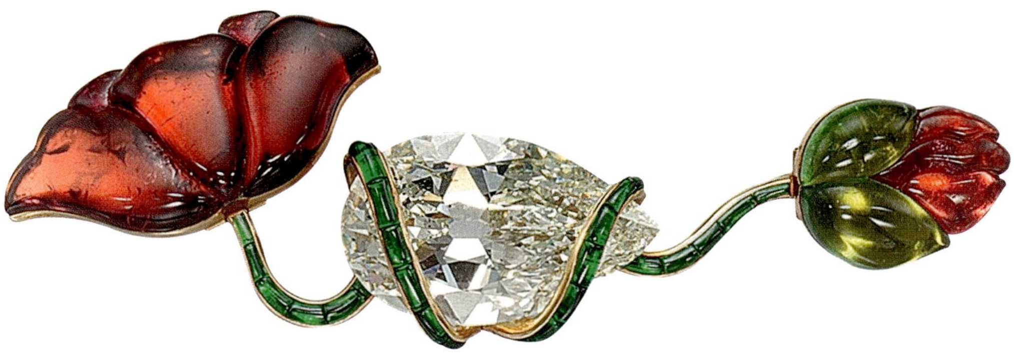

Poppy
JAR
1982

to sketch floral details they saw in the street, on architectural pediments, iron work and stone urns. Cartier created a new modern 'garland style' of perfectly balanced neoclassical compositions of foliages, sprays, petals and blossoms, set in platinum. The 'garland style' did not borrow directly from nature, but was inspired by the Greek and Roman interpretation of flowers.

During the 1930s, Cartier moved towards a more stylised form of geometric and linear motifs, with flowers and leaves created from flat carved emeralds, ruby seed beads and sapphires. Named 'tutti frutti', this was a European rendition of the Mughal Tree of Life, the combination of the stones redolent of heady fragrances of fruit, flowers and colours in a lavish Indian garden.

Gradually, under the influence of its director of fine jewellery, Jeanne Toussaint, Cartier's flowers began to look more figurative, chiming with the new freedom of dress given to women by Toussaint's close friend Gabrielle Chanel. Women were now starting to move away from the strict social codes governing jewellery.

Diamonds and precious stones became the pistils, stems, petals and leaves as the Cartier flower moved away from classicism and towards a naturalistic realism. There was a greater freedom in stone cuts, articulation and subtle movement, allowing flowers to display natural grace and fragility in complex designs of buds, open blossoms, as well as petals, with tear-shaped gaps suggesting they were about to fall. Such was the profusion of flowers that the glamorous muse to Dior, Mitzah Bricard, advised, 'When a man wants to buy you flowers say "My florist is Cartier".'

> *This time they [Cartier] have turned their attention to the fragility of flowers, interpreting this freely, in a style that echoes nature. This work requires volume. Depth without heaviness is obtained in various ways. Raised cabochon stones are used. The metal itself is rolled, folded, teased into shells. It gives the impression of a ribbon, or a malleable fabric. The onlooker expects the designs to move, to come to life!*
>
> *Vogue*, August 1936

Toussaint created floral bouquets with stylish panache and wit each Christmas, such as brooches with tiny posies offered by an outstretched hand carved in lapis lazuli, onyx or coral. One diamond, emerald, round-faceted beaded ruby and sapphire bouquet was tied with twisted gold wire and wrapped in golden paper as if just taken from the florist.

Traditionally, plate-sized yellow sunflowers weren't included in jewellery sprays, as they towered above other summer flowers, their burnished golden flower heads resting on giant stems with coarse leaves. Sunflowers are native to the Americas, cultivated from 3000 BC by American Indians, as a source of medicine, food and body paint. Incas worshipped the flower as a symbol of the sun god, and had depictions of the flower engraved on breast plates of

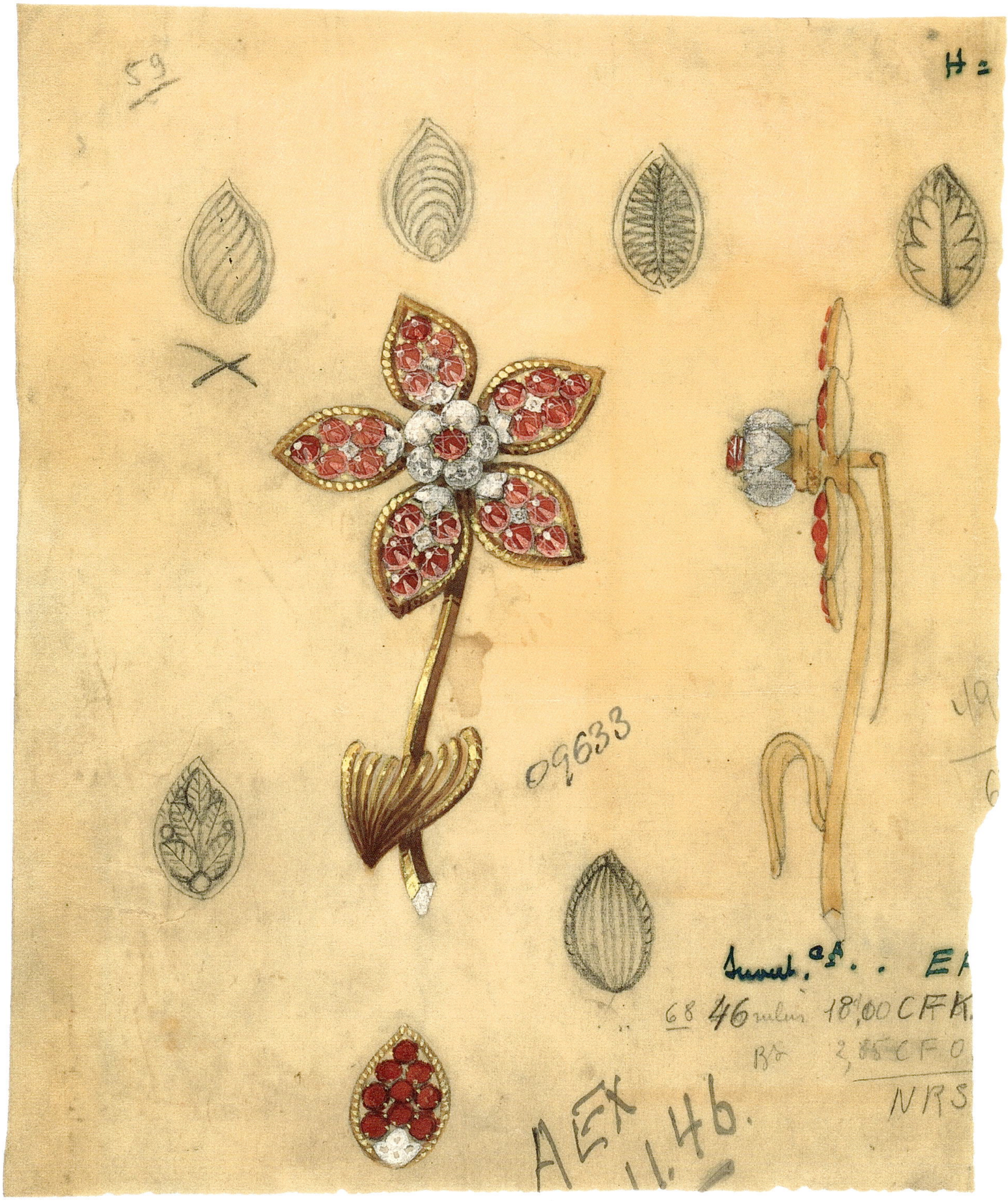

Design for Flower Brooch

Jeanne Toussaint,
Cartier Paris
1947

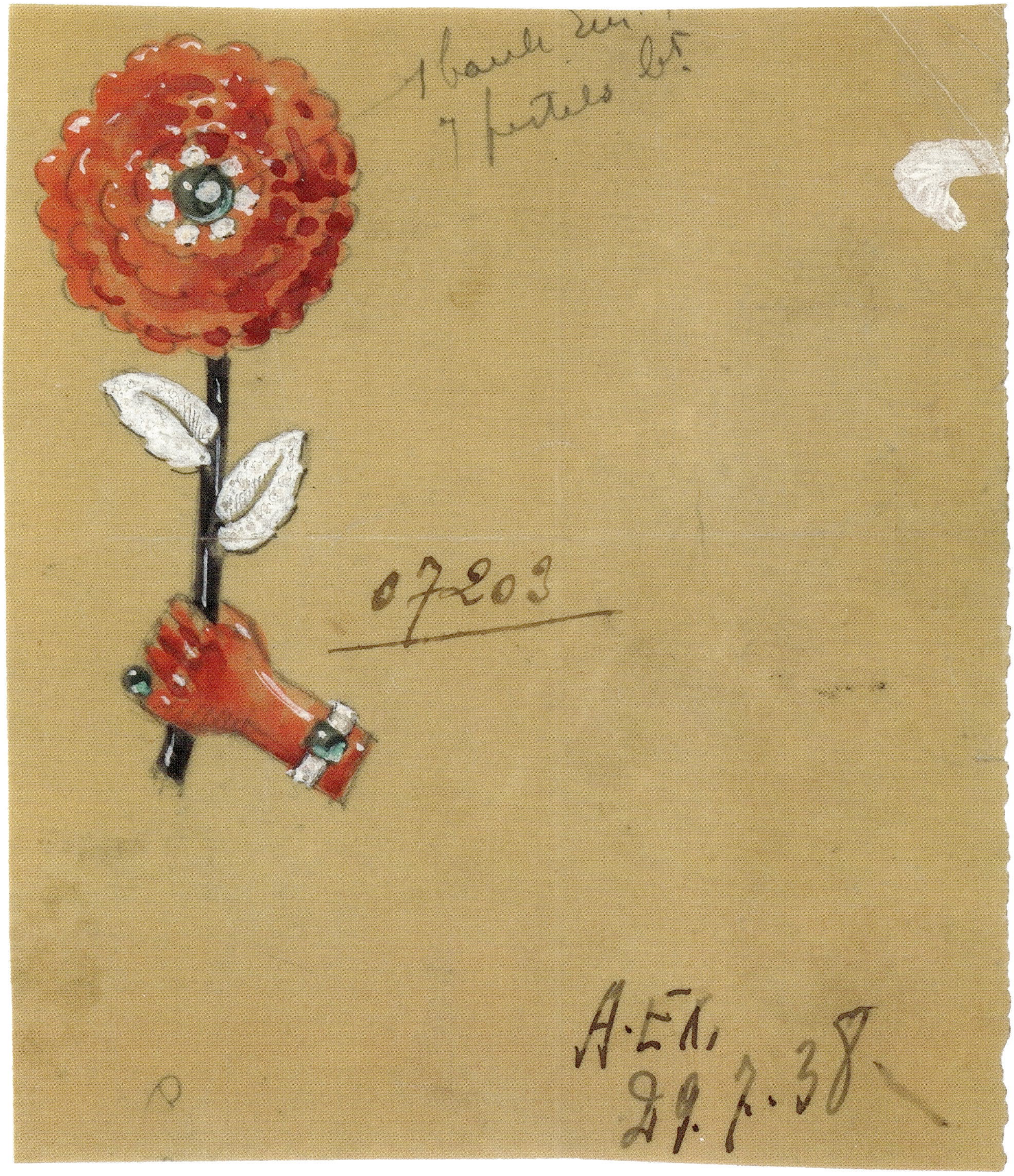

Design for Flower Brooch
Jeanne Toussaint,
Cartier Paris
1938

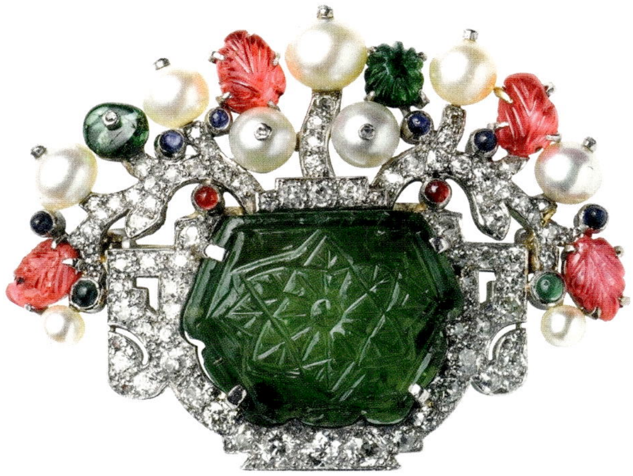

Bouquet
Cartier London
1928

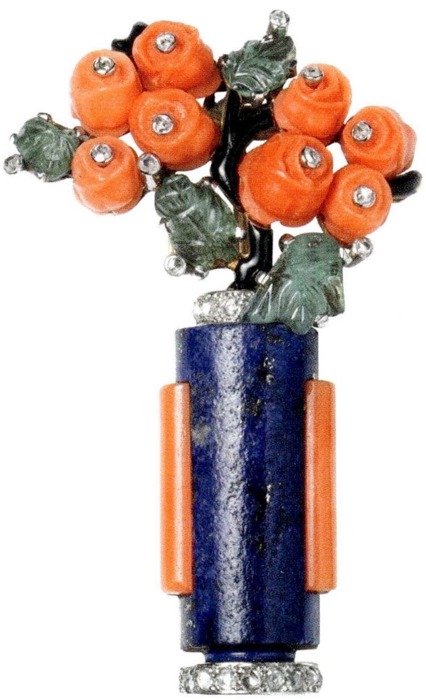

Bouquet
Cartier Paris
1938

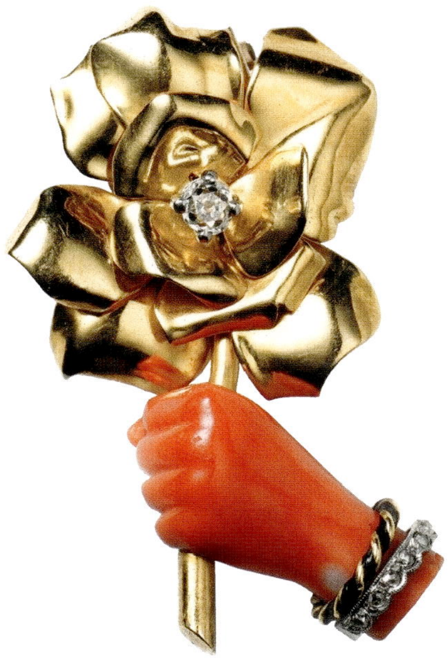

Rose
Cartier Paris
1938

pure gold. Early Spanish explorers took seeds to Europe in the sixteenth century, where the plant dazzled gardeners, couturiers, artists, jewellers and botanical collectors, with its dramatic colour and size.

The sunflower quickly became associated with adoration and marital fidelity because it exhibited 'heliotropism', devotedly following the course of the sun across the sky. The Greeks believed that the water nymph Clytie fell in love with the sun god Helio; for a time the love was reciprocated, but when he tired of her the forlorn Clytie sat day after day slowly turning her head to watch Helio move across the sky in his chariot. The gods eventually took pity on the love-sick girl, turning her into a brilliant flower, always following the path of the sun.

Her gold hair fell on the wall of gold
Like the delicate gossamer tangle spun
On the burnished disk of the marigold,
Or the sun-flower turning to meet the sun

In the Gold Room: A Harmony
Oscar Wilde

Their sunny disposition and simplicity made them an inspirational subject for the artist Vincent van Gogh at different times during his life. He painted them when he first arrived in Paris, where they grew on the slopes of Montmartre, as well as in his final canvas in 1890. He also began a series of sunflower paintings while waiting for his friend Paul Gauguin to arrive in Arles to share his studio, believing that the canvases would brighten up his companion's room.

When Van Gogh paints sunflowers, he reveals, or achieves, the vivid relations between himself, as a man, and the sunflower, as sunflower, at that quick moment of time. His painting does not represent the sunflower itself. We shall never know what the sunflower itself is.

Morality and the Novel
D. H. Lawrence

The symbolic connections of the sunflower with warmth, and its bold yellow colour and shape, which lent itself easily to stylisation, made it the emblem of choice for the nineteenth-century Aesthetic Movement, whose exponents included Dante Gabriel Rossetti, William Morris and James McNeill Whistler.

Flowers have an expression of countenance as much as men and animals. Some seem to smile; some have a sad expression; some are pensive and diffident; others again are plain, honest, and upright, like the broad-faced sunflower and the hollyhock.

Star Papers
Harry Ward Beecher

This coterie of artist friends and poets was dedicated to the 'cult of beauty', sharing a modern set of ideas that challenged existing concepts of art. Their taste for intense colours, exotic subjects and vibrant naturalistic motifs such

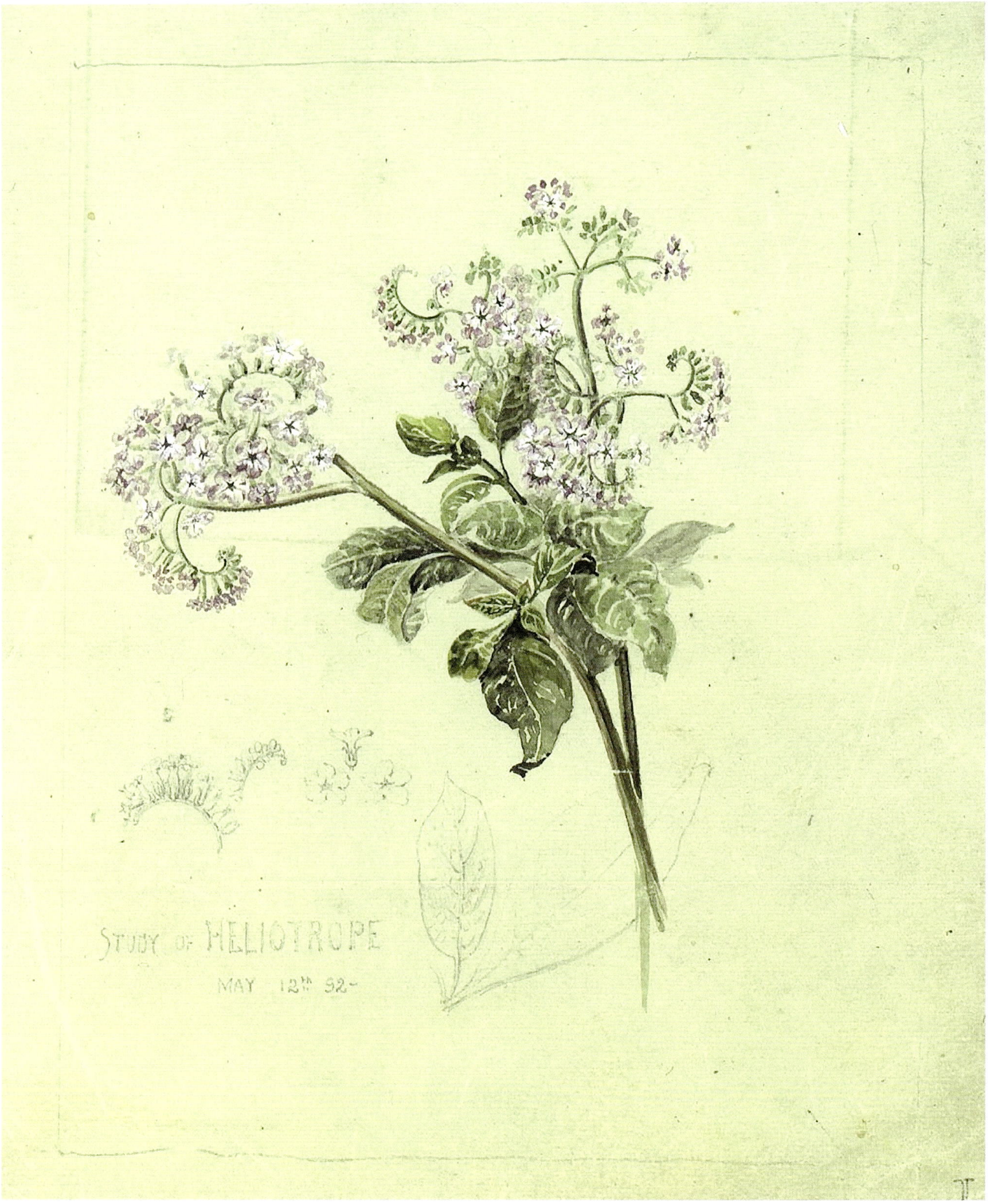

Heliotrope
Tiffany & Co.
1892

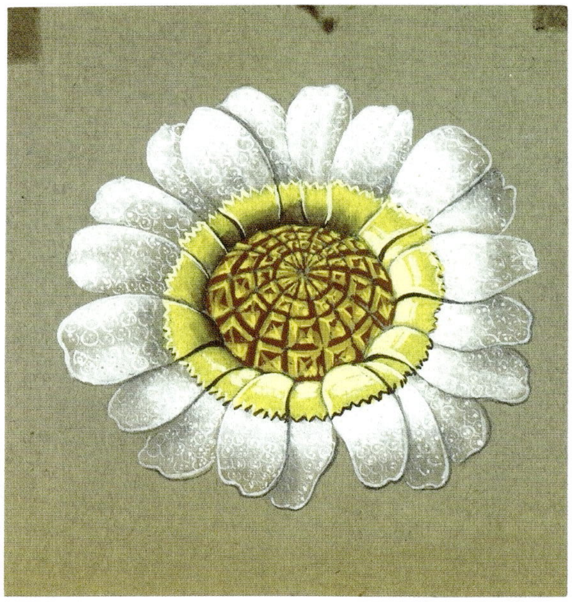

Sunflower
Tiffany & Co.
1940

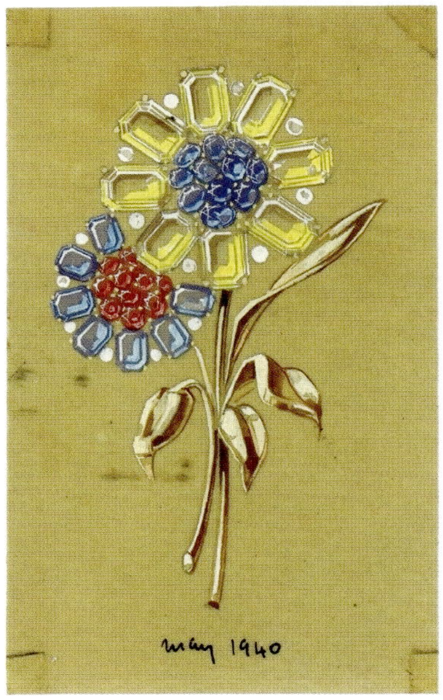

Sunflowers
Tiffany & Co.
1940

as the sunflower caught the public's attention. Oscar Wilde, as a disciple of the movement, frequently carried or wore a sunflower.

The warmth and glow of yellow gold was particularly fashionable during the 1940s, when the vogue in cocktail jewellery was for large pleated and knotted gold pieces featuring three-dimensional naturalistic flowers. Diamonds were in short supply, due to the blocking of trade routes during the war, so bright stones such as yellow citrine emerged from Brazil. Tulle, worked gold and the cheerful-coloured citrine made a perfect combination for the large sunflower clusters. One Cartier sunflower has a large 96.9-carat citrine central floret, with diamonds and quartz leaves that gently fall back like a fringe, as the citrine moves towards the light.

Jean Schlumberger set a rare Ceylon sapphire, known as the Dancing Girl of India, into the centre of a gold sunflower with garnet dust in a terracotta pot for Mrs Paul Mellon, as a witty tribute to her love of gardening.

One summer bloom that needs no tending in the garden and which grows with wild abandon is the pink, purple and blue thistle. The ancient Celtic symbol of nobility of character and birth, it has a stem of prickly thorns adapted to enable the flower to administer punishment on provocation.

The thistle is the order for dignity and antiquity;
the veritable nemo me impune lacessit *of chivalry.*

The Last of the Mohicans
James Fenimore Cooper

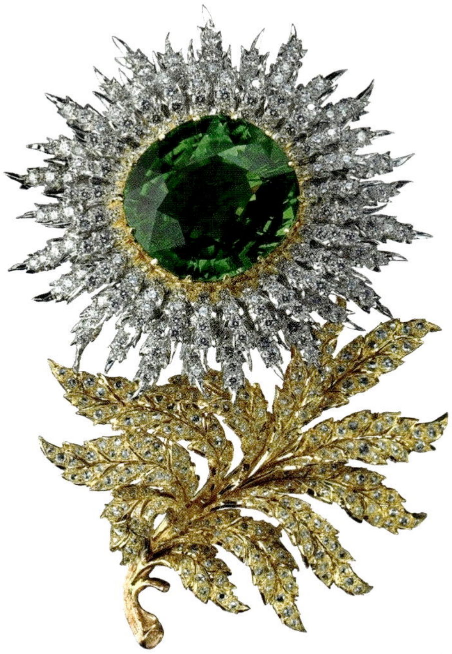

Sunflower
Buccellati
2010

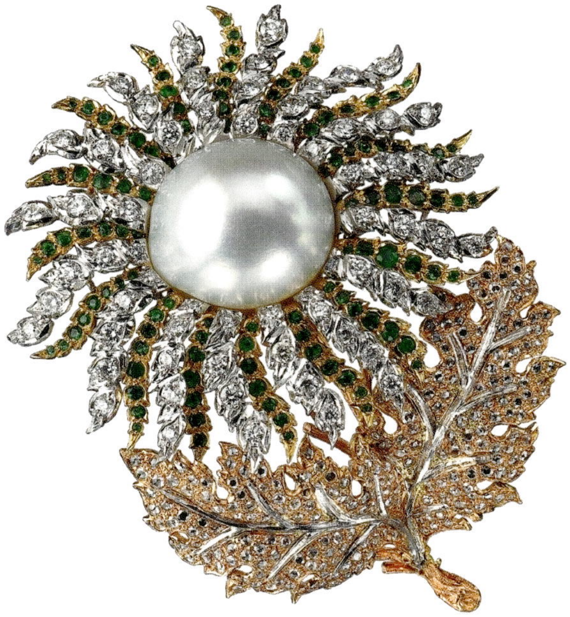

Sunflower
Buccellati
2012

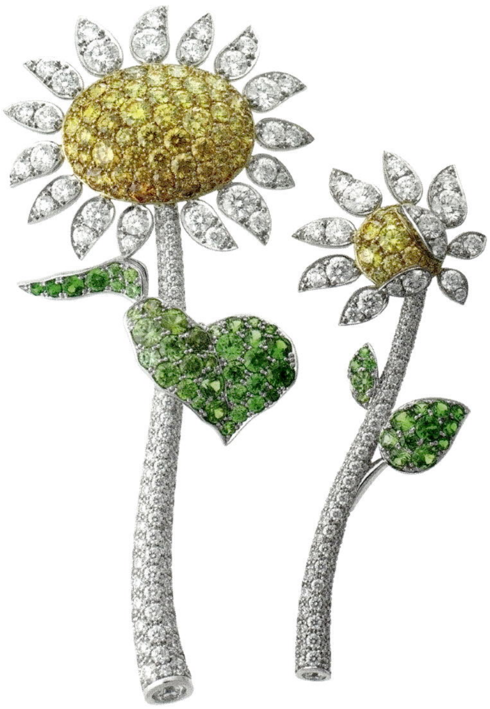

Sunflowers
Gimel
2000 (left) and 2003 (right)

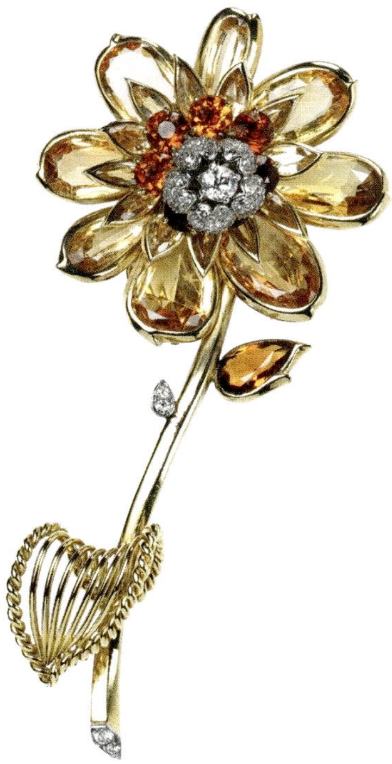

Sunflower
Cartier London
1943

According to legend, an invading Norse army landed in Scotland at night, removing their footwear to launch a silent surprise attack on sleeping Scottish clansmen. One Norse soldier, stepping on a thistle, cried out in pain, which raised the alarm and saved the sleeping Scots.

Go you to a brook hollow where they grow some late summer twilight at dewfall; and on the still air that rises suddenly to meet you will come a waft of faint, aromatic fragrance, wondrously sweet and evasive the distillation of that despised thistle bloom.

The Golden Road
Lucy Maud Montgomery

The thistle is the symbol of the Scottish monarchy. In 1503, the court poet William Dunbar penned a poem to celebrate the marriage of Margaret Tudor, represented by a rose, to James IV of Scotland, entitled 'The Thissil and the Rois'. It's a dream vision in which Dame Nature comes to inspect the plants and judges the spiked thistle to be 'able for war', crowning it the King of Plants with a 'radiant crown of rubys', representative of the king's ambition to defend his kingdom.

His [Thistledown elf's] purple mantle and doublet of green were embroidered with the brightest thread and the plume of his cap came always from the wings of the gayest butterfly.

Flower Fables
Louisa May Alcott

The thistle, as a metaphor for determination, is perfectly suited to being represented by the diamond, whose name is derived from the Greek *adamas*, meaning invincible. The thistle was the plant most often used by Lalique, who liked the contrast of the coarse stem and leaves with the soft petals and thistledown, often depicting it in frosted glass. The bulb of a Cartier thistle is crowned with baguette-cut diamonds; the elongated shape, set with a sense of disorder, composed of curved leaves, suggests the flower's prickly head.

Van Cleef & Arpels have drawn inspiration from the thistle since 1935, using marquise-cut diamonds in Mystery settings, the large flowering heads set from the back to suggest the plant's prickly nature. Some thistles in their bejewelled garden have diamond bombe flower heads, bordered by sapphires on diamond stems, while other thistles in profile are wrapped around a 9.72 carat pink sapphire in full blossom.

Why don't you… wear a blue sapphire thistle in one ear and a ruby thistle in the other? On each lapel a larger thistle, the colour reversed.

Harper's Bazaar, November 1937
Diana Vreeland

Being an emblem of royalty, as well as being in vogue at the time, thistles became a popular jewel with the Duchess of Windsor. In the 1940s, she owned a white diamond flower head and stem set by Cartier, with dashing pink diamonds exploding out of the top.

Another thistle was made for the duchess by Fulco Verdura, who had heard from various sources that at dinner parties she regularly claimed to have designed it herself. Sometime later, she approached Verdura to see if she could exchange it for a rose-bud pin, in pink topaz and emeralds, with gold-fringed emerald leaves, which had just appeared in a *Harper's Bazaar* feature shot by Richard Avedon. 'Alas I cannot,' he answered, 'you see everything here is designed by me and I understand this thistle is your design.'

They lay on their heathery beds and listened to all the sounds of the night. They heard the little grunt of a hedgehog going by. They saw the flicker of bats overhead. They smelt the drifting scent of honeysuckle, and the delicious smell of wild thyme crushed under their bodies. A reed-warbler sang a beautiful little song in the reeds below, and then another answered.

The Secret Island
Enid Blyton

The tall, stately foxglove was another quintessential wild flower, raised up from deep hollows and woody dells into a fine jewel by René Boivin. The tall spires of tubular flowers, called fairy's gloves, caps or thimbles, blooming in midsummer with speckled throats, were realised in pink tourmaline and amethyst articulated petals with a ruby circular top and olivine leaves in one type of brooch, and in other varieties of brooch with pear-shaped diamonds with emerald leaves. The elegant flower was popularised by the nineteenth-century horticulturist and collaborator of Sir Edwin Lutyens, Gertrude Jekyll, who liked to add the graceful purple and pink bells of the foxglove to her white planting schemes. Jekyll found comparisons between plants and textures, as well as a similar use of colour by painters and gardeners. Had she seen Boivin's foxglove, she would have noted how the colours chimed with the most magnificent purple wild flushed foxglove she could grow.

What is there to say about June, the time of the perfect young summer, the fulfilment of the promise of the earlier months, and with as yet no sign to remind one that its fresh beauty will ever fade.

Wood and Garden
Gertrude Jekyll

The rippled and frilly-edged sweet pea encapsulates the sweet scent of the June garden. All sweet peas are descended from one wild plant, brought to cultivation by a monk called Franciscus Cupani, who was compiling a flora of Sicily and sent seeds to plant collectors in the late seventeenth century. Jeweller Glenn Spiro

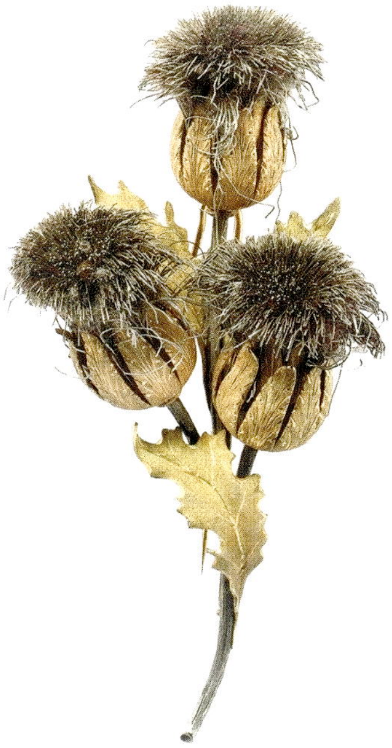

Thistle
Buccellati
Mid 20th century

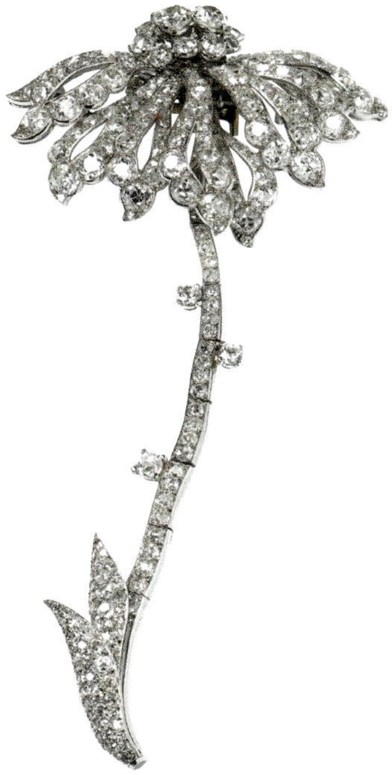

Thistle
Cartier Paris
1941

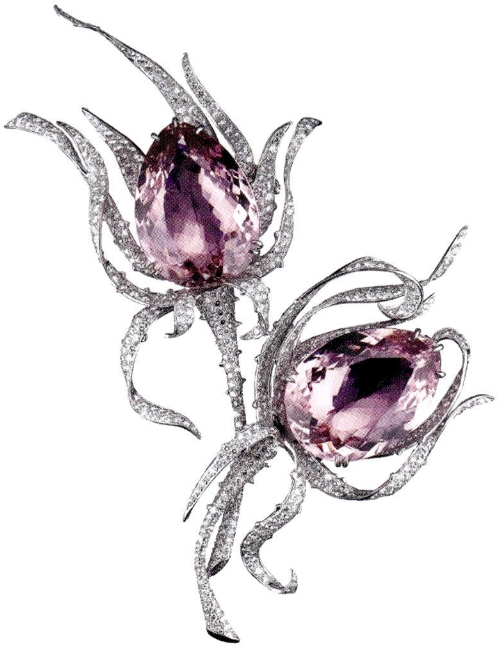

Thistle
Michelle Ong
2000

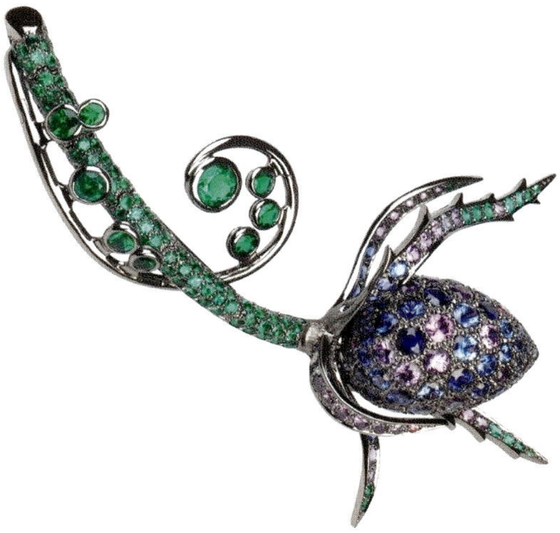

Thistle
Boucheron
2009

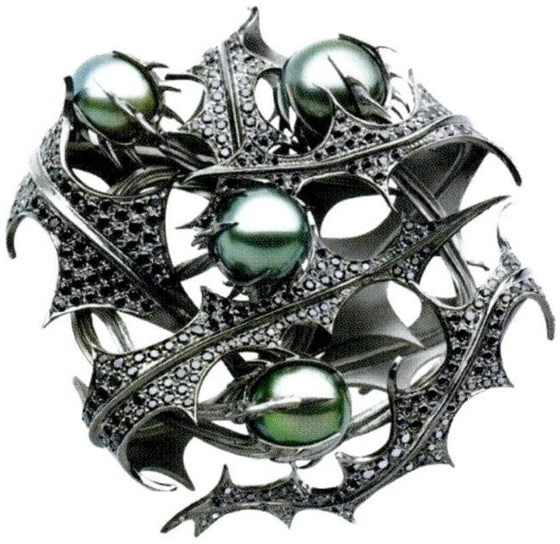

Thistle
Shaun Leane
2006

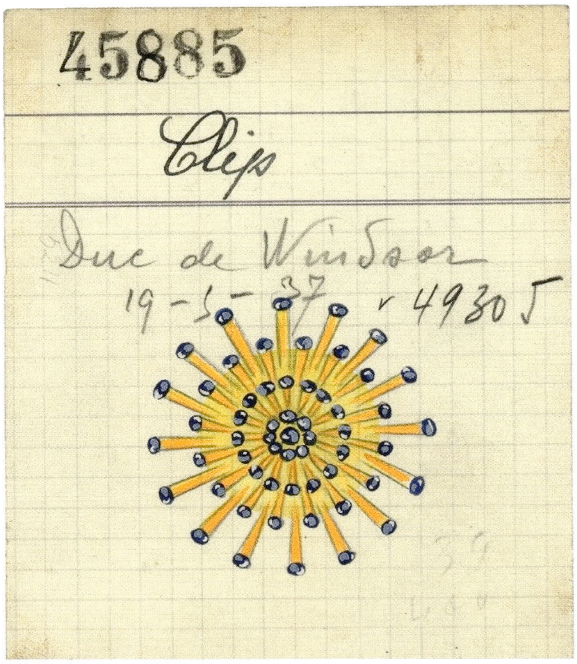

Thistle
Van Cleef & Arpels
1936

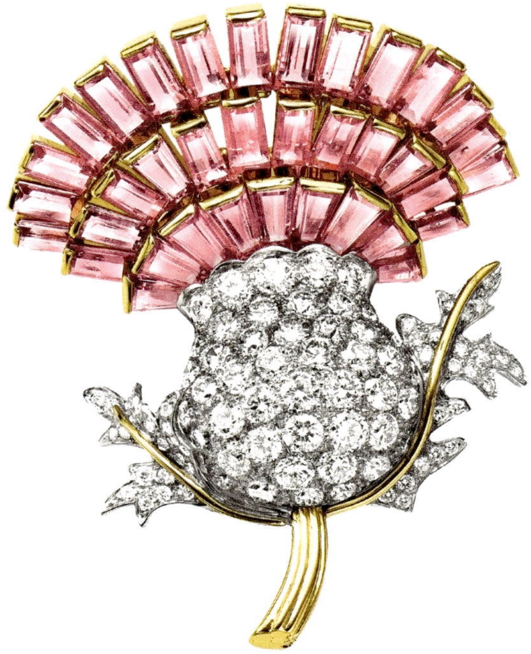

Thistle
Verdura
2005

does not like the frilled and fluted delicate petals of his jewelled sweet peas to be too perfect, setting the stones in a deliberately asymmetric manner.

Here are sweet peas, on tip-toe for a flight:
With wings of gentle flush o'er delicate white,
And taper fingers catching at all things,
To bind them all about with tiny rings.

I Stood Tip-Toe Upon a Little Hill
John Keats

Spiro takes inspiration for his floral creations from his daily walk past the flower stall on the corner of London's Bond Street, as well as his meanderings through gardens when he is on holiday. One local flower on the Caribbean island of Mustique was brought back in a plastic bag, so he could study the white stems and vibrant red and green flowers. 'I don't want to copy the flower as such', he says, 'it gives me an idea and then I sit and play around with stones to find the right combination of colours.' He likes soft pastel shades, much like those in his romantic English garden in the South of France, where beds of fragrant lavender have a 'collar' of white flowers surrounding them, and the delicate pinks of the bougainvillea that covers his Saint-Tropez house.

And then, opening her eyes, how fresh like frilled linen
clean from a laundry laid in wicker trays the roses looked;
and dark and prim the red carnations, holding their heads up;
and all the sweet peas spreading in their bowls, tinged violet,
snow white, pale – as if it were the evening and girls in muslin frocks
came out to pick sweet peas and roses after the superb summer's
day, with its almost blue-black sky, its delphiniums, its carnations,
its arum lilies was over; and it was the moment between six and
seven when every flower – roses, carnations, irises, lilac – glows;
white, violet, red, deep orange, every flower seems to burn by
itself, softly, purely in the misty beds; and how she loved the
grey-white moths spinning in and out, over the cherry pie,
over the evening primroses!

Mrs Dalloway
Virginia Woolf

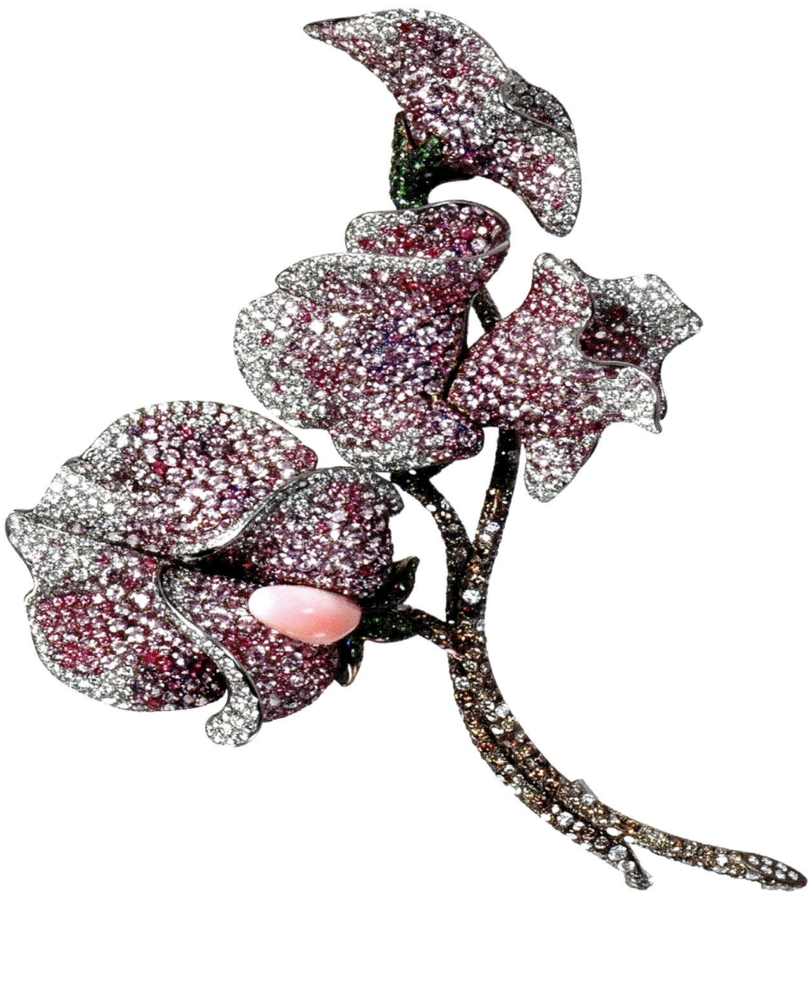

Sweet Pea
Glenn Spiro
2008

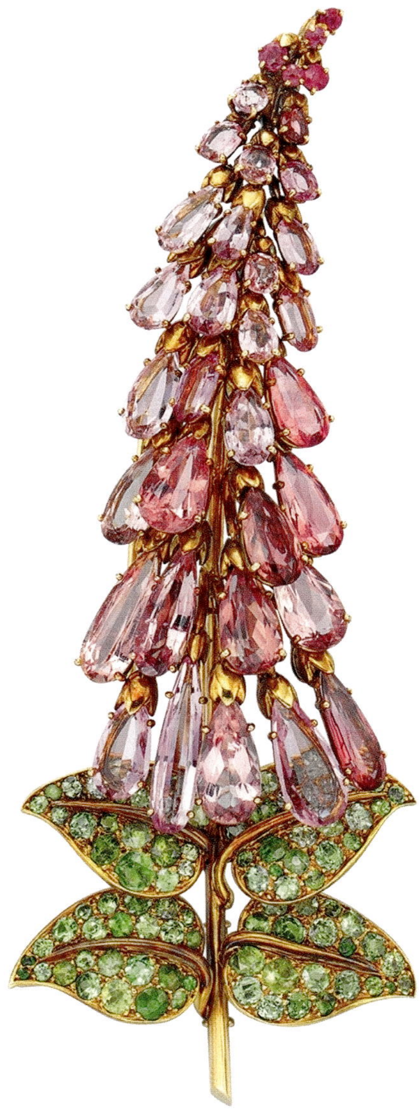

Foxglove
Boivin
1944

The majestic lily also makes a fragrant motif for gemstone brooches in brightly coloured spotted tiger lily styles, with curly petals rendered in vibrant precious stones, or the elegant trumpet of the white Madonna lily in immaculate white diamonds.

We are lilies fair,
The flower of virgin light;
Nature held us forth, and said,
'Lo! My thoughts of white.

Songs and Chorus of the Flower
Leigh Hunt

There are depictions of the flower preserved on frescoes in Pompeii, where they hid their sweetness for centuries under volcanic ash. In Roman legend, when Venus, the goddess of love, rose from the water, she caught sight of a lily; envious of its beauty, she arranged the long pistil at the centre of the flower to make it less attractive. The bright colours of the lily attract pollinating insects, and the long erotic pistils, laden with pollen, have been associated with love, lust and fertility. The Victorians thought the flower was too sexual, so cut out the stamens and pistils.

Paradoxically, although the lily was generally associated with love and lust, the white Madonna lily was symbolic of virgins, as it was believed that lilies sprung from the repentant tears of Eve as she left the Garden of Eden. The flower was grown in the Garden of Gethsemane, so it was given the name the 'white-robed apostle of hope', becoming a potent symbol of purity. Lilies were a much-used floral accessory in Christian art, appearing in Annunciation scenes by artists from Hans Memling to Dante Gabriel Rossetti, where they were often placed in a vase in front of Mary, or presented to her by the Angel Gabriel. The stainless white flower symbolised Mary's purity and the golden stamen her soul.

And the stately lilies stand
Fair in the silvery light,
Like saintly vestals, pale in prayer;
Their pure breath sanctifies the air
As its fragrance fills the night.

A Red Rose
Julia C. R. Dorr

From the late sixteenth century onwards, exotic varieties of lilies arrived from North America, as well as Asiatic lilies from China and Japan. By 1900, the tiger-lily had become a cherished English garden flower. Gertrude Jekyll commented on how familiar it was, 'not only in our gardens, but in old pictures and in the samplers and embroideries of our great-grandmothers'.

The lily is a motif at Parisian jeweller Mellerio dits Meller, famed since 1613 for their naturalism, having created jewels for Marie-Antoinette and, after surviving the Revolution, for Empress Josephine too. As a symbol of the French monarchy, the diamond and pearl jewelled lilies have been crafted in homage to the pieces they made for Marie de' Medici, who was queen of France in the early seventeenth century. Mellerio's designer Édéenne was inspired by a painting by Rubens of Marie de' Medici wearing a royal coat embroidered with golden lily flowers, as well as the angel holding a white lily in Botticelli's *Annunciation*. The precious flowers are created in three floral styles: the lily growing naturally in the garden, a stylised flower and a poetic bud blossoming into a flower. A lily tiara boasts thirty-five diamond lilies and white pearls on a black velvet ribbon, and a high collar necklace is arranged with fifteen Burmese rubies and fifty-five carats of pavé-set diamond buds around three white South Sea pearls.

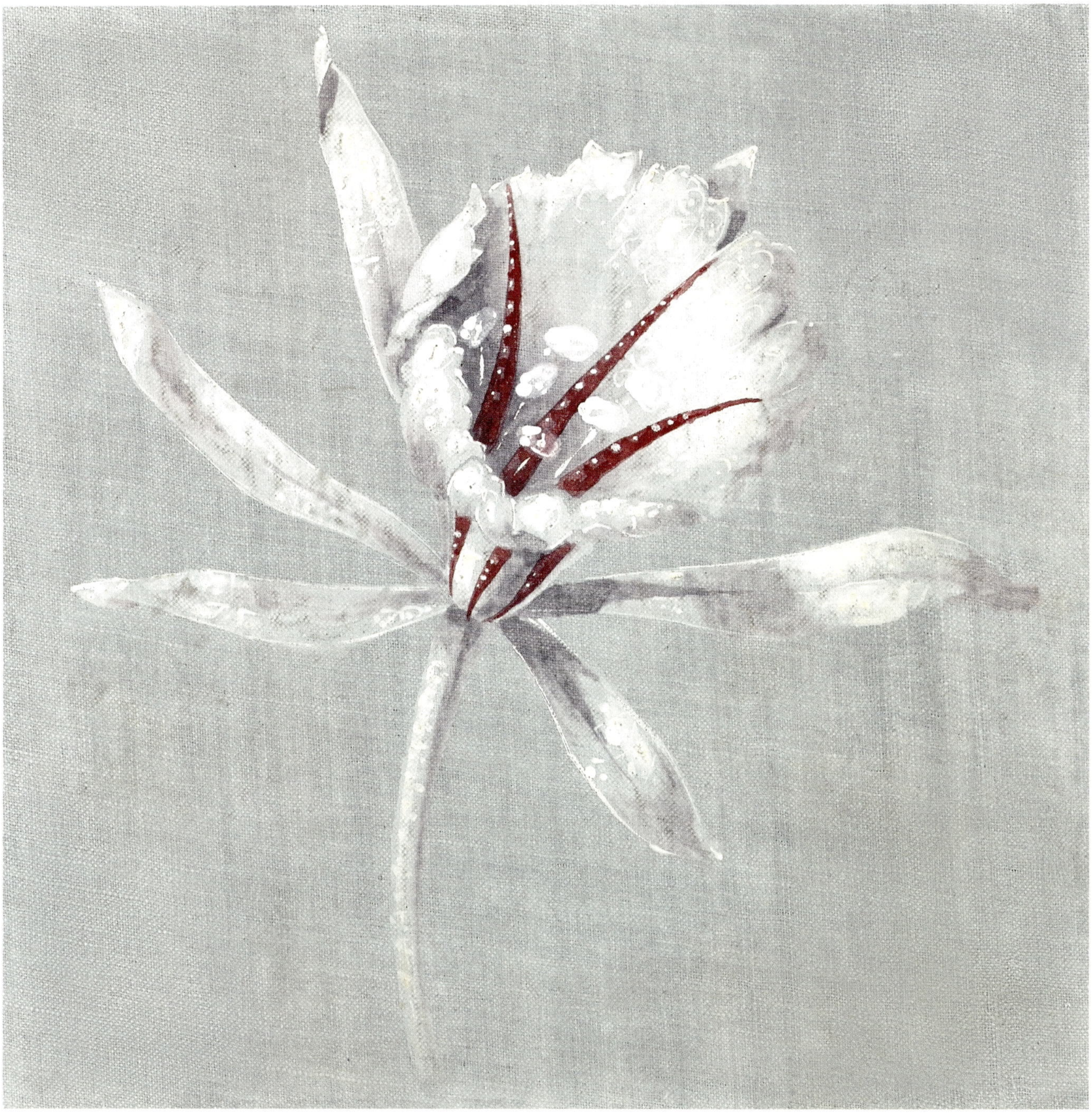

Lily
Chaumet
c. 1890–1900

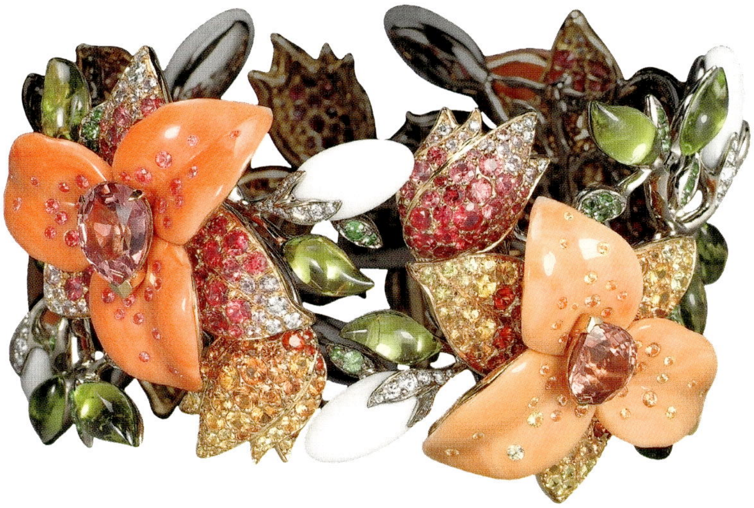

Lily
Lorenz Bäumer
2008

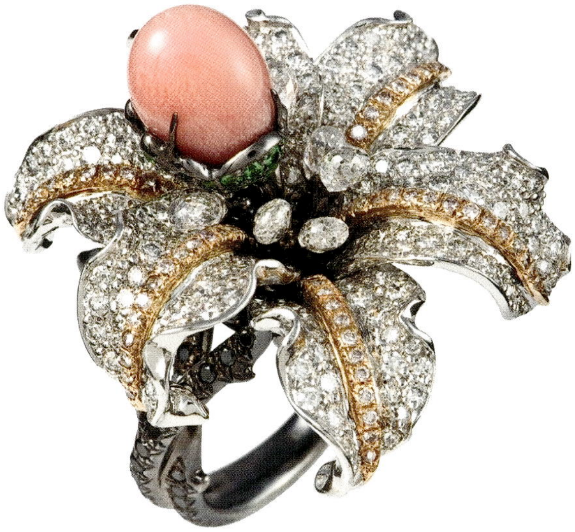

Lily
Cindy Chao
2009

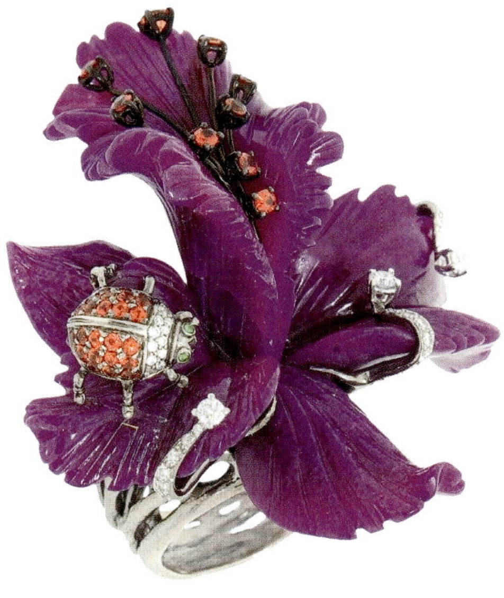

Lily
Lydia Courteille
1998

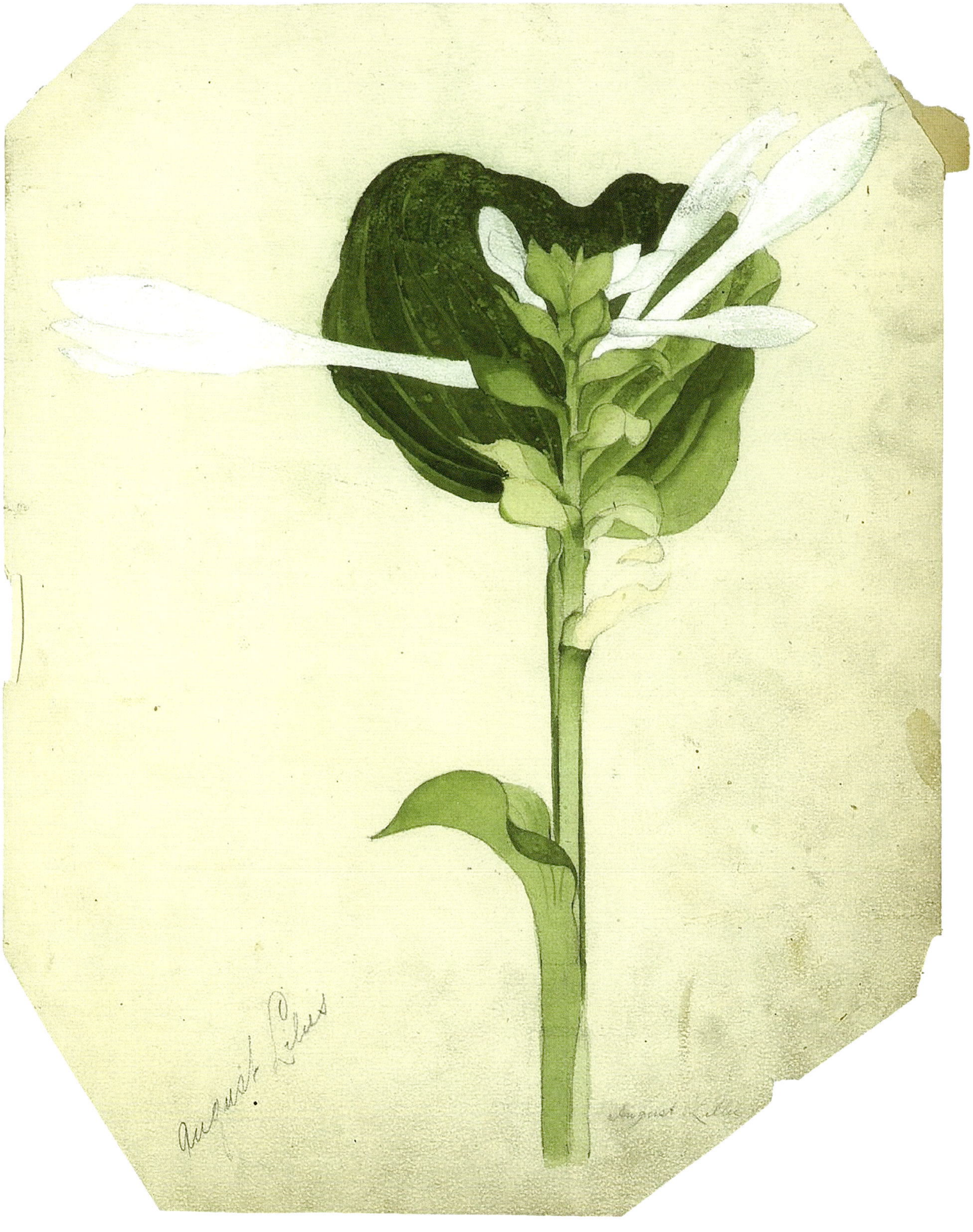

Lily

Tiffany & Co.

c. 1900

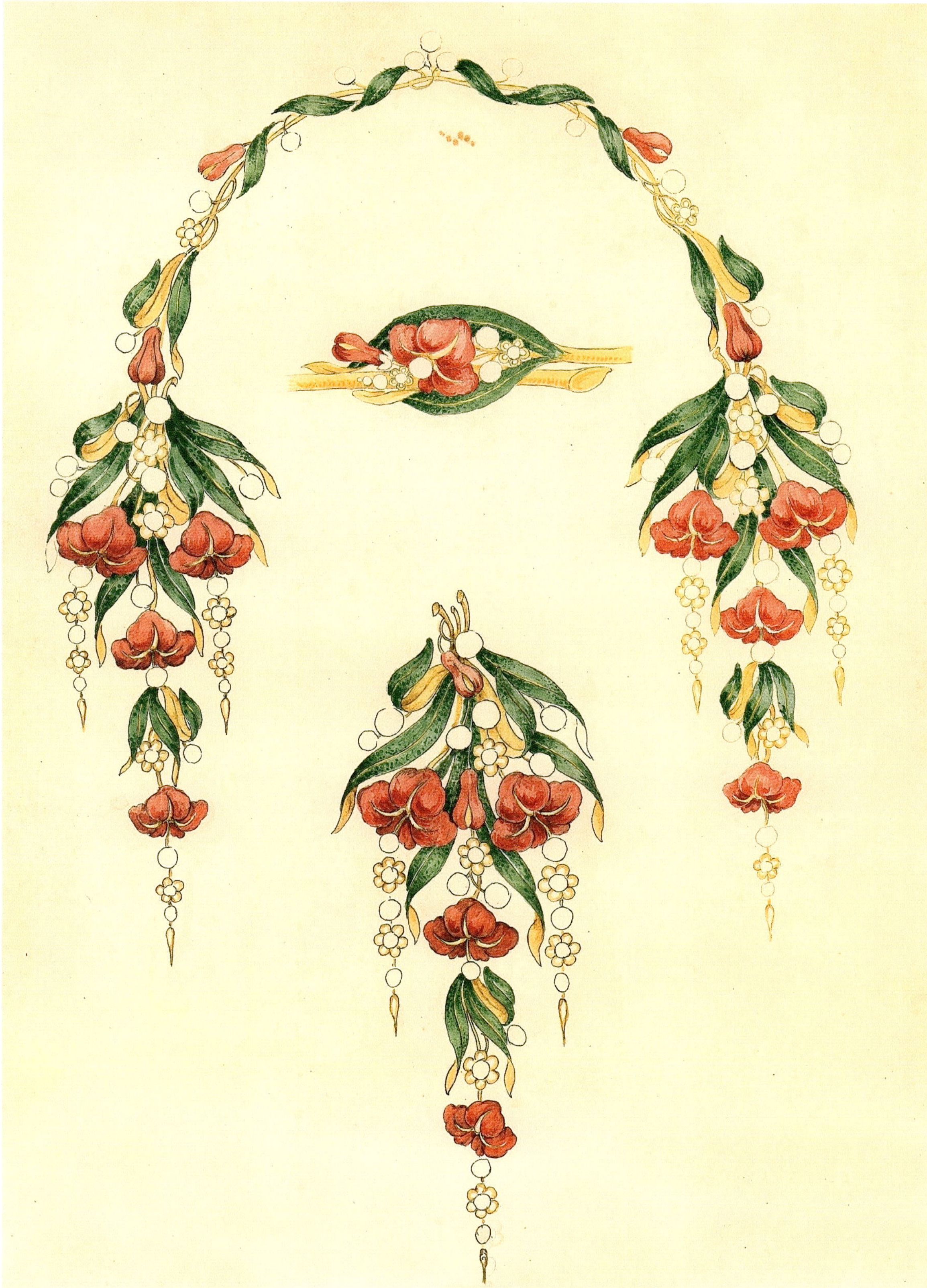

Lily
Mellerio dits Meller
c. 1840

I shall not entirely
Sit emptied of beauties, the gift
Of your small breath, the drenched grass
Smell of your sleeps, lilies, lilies.

The Night Dances
Sylvia Plath

The curling petals of Anna Hu's modern Turandot Lily are set with white and pink diamonds, suggesting translucency, with the anther pollen sacs at the tips of the stamens bursting with marquise-cut yellow diamonds, with natural Afghanistan Panjshir emerald beads in the centre. The calla lilies at Asprey curl their delicate diamond trumpets and coloured sapphire flowers in floral bracts around the finger. Parisian jewellery designer Lydia Courteille likes meadow flowers and herbs, which she picks from the fields around her old shepherd's house in the lavender fields of Provence. This secret garden surrounded by colour, fragrance and shapes inspires her calla lily designs in green turquoise, garnets and peridots, often with a small bug or ladybird hiding amongst the leaves, attracted by her vivid colours.

The reason we love the lily and the sunflower... is because these two lovely flowers are in England the two most perfect models of design ... the gaudy leonine beauty of the one and the precious loveliness of the other giving the artist the most entire and perfect joy.

Essays and Lectures
Oscar Wilde

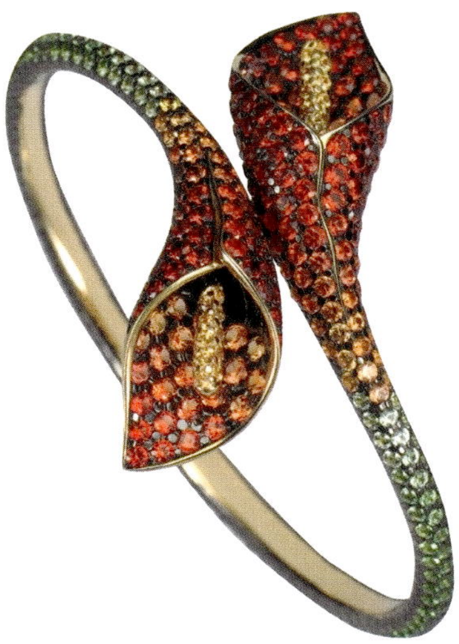

Calla Lily
Asprey
2010

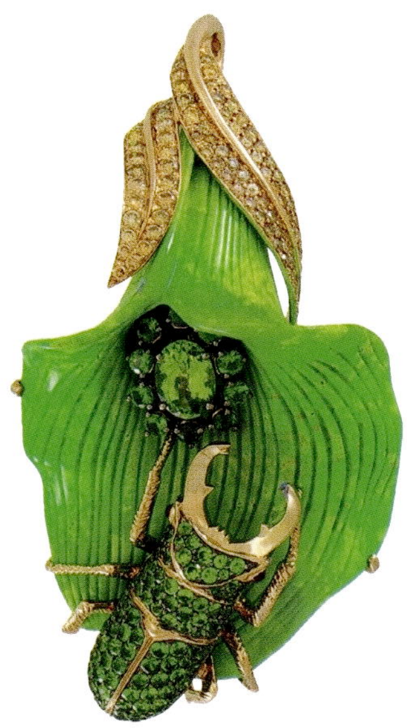

Calla Lily
Lydia Courteille
2010

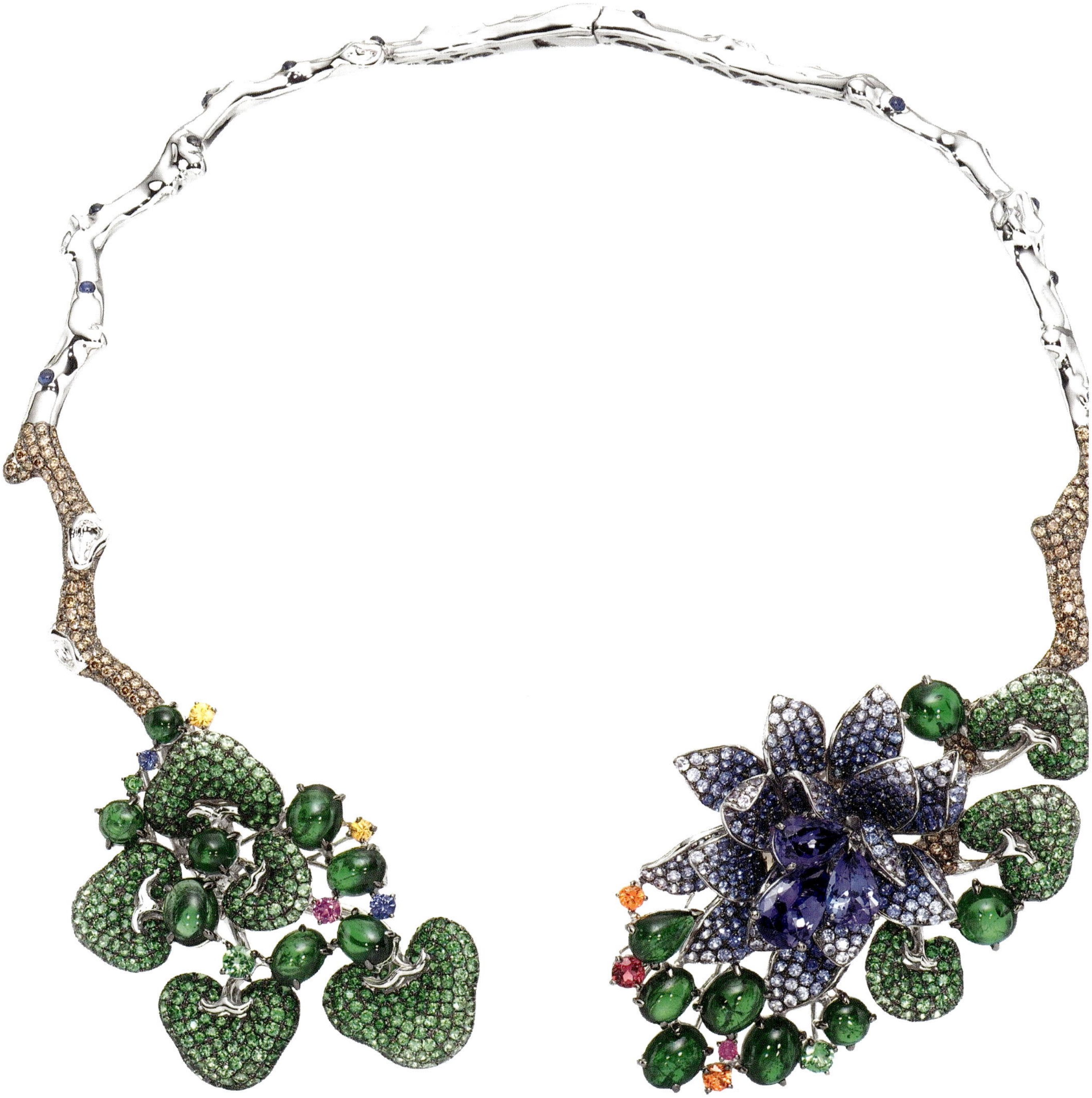

Blue Lotus
Wendy Yue
2013

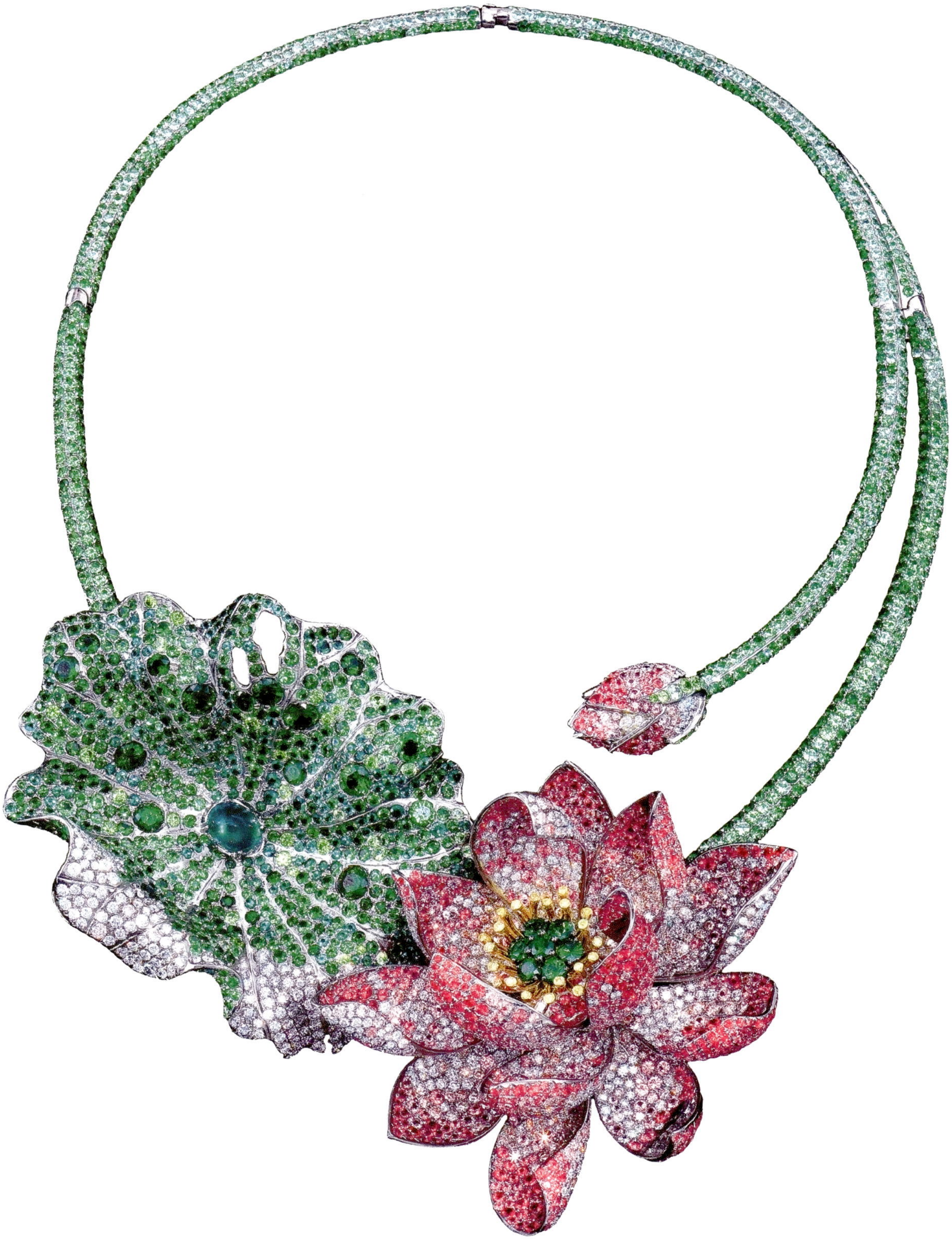

Celestial Lotus
Anna Hu
2010

The white Madonna lily is Europe's answer to the lotus flower, which originally bloomed along the Nile, painted on the walls of the temple of Karnak, signifying rebirth and transformation. Its roots are planted in the soil of a pond or at the bottom of a riverbed, whilst its buds rise to float on the surface. Attaching great significance to the symbolic meanings of plant life, Egyptians took the flower, often represented in lapis lazuli, carnelian and gold, to their burial chambers to sweeten the journey into the afterlife.

The lotus plant has been used in Chinese medicine for thousands of years to improve mental alertness, the petals and leaves suffused in tisanes, the rootlets pickled with rice vinegar and sugar, the seeds dried or boiled and sweetened with rock sugar.

The lotus flower is the symbol of Buddhism. Legend has it that wherever Buddha stepped a lotus flower blossomed; rather than footprints, he left a trail of flowers whose unfolding petals signified expansion of the soul. In meditation, the mystical union of energies is referred to as the 'jewel in the lotus', representing purity of mind and spiritual growth. In Hindu iconography, deities such as Ganga and Ganesha are depicted seated on opening lotus flowers, associating the flower with both the spiritual and decorative allure of the East.

I love the lotus because, while growing
from mud, it is unstained.
Zhou Dunyi

Queen Elizabeth the Queen Mother was given a lotus flower diamond and pearl tiara by Queen Mary, designed with stylised Egyptian-inspired blossoms, overreaching arches and graduated pinnacles surmounted by a single pearl. In 1934, a fascination with Egypt inspired a diamond lotus blossom and platinum tiara bought from Cartier by the Aga Khan. More recently, De Beers diamond jewellers have cultivated large exotic Asian varieties in stylised openwork diamond-set blossoms. In the Bal de Légende by Van Cleef & Arpels, an Asian jewelled fairy stands on a carved stone lotus leaf holding a lotus flower. For their 'Les jardins' collection, the same jeweller created an exotic Asian garden with a Zen-like serenity of precious pieces, featuring streams of sapphire beads with a pathway of diamonds, leading to a golden miniature temple, overflowing with precious-set lotus flowers. Heavy bunches of natural coloured pearls, vibrant orange garnets and rubies swung decoratively from miniature pagodas in oriental scenes.

'The images of the pond, the water and the interplay of light and shade have been an integral part of my memory ever since', says Anna Hu of a visit to Claude Monet's Giverny garden, which inspired his *Water Lilies* series of paintings. Hu designed a Water Lily necklace set with 2,000 deep pink sapphires, tsavorites, tourmalines, morganites, alexandrites, natural-coloured sapphires and pastel diamonds in pink, white and grey with a 45.22-carat tanzanite. Her Celestial Lotus necklace celebrates the East, depicting a lotus bud, leaf and flower using intense vivid yellow, grey and white diamonds with demantoid garnets, Colombian emeralds and Burmese red ruby blossom.

Another flower whose sweet heady fragrance drifts on light summer breezes is the rose, which entwines itself over arches, stone walls and pergolas, compelling comment on its showy beauty. The abundant blossoms in delicate colours with the textures of velvet and satin have captured the imagination of poets such as Blake, Browning and Keats. Artists and jewellers likewise express the romance of the rose – the round shape and softness has become the quintessential expression of femininity – and its long association with the profoundest of human emotions.

The rose looks fair, but fairer we it deem
For that sweet odour which doth in it live.

Sonnet 54
William Shakespeare

The rose has an ancient history, as evidenced by the existence of forty-million-year-old fossilised remains. Cleopatra filled her pillows with rose petals and strew them on the ground before Mark Antony. The flower first captured the West's imagination when it was introduced from China in the late eighteenth century. Rose parties became all the rage in Britain and America, where wealthy families such as the Vanderbilts would boast 50,000 different varieties of roses at a mid-winter party in New York during the 1880s.

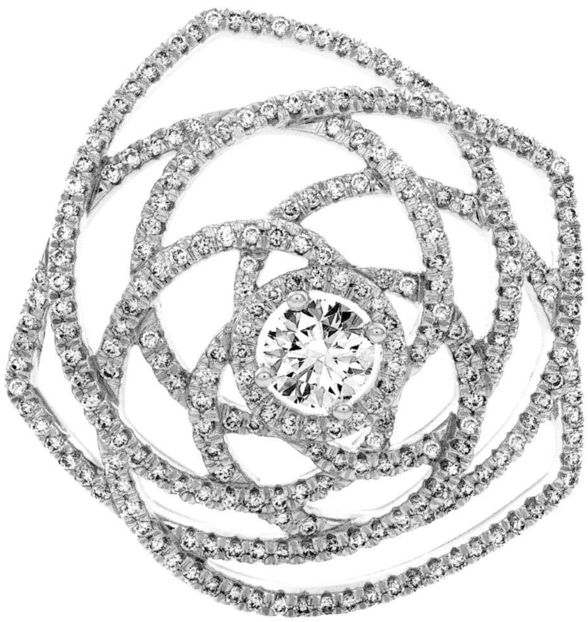

Lotus
De Beers
2009

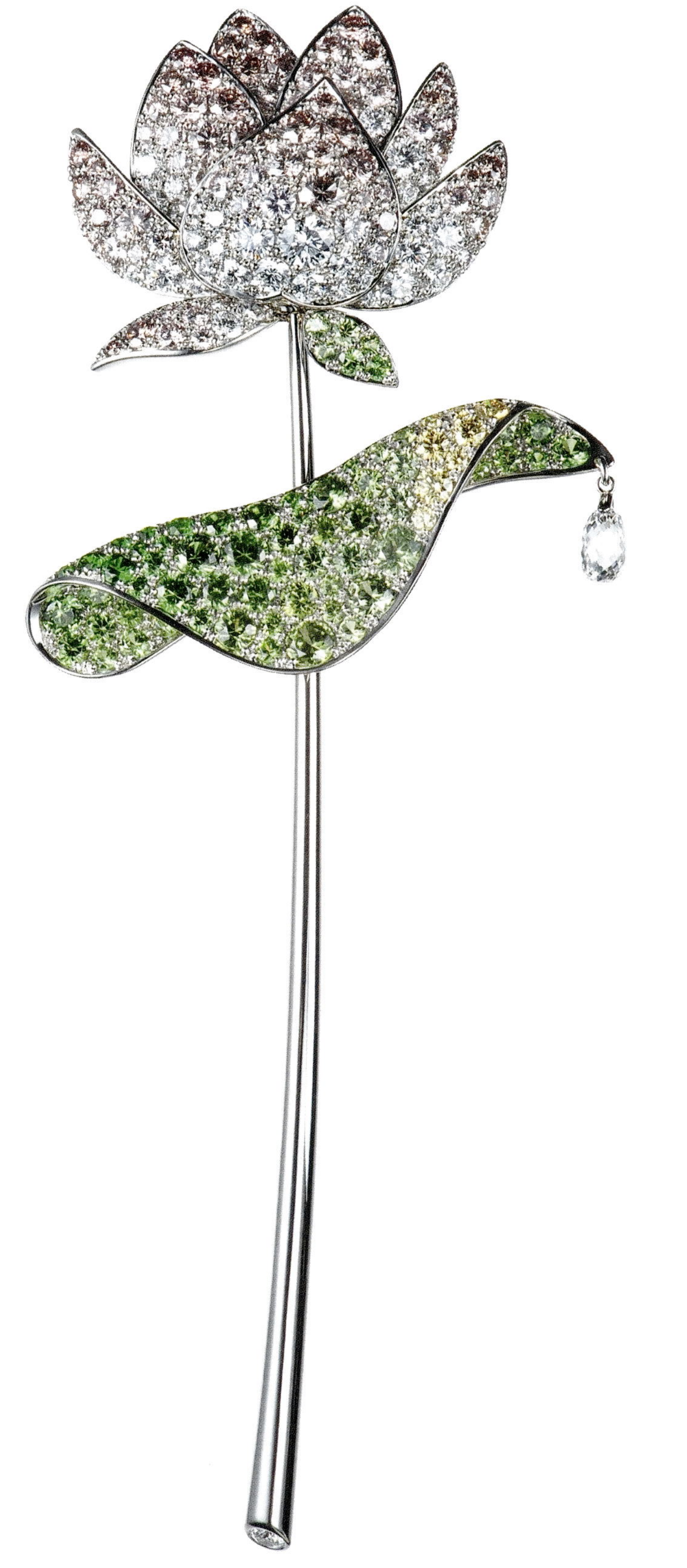

Lotus
Gimel
2001

Medieval Christians identified the rose with the Virgin Mary, whose epithets included Rose of Sharon and Queen of the most Holy Rose Garden, because she personified the first pure rose grown in the Garden of Eden. She was the rose without thorns, the red petals symbolic of her sorrow and the white her joy. Many medieval paintings depict Mary in a walled rose garden beneath a rose arbour or wreathed with a rose crown. These medieval gardens were laid out in a four-square design, mirroring the original harmony in the Garden of Eden, where four streams flowed out from the central Tree of Life.

The *Roman de la rose* (Romance of the Rose) is a French poem written in the thirteenth century that established the garden as a *locus amoenus*, an idealised place. The poem's young hero dreams of entering a large walled garden where 'no summer flower was absent, not broom nor violet nor periwinkle, not yellow nor indigo, nor white, while intertwined in places were great, broad, rose-leaves'. He enters in search of a beautiful rose he desires, which symbolises the lady of his obsession.

When I approached the rose, I found that it was a little
larger and saw that it had grown since the time I first saw it.
The rose was a little larger on the top, but I was pleased that
it had not opened enough to reveal the seed but was still enclosed
by the rose leaves, which stood up straight and filled the place
within, so that the seed with which the rose was full could
not appear. May God bless it, it was even more beautiful
and redder as it opened than it had been before, and I was
astounded at the wonder of it. Love bound me more and
more fairly as its beauty increased, and continually
tightened his knots as I experienced greater pleasure.

Roman de la rose
Guillaume de Lorris and Jean de Meun

Gothic cathedrals in medieval cities displayed circular rose windows, often dedicated to Mary, and during the sixteenth century the rose-cut or rosette diamonds with triangular facets arranged in symmetrical radiating patterns in circular shapes were created in the manner of a rose window to resemble the opening of a rose-bud.

Marie-Antoinette planted a rose garden at Le Petit Trianon in the grounds of Versailles, pruning prickly rose bushes wearing a sheer muslin gown. She spent extravagantly on landscaping and importing exotic plants, like her favourite tuberose from Mexico. According to Élisabeth de Feydeau, author of *From Marie-Antoinette's Garden: An Eighteenth-Century Horticultural Album*, 'The Temple of Love, in the dappled shade of two weeping willow trees, was built in the middle of an island planted with "paradise" apples, white pelote de neige roses, and lilacs...'

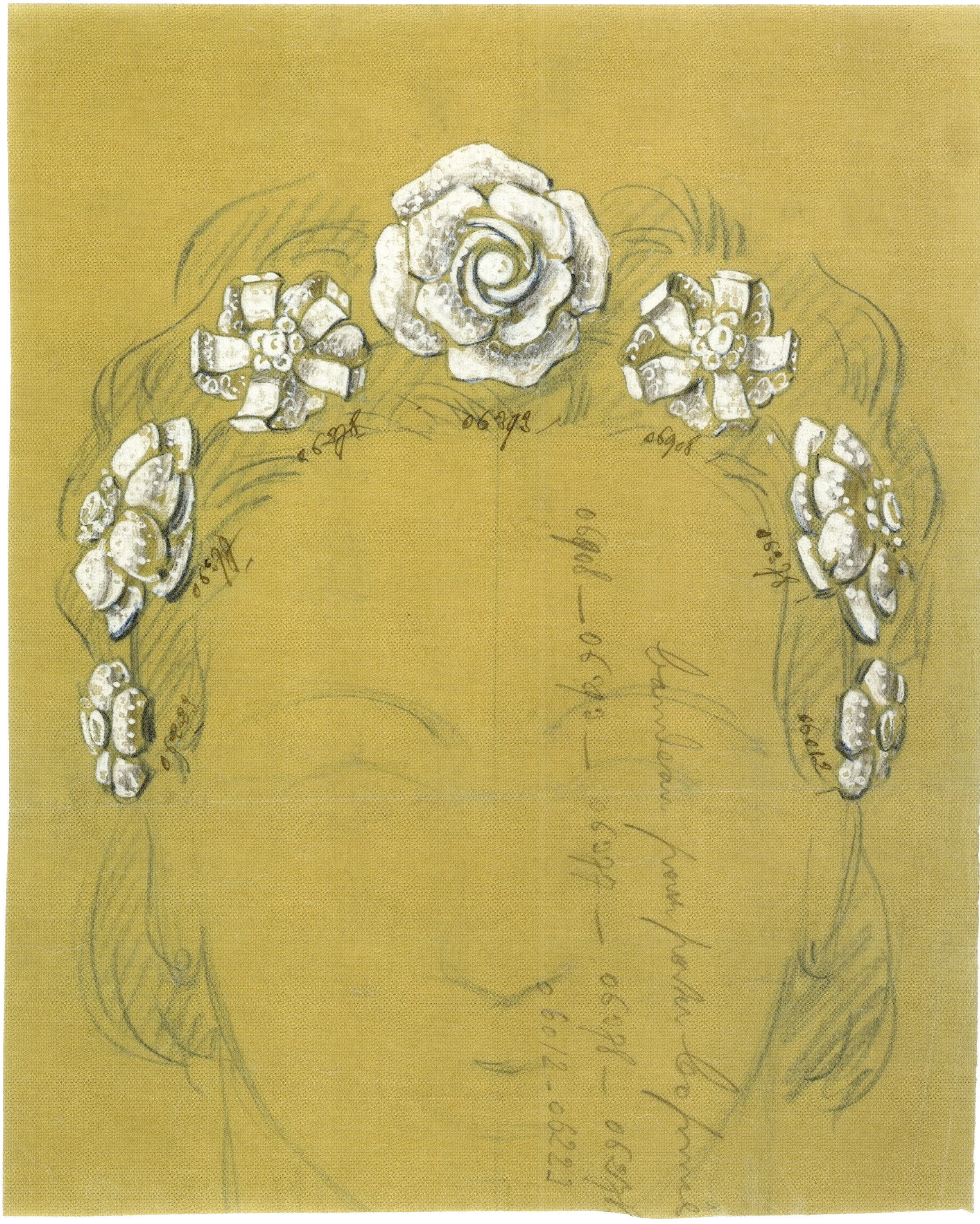

Rose
Cartier Paris
1938

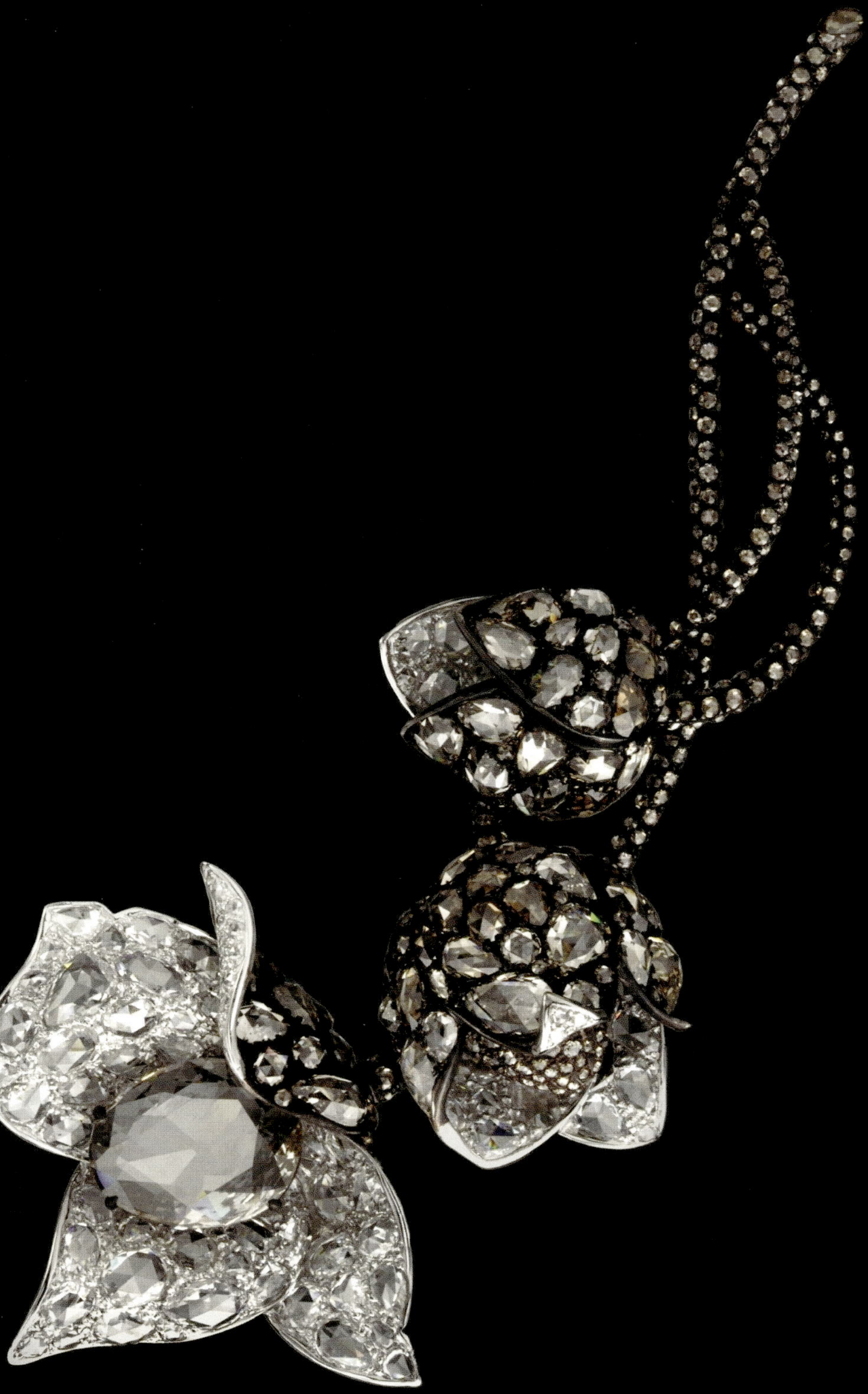

Wood Rose
Michelle Ong
2010

Marie-Antoinette wore floral scent distilled from rose petals, had the flower embroidered onto pastel-shaded sea-green, lilac and soft blue silks, and was holding a pale pink rose when she had her portrait painted by Élisabeth Vigée-Le Brun. The queen's decorative surroundings featured arbours of roses on wallpapers, rose wreaths carved on armchairs, roses painted onto furniture, the panels of coffers and her Sèvres porcelain. Her jewels were diamond swags, ribbons and floral sprays of rose-cut diamonds. The sale of the French crown jewels in 1887 included several diamond wild roses set with hundreds of carats of rose-cut diamonds designed by Alfred Bapst for Empress Eugénie in the style of Marie-Antoinette.

As close to the French Revolution as 1786 Queen Marie-Antoinette ordered a bouquet of wild roses and hawthorn blossom from the jeweller Bapst.

Jewels and Jewellery
Claire Phillips

Following in the floral footsteps of Marie-Antoinette, Empress Josephine was also captivated by roses, creating a famous rose garden in 1799 at the Château de Malmaison, a country estate she shared with Napoleon seven miles west of Paris. She also shared a love of extravagance, wanting always to appear as Napoleon instructed, at her dazzling best, in jewels and dress. She ordered spectacular gowns, such as a pink crepe dress covered in rose petals or toucan feathers, adorned with pearls, purchasing over 1,000 pairs of gloves each year. Her intention was to create 'the most beautiful and curious garden in Europe, a model of good cultivation'. A 165-foot-long orangery was heated by coal-burning stoves housing tropical flora, fruit trees, dahlias and amaryllis, 300 pineapple plants, and a collection of heather and jasmine from her native Martinique. Even while France was at war with England, she bought huge quantities of rose plants from London, obtaining a passport for her nurseryman to travel back and forth. Napoleon instructed the French navy to seize any rose plants, seeds or flora they found, searching ships to take back to his waiting empress.

Malmaison was a fiefdom of rare and exotic plants from all over the world. She [Josephine] grew many species for the first time in Europe, some of which are now common in our gardens, including cactuses, rhododendrons, tulips, dahlias and double jacinths.

Josephine: Desire, Ambition, Napoleon
Kate Williams

From 1804, Josephine grew fifty varieties of rose, documented as the most important work of rose hybridisation of the early nineteenth century, and once spent 3,000 francs on a single bulb. Pierre-Joseph Redouté, formerly the flower painter and drawing master to Marie-Antoinette, produced colour plates to record the garden in *Jardin de la Malmaison* (1803–5), and many of his flower pictures covered the walls of her bedroom.

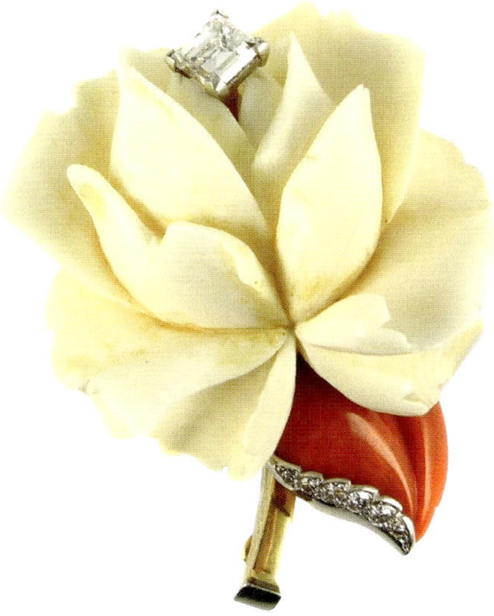

Rose
Cartier London
c. 1950

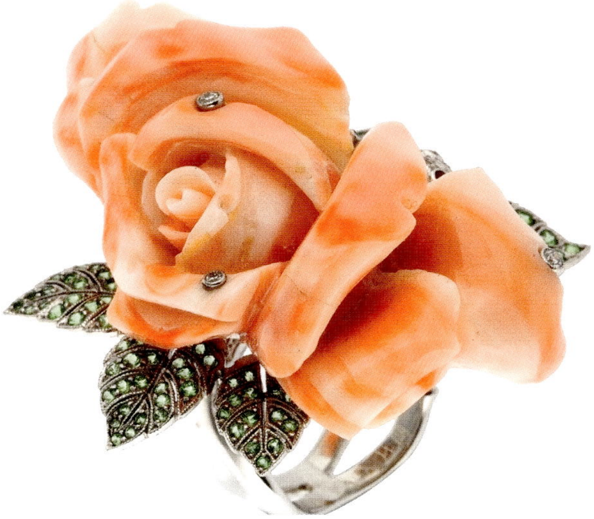

Rose
Lydia Courteille
1990

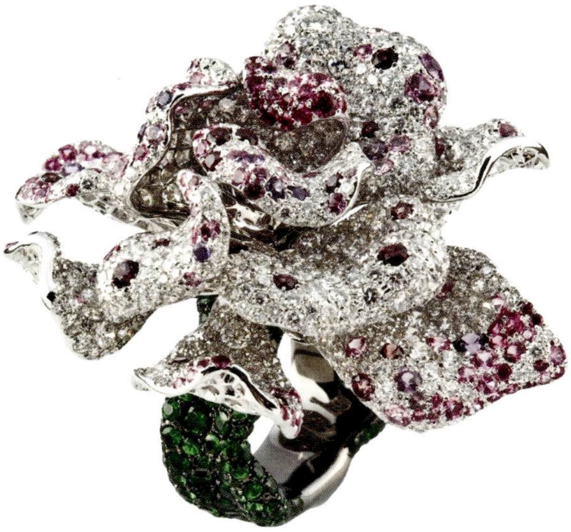

Rose
Cindy Chao
2012

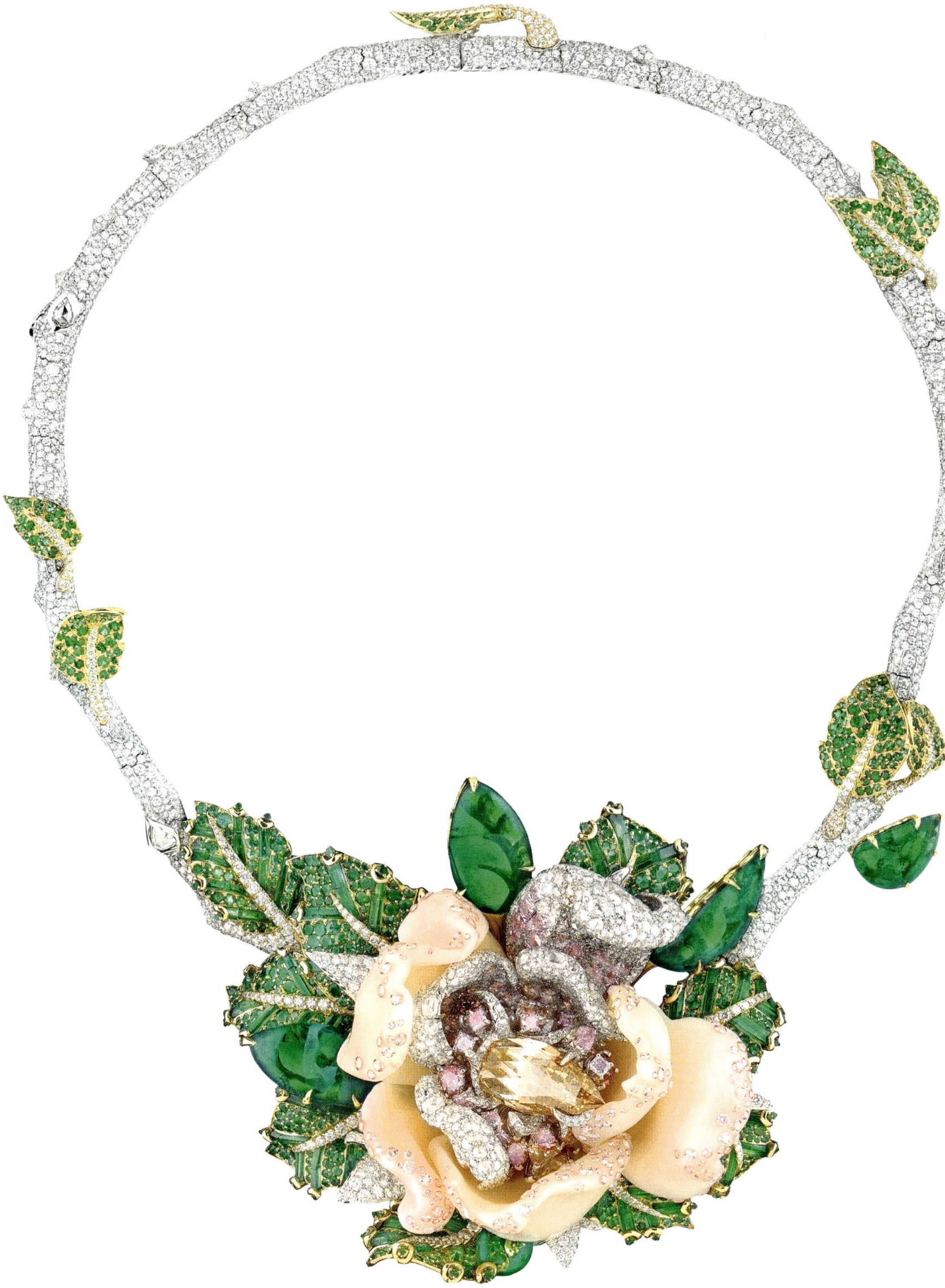

Bal de Mai
Victoire de Castellane,
Dior High Jewellery
2011

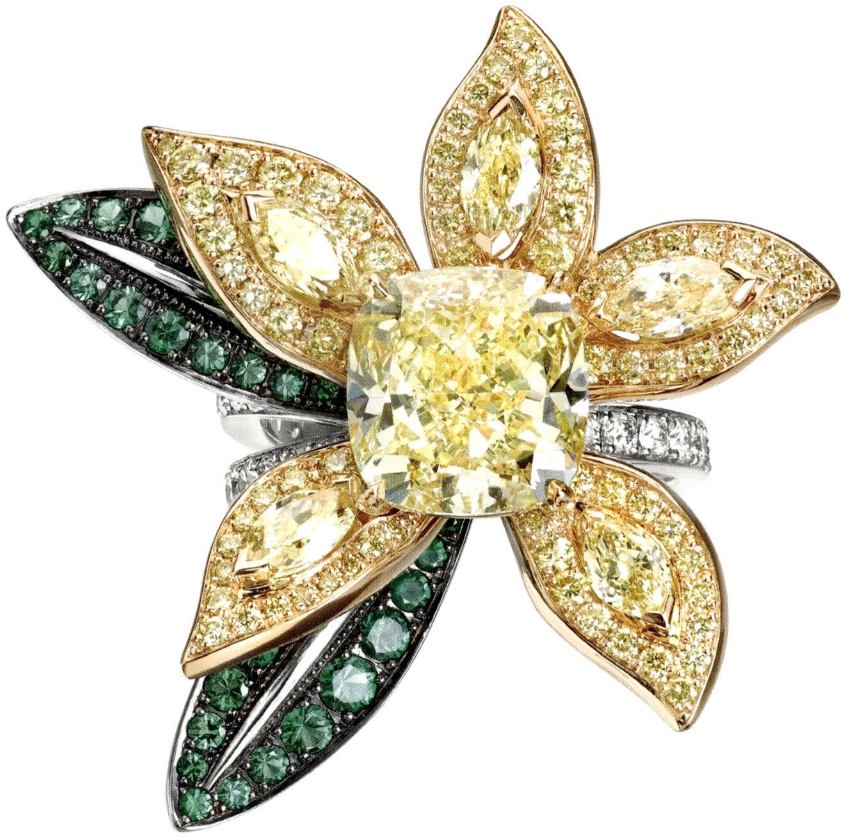

Vanilla Flower
Piaget
2014

Rising out of the grass, tangled round the sun-dial,
wreathing the tree trunks and hanging from their branches,
climbing up the walls and spreading over them with long
garlands falling in cascades – they came alive day by day,
hour by hour. Fair fresh leaves, and buds – and buds – tiny at
first but swelling and working Magic until they burst and
unfurled into cups of scent delicately spilling themselves
over their brims and filling the garden air.

The Secret Garden
Frances Hodgson Burnett

Using Napoleon's riches, Josephine rescued jewellery artisans who had lost their livelihood in the aftermath of the French Revolution. Marie-Antoinette's jewellery box proved too small for the empress's diamonds. In addition to the French crown jewels, her diadems, tiaras, a favourite necklace of twenty-seven large diamonds and bracelets jostled for position amongst gifts brought back from Napoleon's expeditions, including oriental rubies, ropes of pearls and precious stones from Brazil. An incredible thirty-drawer jewel cabinet, now displayed in the Louvre, the size of a modern wardrobe, with gilt bronze plaques and inlaid mother-of-pearl, was made to house her treasures.

> *In 1811 an inventory was made of Josephine's jewels,*
> *which assessed them as worth over five million francs.*
> *The good 'easy going woman', the Martinique plantation*
> *daughter, had become the Imperial Empress,*
> *bowed under the weight of precious stones.*
>
> *Josephine: Desire, Ambition, Napoleon*
> Kate Williams

Using the botanical drawings and archives of Redouté, fine jewellers Piaget are helping to fund the renovation of the gardens at Malmasion, which in turn has inspired their own jewellery collection. A yellow diamond vanilla flower, with vibrant emerald leaves, has been created as a memento of the exotic island flowers that Josephine grew up with on Martinique.

Two centuries after the death of Empress Josephine, Place Vendôme jeweller Lorenz Bäumer is experimenting with the breeding and cultivation of jewelled flowers. 'I use hybridisation of form and colour in my drawing to bring pieces to life like in the world of flora', he explains of his drawing prior to the search for stones. 'I look for precious stones and pearls in the depths of the ocean and darkest recesses of the earth's caves,' he continues, 'which makes me feel at harvest time like a gardener of the world.' Bäumer aims to work in a similar vein to the painters of the Dutch Golden Age, who assembled amazing bouquets of poppies, roses, wall flowers, tulips, narcissi, anemones and most garden blooms for their art. Freeing himself from the rules of nature, he likes to create strange new varieties of psychedelic blooms, as well as coral, diamond and multi-gem bangles and traditional old blush pink roses on diamond stems with glistening briolette diamond drops of dew as if freshly picked from the garden that morning.

In bejewelled botany anything is possible: sapphire blue roses have bloomed at Cartier alongside the more traditional colours of yellow jonquil diamonds on emerald leaves. Dior too have cultivated a hybrid blue in the Bal Bleu Nuit ring, with grey diamonds, blue sapphires, blue chalcedony and tanzanites.

Christian Dior developed an encyclopaedic knowledge of roses, and used to recite their names in Latin, his life-long passion for the flower being sparked by his love of the rose garden at the two-acre park around Les Rhumbs, his childhood home at Granville. The tender hues of the soft delicate petals and their sensual curves were cultivated in his couture, appearing embroidered, printed and brocaded on evening dresses.

In homage to Monsieur Dior's love of roses, Victoire de Castellane designed a few pieces of floral jewellery as if they were the personification of a couture client dressed for an extravagant ball. Each one named after one of the fashion house's 1950s ball gowns, the petals of the flowers in white stones are set like the softest satin with coloured gemstone embroidery. Similar to the creation of a couture gown, great attention was paid to what de Castellane described as the hidden stone 'linings' underneath the jewels.

Your slightest look will easily unclose me
though I have closed myself as fingers,
you open always petal by petal myself as Spring opens
(touching skilfully, mysteriously) her first rose.

LXII
E. E. Cummings

The Bal de Mai necklace is elaborately set with fancy brown, pink, lilac and mauve diamonds, with pink opals and emeralds, while the Bal de l'Opéra has texured petal-shaped rubellite stones and a shiny lustre, polished to emphasise the velvety softness of each petal. The anatomy of a rose has been carefully observed as the gold is etched with intricate vine motifs, life-like textured branches, chiselled stems and curving soft tendrils.

It [Madame Plantier, a climbing rose] is fifteen feet high
with a girth of fifteen yards, tapering towards the tip like
the waist of a Victorian beauty and pouring down in a
vast crinoline stitched all over with its white sweet-scented
clusters of flowers... I go out and look at her in the moonlight;
she gleams, a pear-shaped ghost, contriving
to look both matronly and virginal.

A Joy of Gardening
Vita Sackville-West

During the nineteenth century, the splendour of roses made them a perfect subject for tiara design, their long tendrils able to catch each other, forming bridges like hazy mantles of diamonds and pearls. Queen Therese of Bavaria had a flower-head tiara set with turquoise, emeralds, pink topaz and pearls. The Strathmore tiara was created in the form of wild roses, set with rose-cut diamonds, and Chaumet designed the Bedford tiara of large blossoms of diamond-set roses with wild flowers. In 1973, Garrard, as the crown jeweller, created a new tiara for Her Majesty the Queen, in the form of a wreath of roses, with clusters of rubies in the centre of diamond petals and curving sprays of cushion-cut stones linked by festoons of rubies and diamonds. The ninety-six rubies were a gift from the people of Burma and symbolise the ninety-six diseases that can afflict the human body, as the Burmese regard the ruby as a charm against illness.

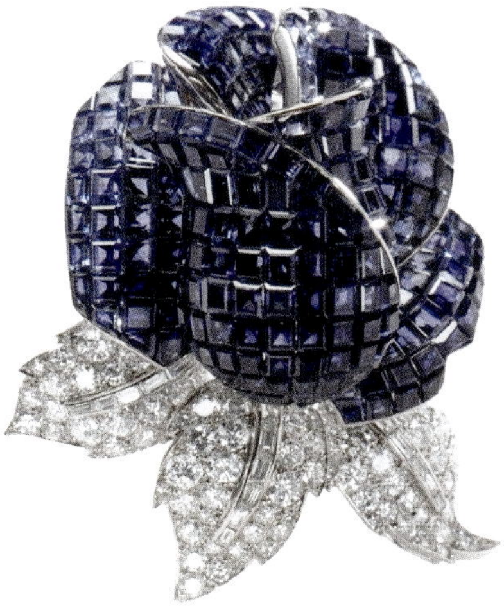

Rose
Cartier Paris for New York
1959

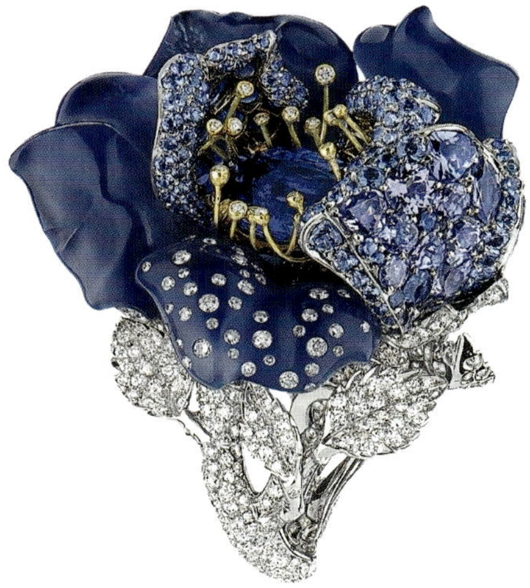

Bal Bleu Nuit
Victoire de Castellane,
Dior High Jewellery
2011

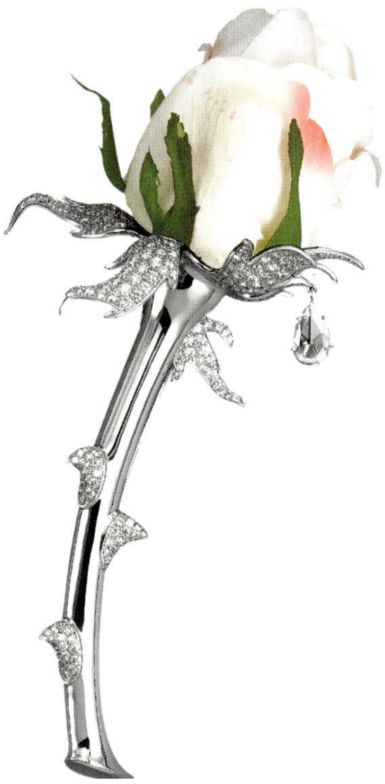

Rose
Lorenz Bäumer
2004

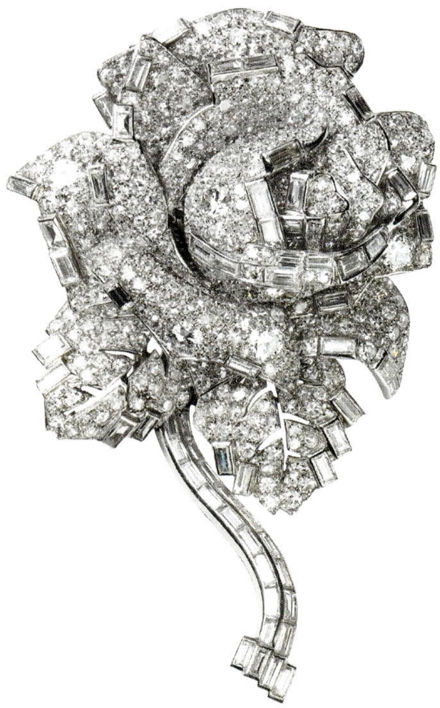

Rose
Cartier London
1938

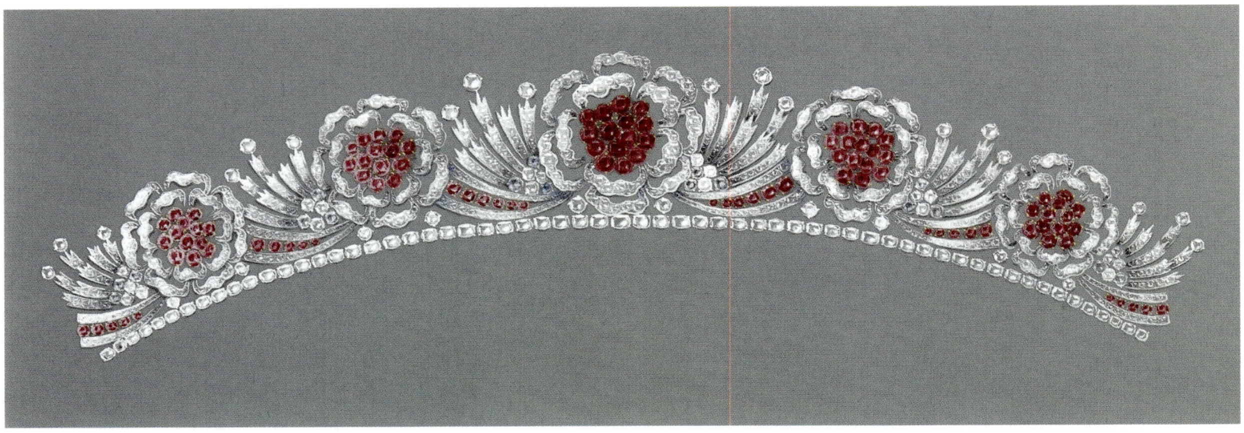

Roses

Garrard

1973

From the oval-shaped flower-bed there rose perhaps a hundred stalks spreading into heart-shaped or tongue-shaped leaves half way up and unfurling at the tip red or blue or yellow petals marked with spots of colour raised upon the surface; and from the red, blue or yellow gloom of the throat emerged a straight bar, rough with gold dust and slightly clubbed at the end. The petals were voluminous enough to be stirred by the summer breeze, and when they moved, the red, blue and yellow lights passed one over the other, staining an inch of the brown earth beneath with a spot of the most intricate colour… the breeze stirred rather more briskly overhead and the colour was flashed into the air above, into the eyes of the men and women who walk in Kew Gardens in July.

Kew Gardens
Virginia Woolf

Growing in the wild, a simple briar rose is remarkable for the way it clings to life in inhospitable circumstances, with pollinator-attracting scent and spiny protective prickles enabling it to hybridise in the wild to produce bigger and better blooms with an even headier scent.

Here the rose appears in a subtle metaphor, evoking the dual nature of love. As the 18th-century saying goes one cannot have the rose without the thorns.

René Lalique

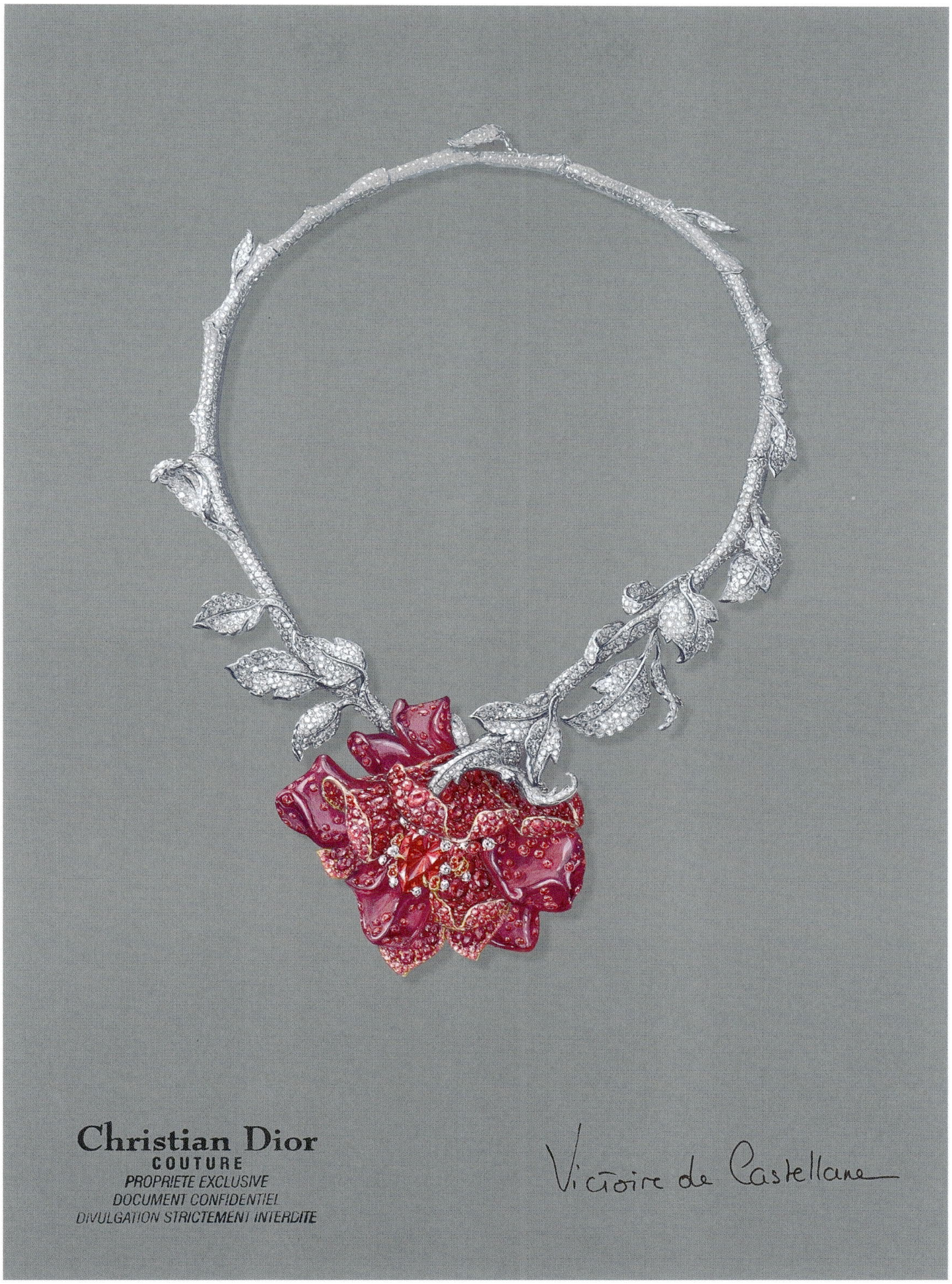

Bal de l'Opéra
Victoire de Castellane,
Dior High Jewellery
2011

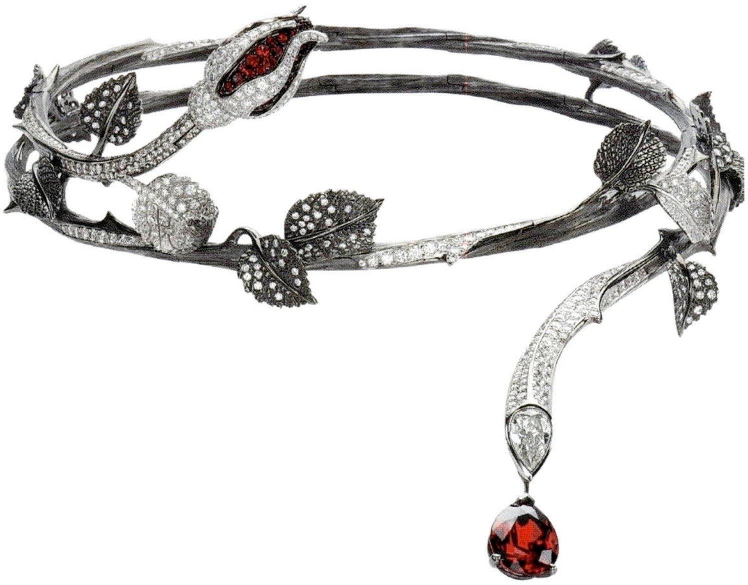

Noces de Sang
Victoire de Castellane,
Dior High Jewellery
2002

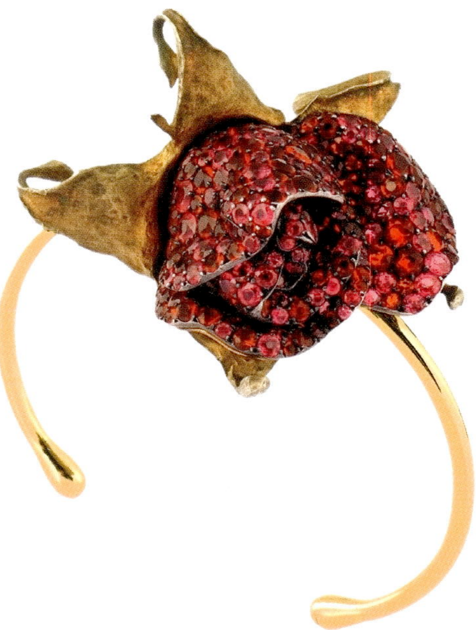

Rose
JAR
1996

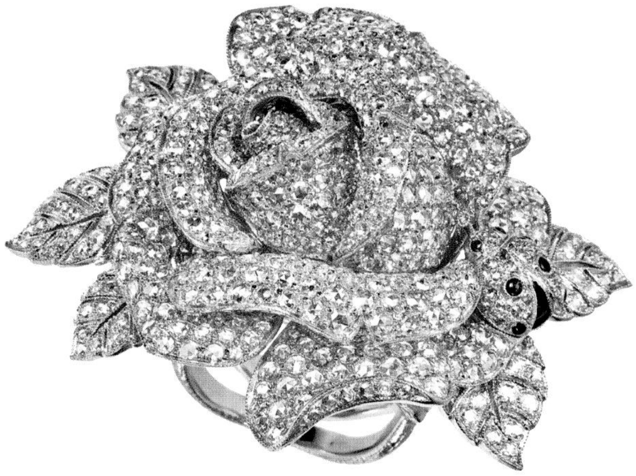

Rose
Lydia Courteille
2007

A magnificent rose stem by JAR encircles the neck in graduated green tourmalines and garnets, gently opening into a diamond dew-dropped bud of pink sapphires and rubies. The stem is covered with jewelled thorns, prickly enough to prevent anyone attempting to touch the swan-like neck on which it rests, making the piece beautifully intimidating. Five eglantine roses with sculpted petals in different bronze shades around a central pearl are made to be worn as a rose garden pinned high on the shoulder, and his wild rose brooches set with sapphires, tourmalines, citrines and garnets have realistic random patterns of protruding enamel stamens.

The Noces de Sang dark rose necklace also has a thorny stem, with blood-red rose-bud gems designed by Victoire de Castellane for Dior, with gothic romance in mind. She imagined a young maiden offering her neck to a vampire to become immortal, the vibrant red Technicolor of the spinel stones dramatically contrasting with the imagined pearly pale neck.

But he that dares not grasp the thorn
should never crave the rose.

The Narrow Way
Anne Brontë

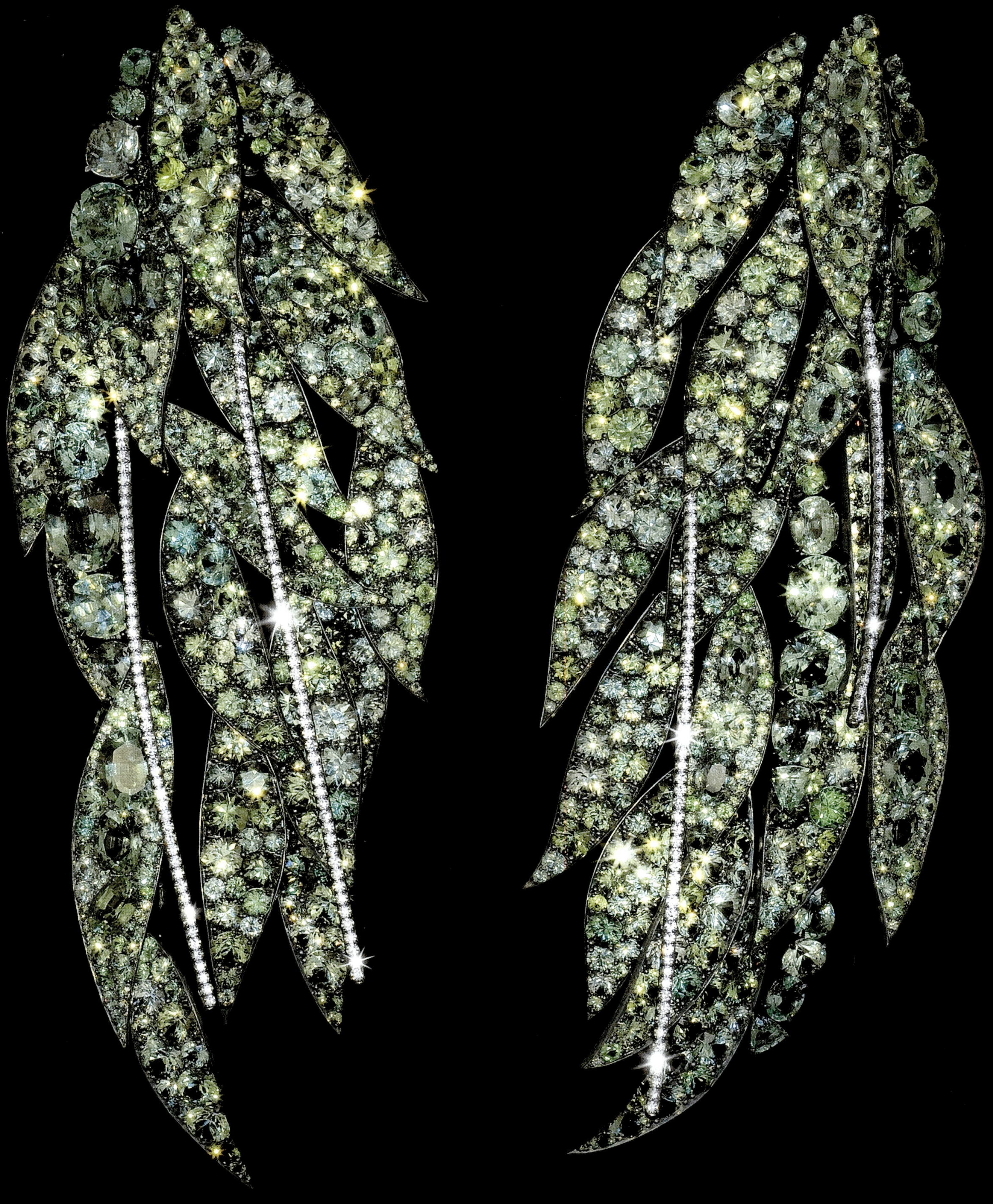

Weeping Willow
JAR
2011

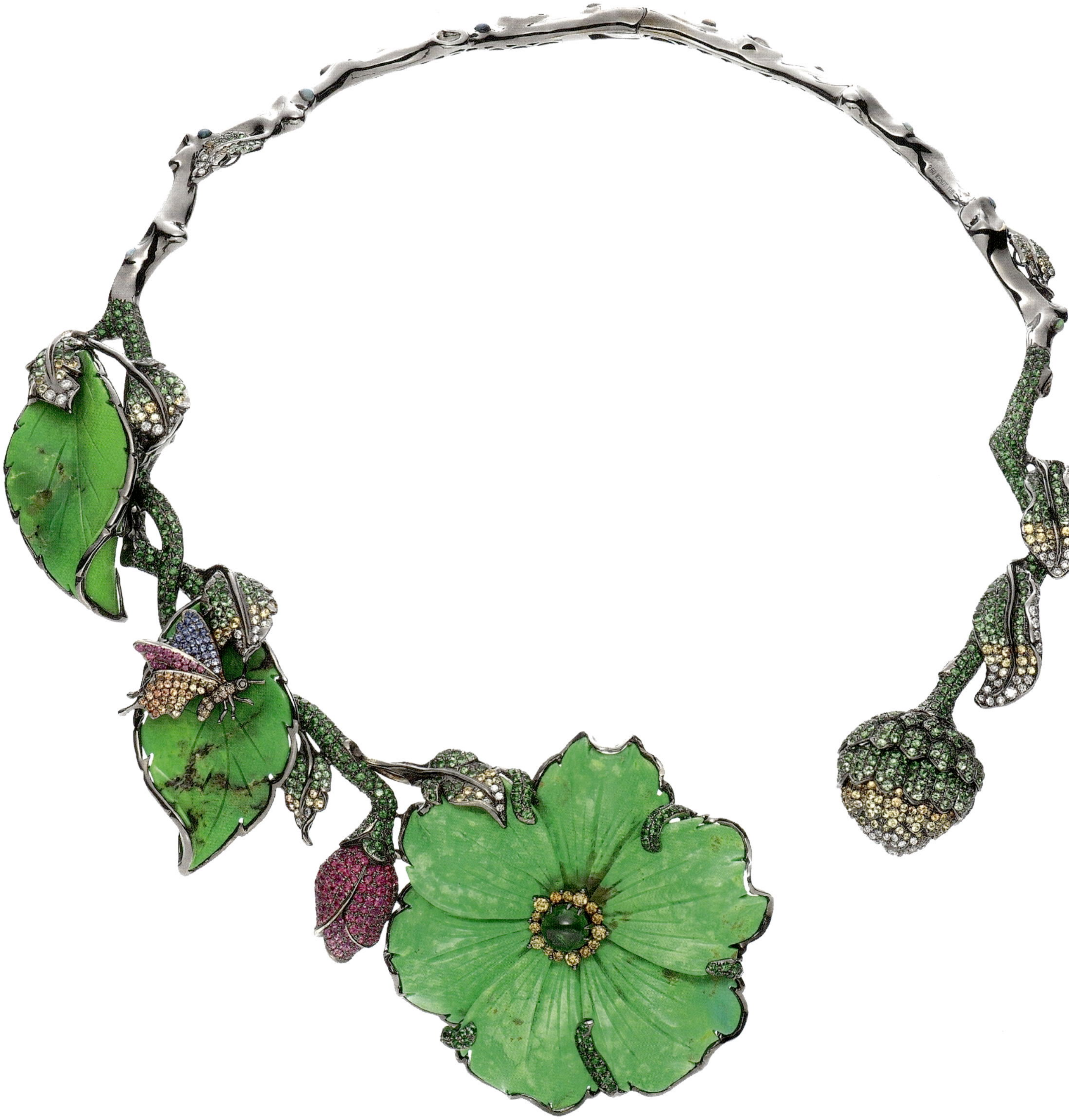

Chinese Hibiscus
Wendy Yue
2013

poppy • peony • sunflower • sweet pea • vanilla flower • weeping willow • camellia • hellebore • holly • ivy • winter plum • ivy

• snowdrop • orchid •

blossom • dandelion • lily of the valley • narcissus • pansy • peony • tulip • violet • calla lily • foxglove • heliotrope • iris • morning glory

camellia • edelweiss • hellebore • holly • ivy

hawthorn • hydrangea • orchid • wild oats • camellia

blossom • dandelion • lily of the valley • narcissus • pansy •

ulip • violet • calla lily • foxglove • heliotrope • iris • morning glory

heliotrope • iris • lily • lotus • morning glory • rose • lily • sunflower • sweet pea • thistle • vanilla flower • foxglove • wild oats • chrysanthemum • hawthorn • hydrangea • poppy

hellebore • holly • mistletoe • snowdrop • winter plum • anemone • blossom • daisy • dandelion • lily of the valley • narcissus • iris • lily • lotus • morning glory • poppy • rose • sunflower • sweet pea

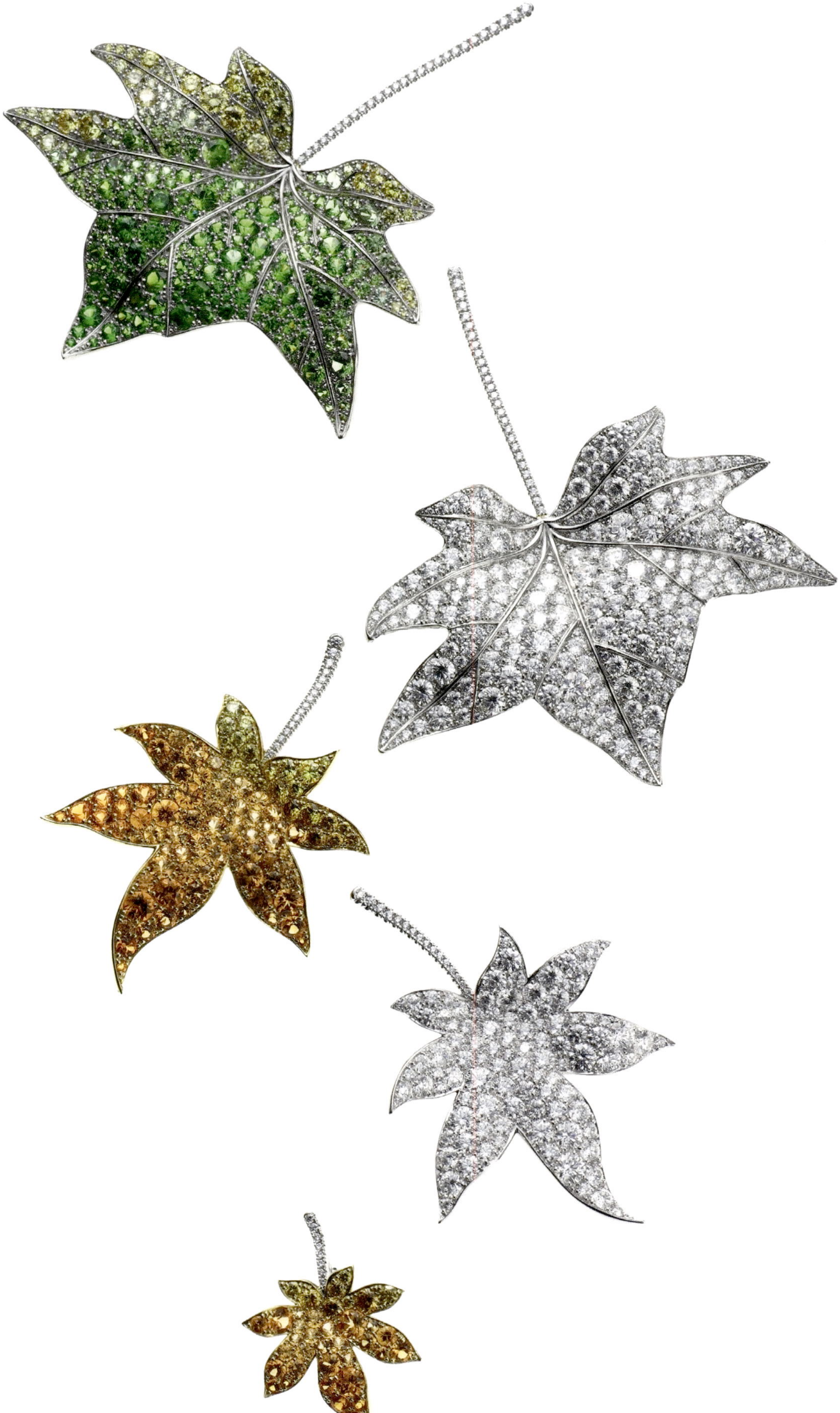

Maple Leaf
Gimel
2003 and 2006

Autumn

Autumn is a second spring when every leaf is a flower.
Albert Camus

Autumn is the season of falling leaves, as the trees' petals crunch underfoot in shades of crisp crimson, flecked apricot and cinnamon sunset. Earthy tapestries of dark conker brown diamonds, redcurrant spinels and mandarin garnets thread through the landscape, gradually fading into tawny-coloured topaz. The countryside is seized by a magical autumnal burst of activity, as every breath of wind, stirring through the woods, carries with it a flurry of leaves; hedgerows prepare for hibernation and ripe fruits are harvested in fields of gold. The last noble patches of colour sprouting from the earth, pumpkin-coloured diamonds and gentle rich red garnets burn like fiery embers, flickering in a last flaming burst of beauty from a November bonfire before it falls to ash.

The leaves from the Rokko Mountains in Japan fall in the breeze around the studio of Kaoru Kay Akihara; the glass walls of her atelier give her a close view of nature. 'Outside our atelier is full of autumn colours of dark red and yellow', says Akihara. She recreates leaves with a compelling simplicity, using strong green demantoid garnets, shaded with veins, and golden yellow diamond edges to denote the leaf changing into an autumn hue; white diamond and blue sapphire leaves with a fresh dew droplet of a briolette-cut diamond swaying on its tip; as well as burnt orange-coloured diamond maple leaves, sparkling as they silently fall from the bough, as the cold north wind blows.

Rhythmical cosmos spray the autumn fields
Maple deepens its red, smiling in the tranquil sunshine.
Acknowledging the approaching winter
The earth falls slowly to sleep as white crystals descend from heaven.
Kaoru Kay Akihara

Taking her dogs on long walks in the woods around her Geneva home inspired Caroline Scheufele, co-president of Chopard, to design an oak tree branch necklace, pavé-set with autumnal coloured diamonds and citrine acorns, nestling in tsavorite leaves that are home to a gem-set spider, seeking shelter from the cold winds. Throughout his long career, Verdura created brooches in the shape of oak or maple leaves using sapphires in autumnal colours, warmed by the season's last sunbeams, ranging from golden yellow to rich brown. Showers of autumn leaves fall in single and double clips at Van Cleef & Arpels in the shape of vines, American sycamore and horse-chestnut, wrought from Mystery-set precious gemstones. In 1937, the firm exhibited a ruby, gold, platinum and baguette-cut diamond chrysanthemum brooch using their patented Mystery setting, which allowed them to play with light and shadow across the surface, and thus create the spidery elongated curling motion of the petals coming out of the round flower head.

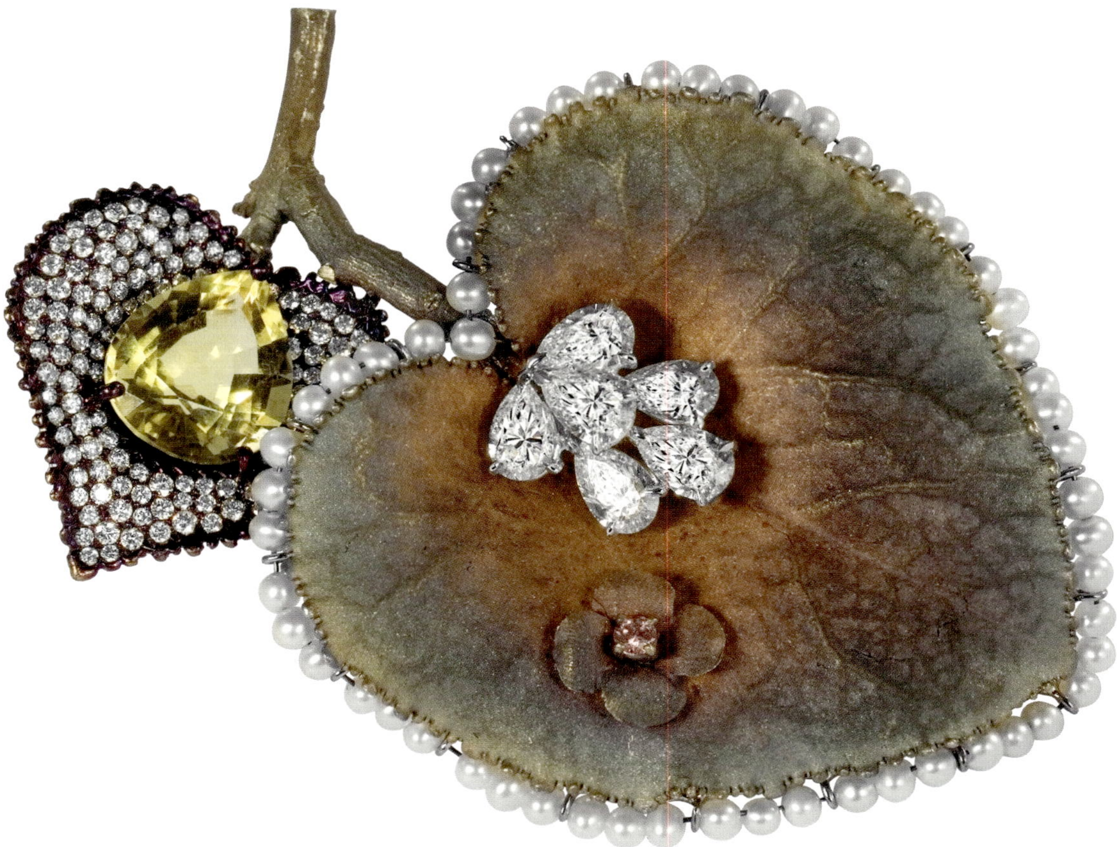

Leaf
Chatila
2010

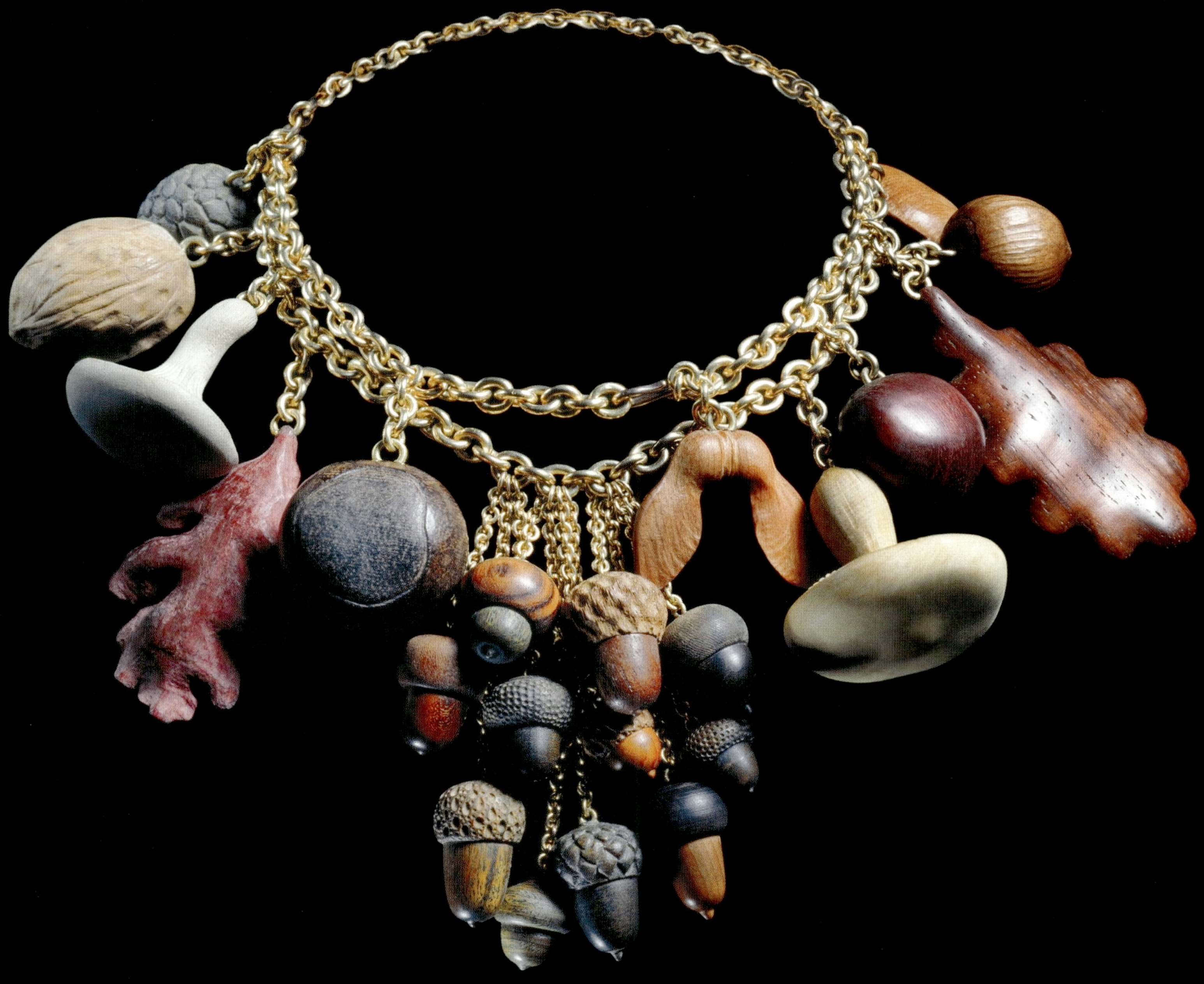

Autumn
JAR
1999

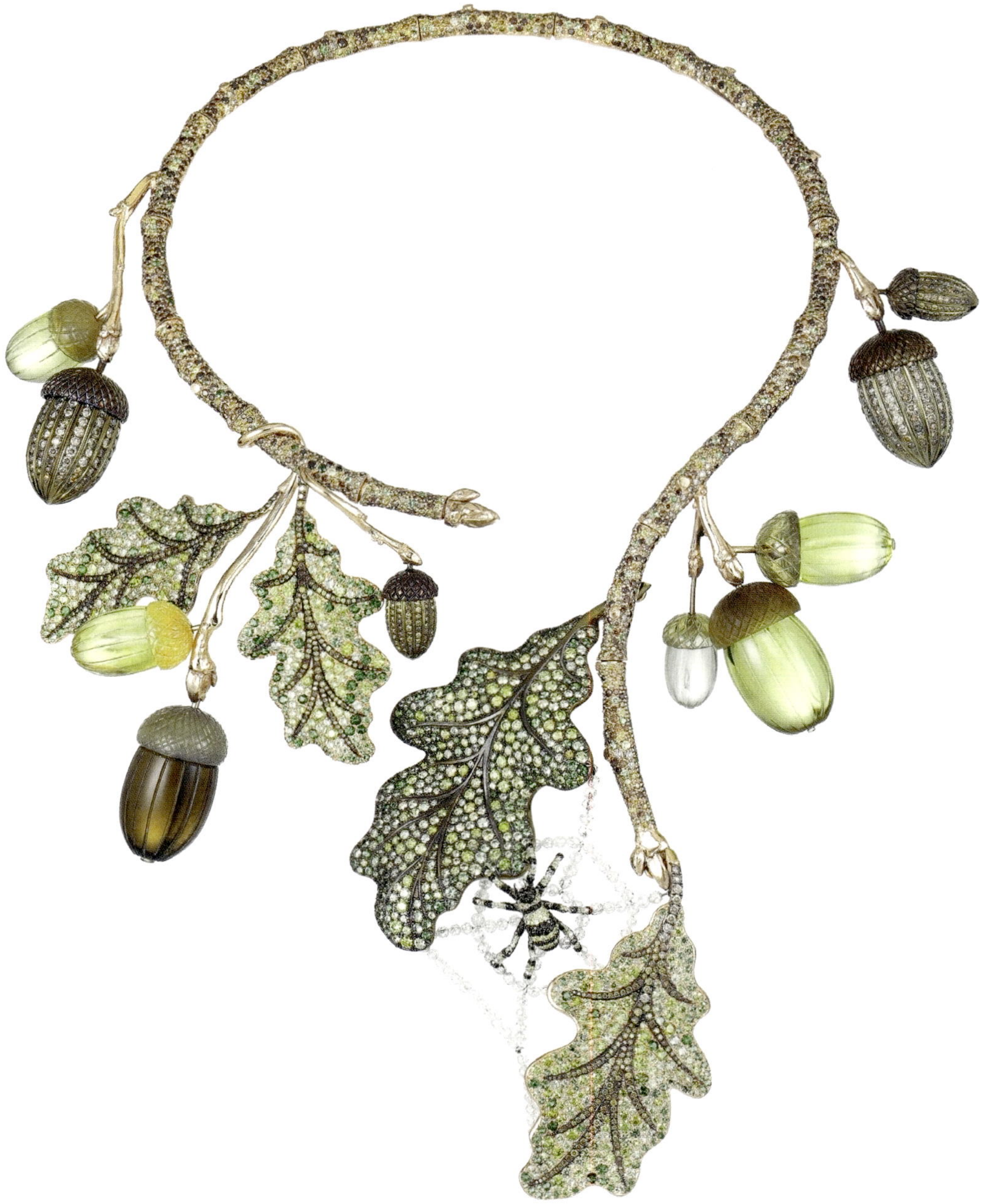

Oak Tree
Chopard
2013

John Steinbeck described the chrysanthemum flower, in the short story *The Chrysanthemums*, as 'a quick puff of coloured smoke'. The chrysanthemum, which originated in East Asia, adds a softer palette of colour to the autumn landscape, blossoming in blush pink, white and soft yellow petals, rolled around a central golden eye. The flower was cultivated 2,500 years ago in China as a flowering herb, its name being derived from the Chinese word 'chu hua', meaning 'October flower'. It retains its graceful shapes and subtle colours long after other flowers have faded. In China, the plant was originally reserved exclusively for the nobility, the lower classes being strictly forbidden to grow it. Once the flower was introduced to Japan by Buddhist monks in the eighth century, it was adopted by the Japanese imperial family for their official seal and the name of their throne.

Confucius suggested putting one chrysanthemum petal in the bottom of a glass of wine for a long and healthy life, and the poet Qu Yuan (340–278 BC) wrote about the arrival of autumn thus: 'Drink dew from magnolia in the morning and take autumn chrysanthemum's falling petals as food in the evening.' One inscription in an early nineteenth-century Japanese scroll refers to a fabled river, flowing with the essence of chrysanthemum dew as the petals fell high in the mountains and were carried downstream, where the people who drank from the river lived a long and healthy life.

> *The Real Thing is enormous, entertaining, personal and witty – flora and fauna immortalised, sea lions, nails, thistles, toadstools, grapes, roses, chrysanthemums. The road to glitter in 1937 is paved with huge and humorous jewels.*
>
> *Vogue*, December 1938

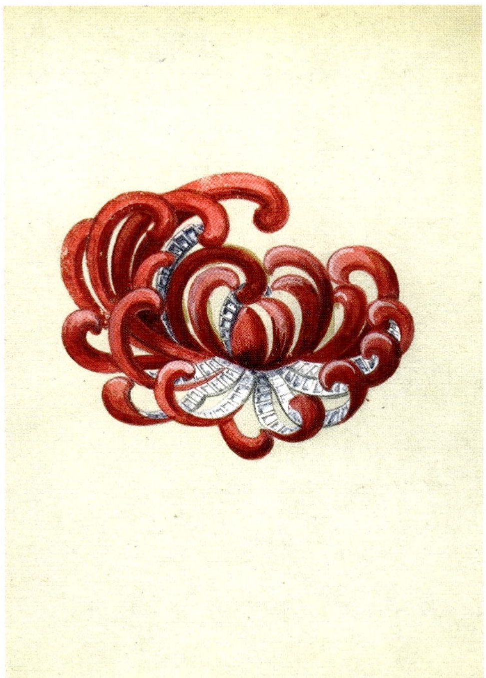

Chrysanthemum
Van Cleef & Arpels
1937

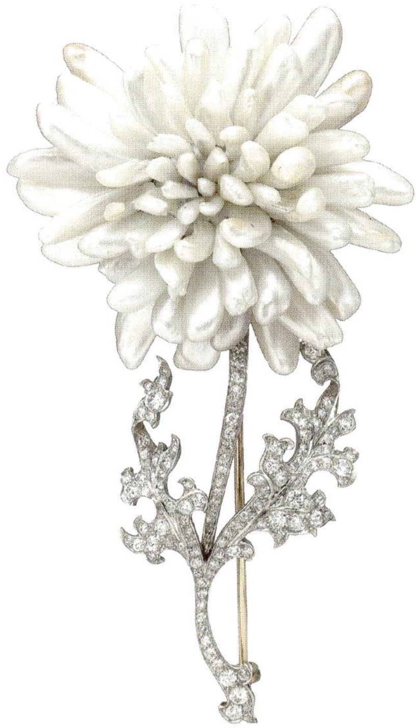

Chrysanthemum
Tiffany & Co.
1905

The flower was introduced to America in the nineteenth century, when Tiffany recreated the dainty buttery pom-poms and long rolling petals in patterns on silver tea services during the Gilded Age. One was bought by the celebrated performer Lillian Russell, who also bought a Tiffany chrysanthemum brooch, set in a large cluster of freshwater dogtooth pearls and diamond leaves. Moira in London create their own colour ranges for the flower, using coloured *plique à jour* enamel, with chrysanthemum petals in striking blue and green, unfurling around a diamond and ruby centre.

Another autumn flower native to Asia with a similar puffball showy beauty is the hydrangea, often referred to as mopheads or lace caps, due to the abundance of tiny star-shaped flowers that combine to make one lavish globe-like shape. During the late Yuan and early Ming dynasties, the hydrangea was depicted using golden thread on silken tapestries, as embroidered flower balls.

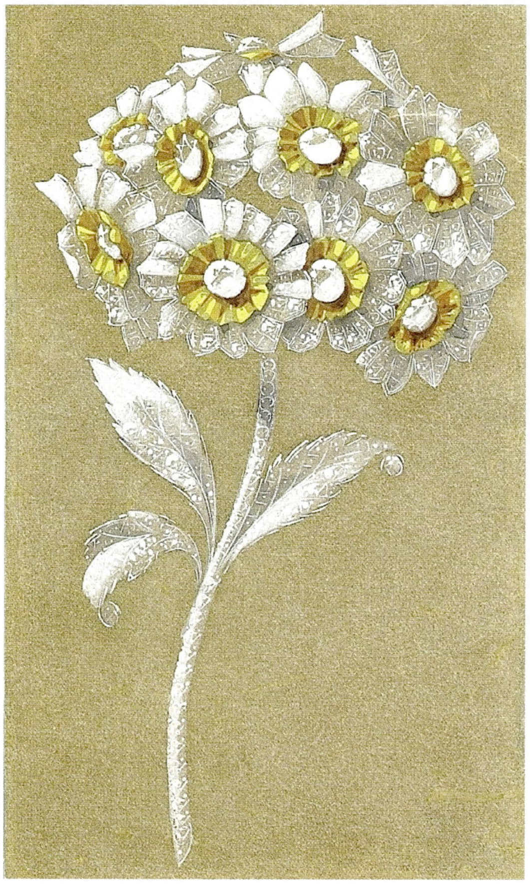

Hydrangea
Chaumet
c. 1890–1900

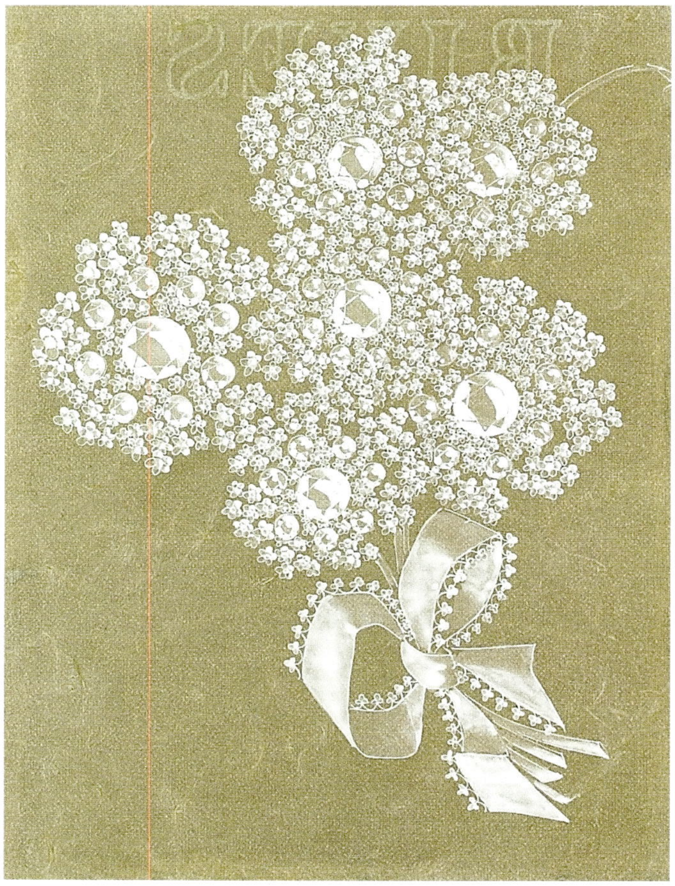

Hydrangea
Chaumet
c. 1890–1900

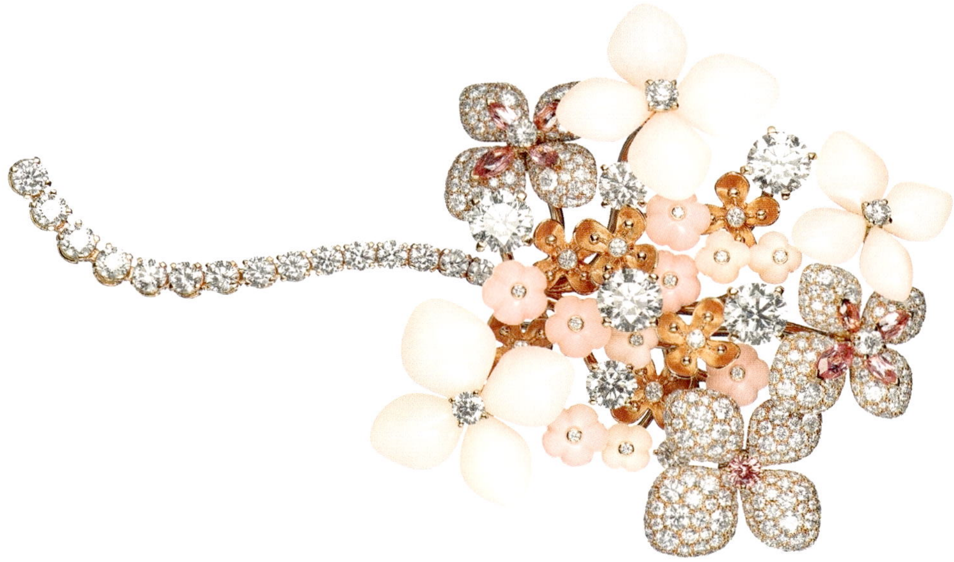

Hydrangea

Chaumet
2013

My eyes were full of colours:
Saffrons, rubies, the yellows of beryls,
And the indigo-blue of quartz;
Flights of rose, layers of chrysoprase,
Points of orange, spirals of vermillion,
The spotted gold of tiger-lily petals
The loud pink of bursting hydrangea

The Captured Goddess
Amy Lowell

Hydrangeas were mentioned in Japanese literature from the eighth century as a 'gathering of blues', because before the breeding of different varieties became popular the flowers were commonly pale pastel blue. The flower can change colour according to the chemical make-up of the soil, which is why they came to be associated with wavering loyalties, and were consequently shunned by brave warriors. Still popular in modern Japan, pink hydrangeas stand for heartfelt emotions, sending the message 'you are the beat of my heart'. The petals of a hydrangea don't fall, they wilt, allowing the flower to keep its structure at every phase of its life. In the hands of jewellers, they become eternal puffs of diamonds.

A dead hydrangea is as intricate and lovely as one in bloom.
Bleak sky is as seductive as sunshine, miniature orange trees
without blossom or fruit are not defective; they are that.

Tar Baby
Toni Morrison

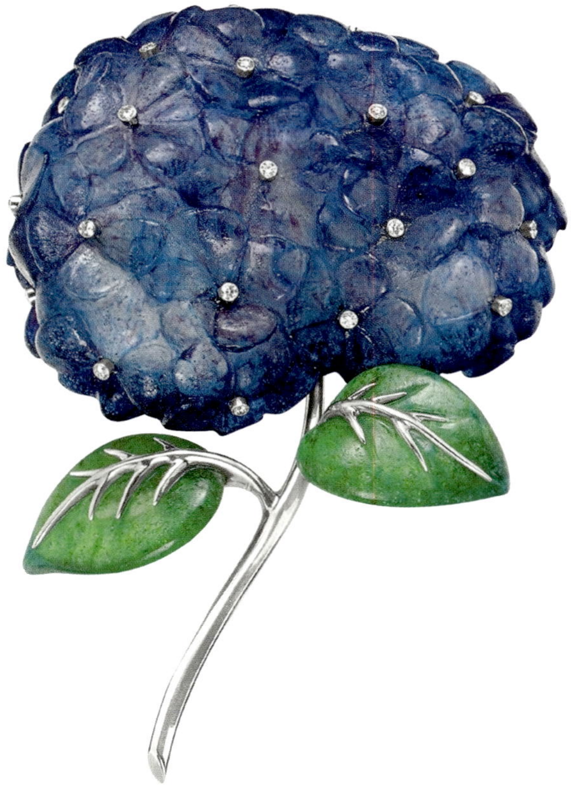

Hydrangea

Tiffany & Co.
Early 20th century

Hydrangeas adorn the garden created by horticulturist Gertrude Jekyll for the mullion-windowed Arts and Crafts manor house, Le Bois des Moutiers, built by her long-term collaborator Sir Edwin Lutyens in Varengeville-sur-Mer in Haute-Normandie. There are luminous lawns, dense woodland gardens, and a formal English-style garden of flagstones and flowers, with paths cut through luscious crimson rhododendrons, azaleas, magnolias and Japanese maples overlooking the sea. 'It's a little like a Sussex garden on vacation on the French Coast', writes Hugh Johnson. During the Belle Époque, Parisians flocked to the area on the new railway line; amongst the visitors were many artists attracted by the soft light, including Claude Monet and Georges Braque.

A nearby house owned by Béatrice de Plinval, artistic director of Chaumet, has a hallway painted by Miró and a garden planted with many rare varieties of oriental hydrangeas. 'It was always a famous place for botanics', explains de Plinval, who has created her own woodland garden in keeping with the history of the area. Fascinated by the movement, softness and diversity of the shapes of the petals of hydrangeas, she grows rare plants such as Japanese-style flat-head flowers, with the coloured appearance of shiny copper red metal. 'I love them because they can be a puffball of a flower', she explains, 'or have a geometric structure.'

It's these specimens, residing in glass vases on de Plinval's gilt neoclassical desk in the magnificent seventeenth-century Musée Chaumet in the noble Place Vendôme in Paris, which have inspired the 'Hortensia' collection ('hortensia' deriving from the Latin for garden) of pale pink opaque angel-skin opal, and translucent tourmaline, ruby, diamond and white agate brooches and necklaces. Next door to her office is the gilded grandeur of the magnificent Tiara Room, displaying many maquettes of the 1,500 diamond scrollwork and bow-knot diadems, tiaras and aigrettes made by Chaumet from the 1780s, as well as large reference books of sketches, gouaches and drawings of both floral tiaras and traditional hydrangeas, drawn by the firm's designers. Dainty sapphires, rubellites, rubies, garnets and diamonds in clusters of small stones, like tiny buds, are gathered to replicate the intricate nature of the volumes and layers of the petals, with as little visible metal used as possible so as to recreate the lightness and suppleness of the articulated puffs of colour. The hortensia brooch is created with a lace-like composition that plays with a contrast of colours, the light gently moving to dark in an asymmetric setting; a cuff represents the geometric nature of the flower, with large openwork lapis lazuli, sapphire and diamond hydrangea florets.

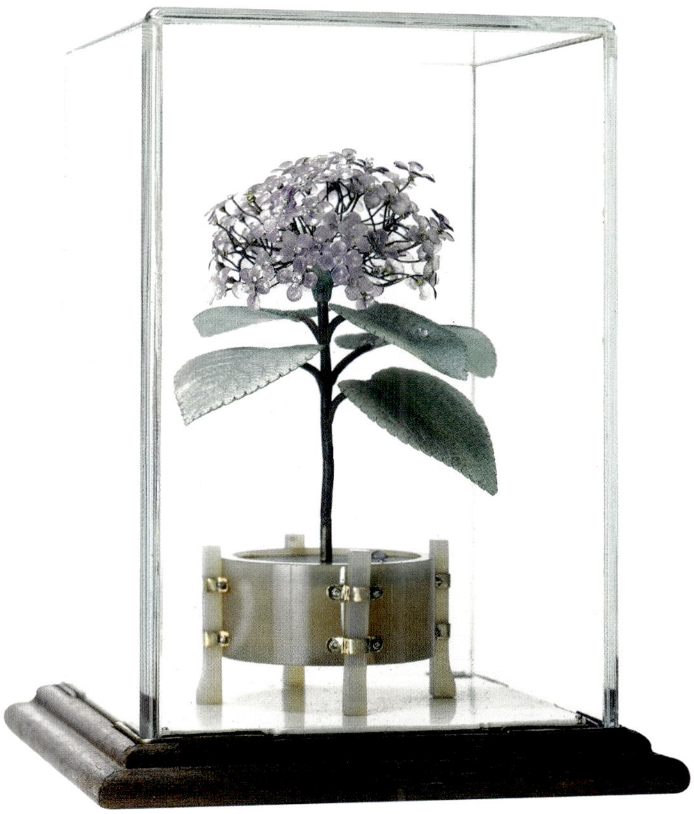

Hydrangea
Cartier Paris
1910

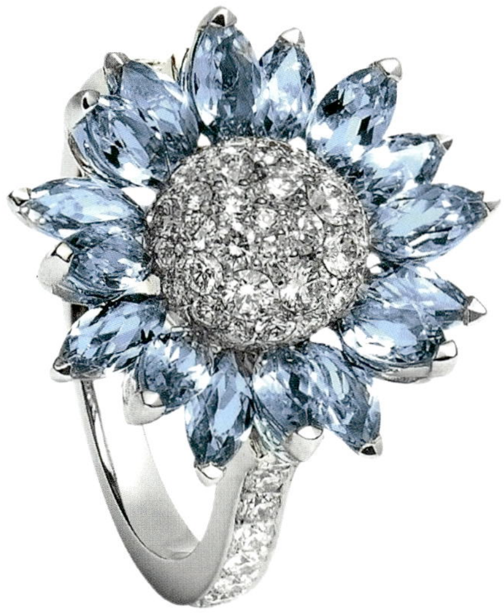

Michaelmas Daisy
Asprey
2012

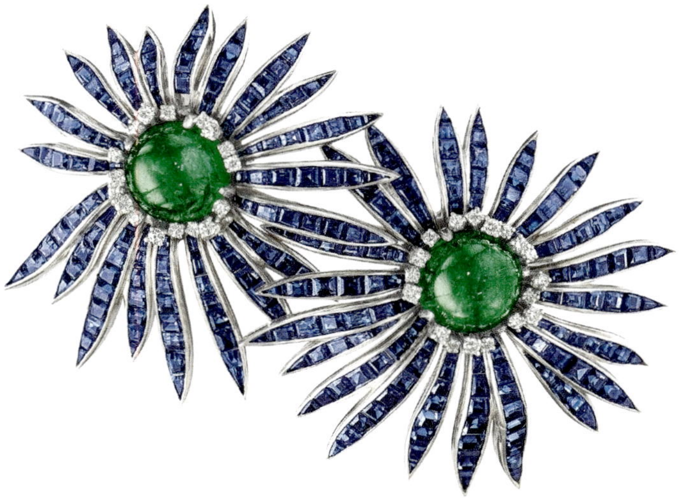

Michaelmas Daisy
Verdura
1965

...Cartier's dainty hothouses in which fairy-tale trees with gold and silver trunks sprout leaves of jade. On a coral branch a bird begins to sing, just like something out of Schéhérazade.

Vogue, 1916

In 1910, a hydrangea was the subject of one of Cartier's hothouse flowers, created with a flower head of mauve enamel glass and rose-cut diamonds with realistic veined aventurine green leaves on which rest tiny dew drops of moonstone cabochons. It's possible to see the influence of *ikebana*, the Japanese art of flower arranging, in the style and presentation of the delicate bloom, entwining above its ivory, glass and wood case. In another jewelled pot plant, the individual blossom petals from sprays of cherry or lilies lie detached from the plant, illustrating the melancholy charm of the transitory nature of life. The flowers imitated the colours of nature through the use of enamel, opaline, jade, agate and moonstone, planted in hardstone vases and bases of ivory, lapis lazuli or crystal.

Warm & mild after a fine night of rain. Transplanted radishes after breakfast. Walked to Mr Gells with the Books – gathered mosses & plants. The woods extremely beautiful with all autumnal variety & softness – I carried a basket of mosses & gathered some wild plants.

The Grasmere Journals
Dorothy Wordsworth

Following the feast of St Michaelmas on 29 September, garden herbaceous borders have a sprinkling of late-season gaiety, in the form of the Michaelmas daisy, which is always associated with the start of autumn. Bushy green clumps sprout white daisy-like flowers with centres of burnished gold florets and star-shaped petals, which graduate into a spectrum of shades, from pale pink to violet, purple, vibrant magenta and flashing indigo, the colour of tanzanite.

At the turn of the nineteenth century, René Lalique was the greatest artist of the Art Nouveau movement. He was attracted to 'modest' aspects of nature, having been captivated by the beauty of the Champagne region of France, where he holidayed as a child. On walks he studied bees closely, as they sipped nectar from wild flowers, keenly interested in all aspects of plant structure, stalks, leaves and blossoms. He collected withered leaves in autumn, storing the feel of their fragile nature and ribbed veins in his memory. By the age of fifteen, he had begun painting flower miniatures in gouache, the theme of nature going on to dominate his jewelled creations.

*He [Lalique] focused also on the decay and rebirth of
the natural world, choosing wilting leaves and petals,
world-weary anemones or poppies, over-blown roses,
or the humblest field flowers, like cow parsley or thistles,
so light and ephemeral with their soft seedheads
about to disintegrate with the next breath of wind.*

The Master Jewelers
A. Kenneth Snowman

Until that time, traditional jewellery making had placed a greater emphasis on precious stones than on the artistry of design, but Lalique used his skill to find new expressive forms that introduced a lightness of movement and non-precious materials, thus giving rise to a new style of modern jewellery. He used unconventional materials, including real hazelnuts along horn hair combs, trailing branches of fragile fading enamelled flowers, hawthorn, willow catkins and sycamore seeds, documenting all stages of floral life, including nature's uglier side, in a naturalistic style. Amongst the autumn branches and translucent enamel foliage in fluid golden shades, evoking the dappled evening sun filtering through into a woodland garden, there were also elements of nature's cycle of decay and death.

*Lalique spent his day sitting at this worktable, a paintbrush
or roughing chisel in his hand. Around him, on every piece
of furniture and in every corner, was a constant profusion
of the flowers that he had loved from his childhood,
their delicate colours and elegant forms analyzed by
him with exquisite taste.*

French Jewelry of the Nineteenth Century
Henri Vever

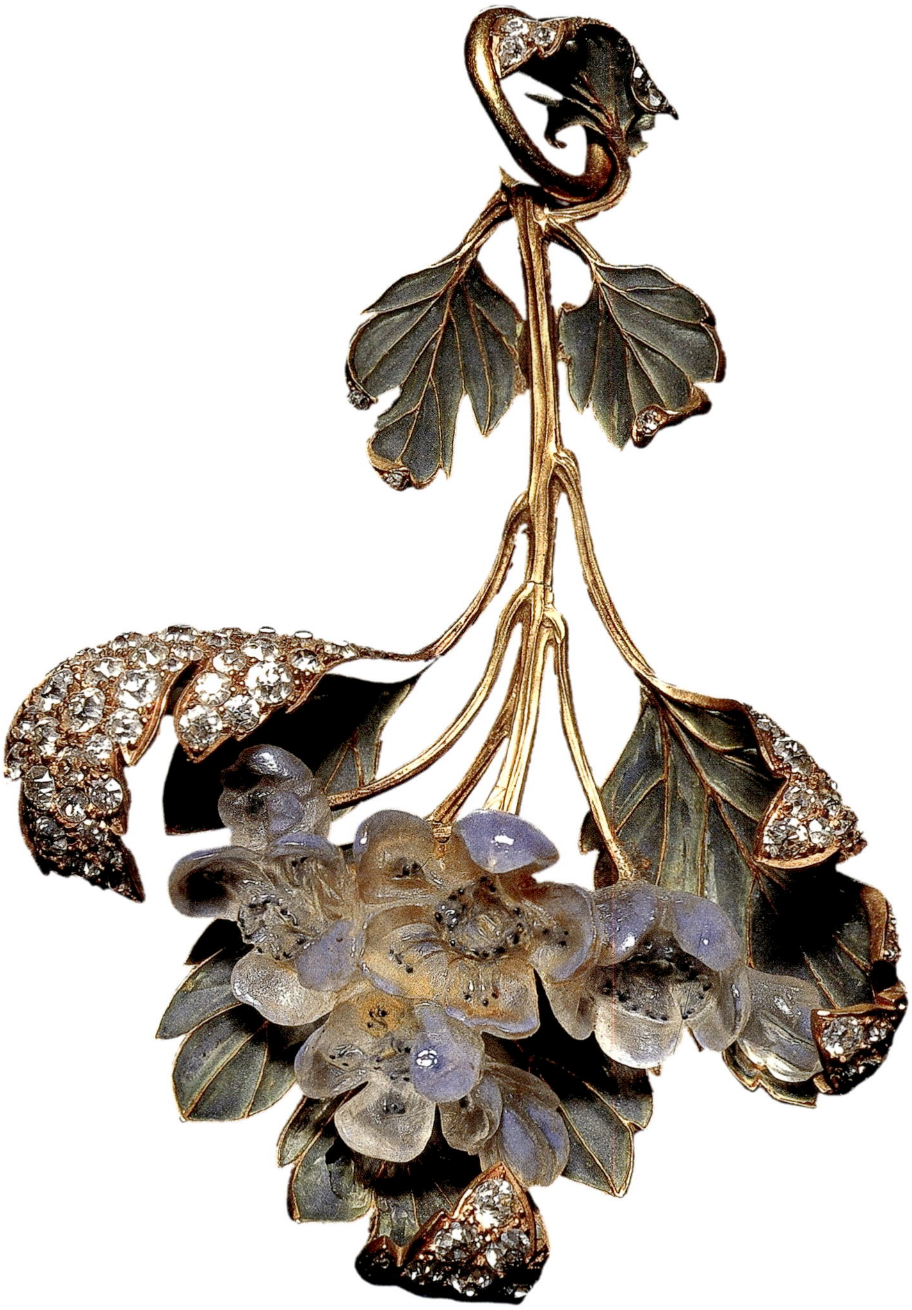

Hawthorn
Lalique
c. 1899–1901

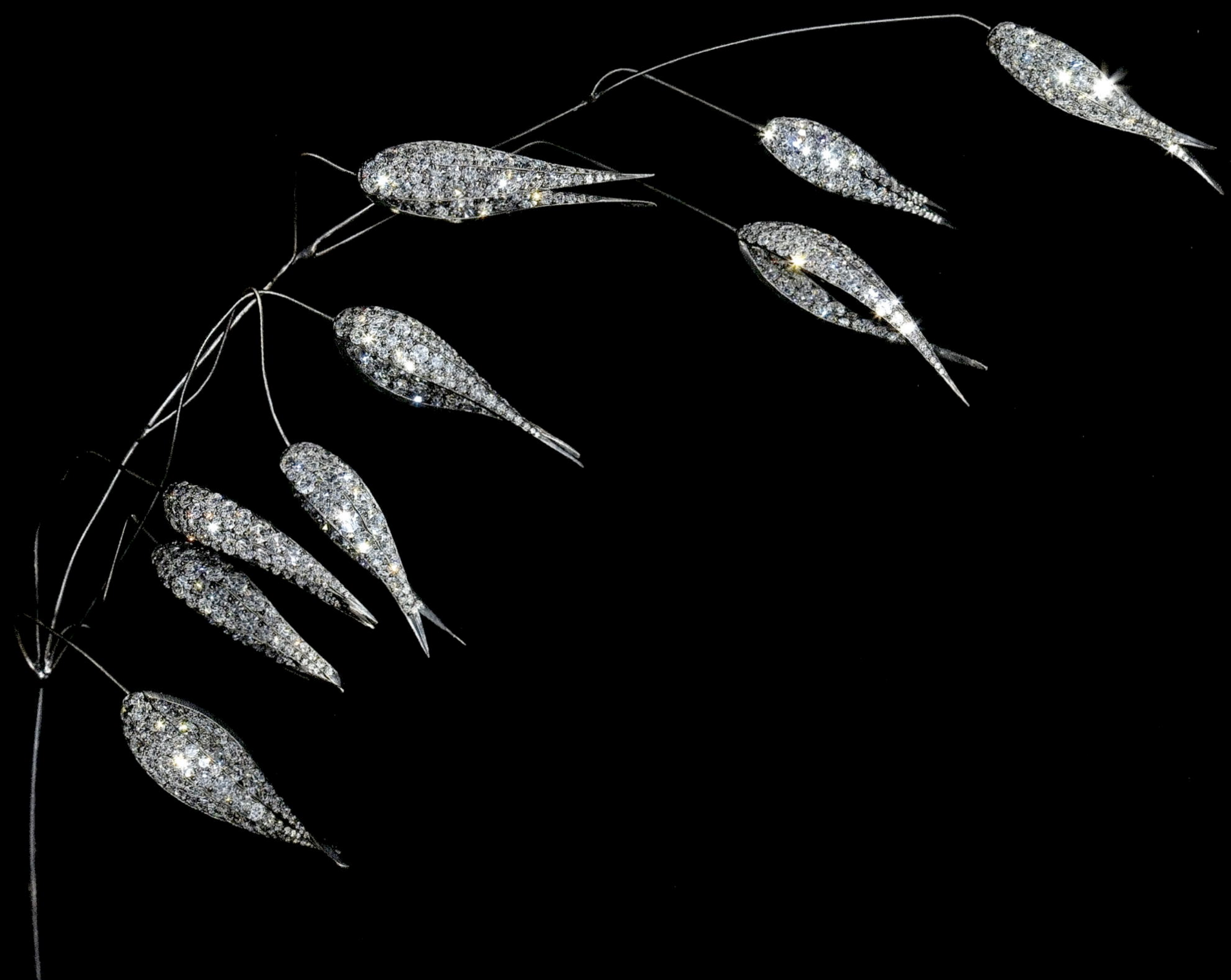

Wild Oats
JAR
2010

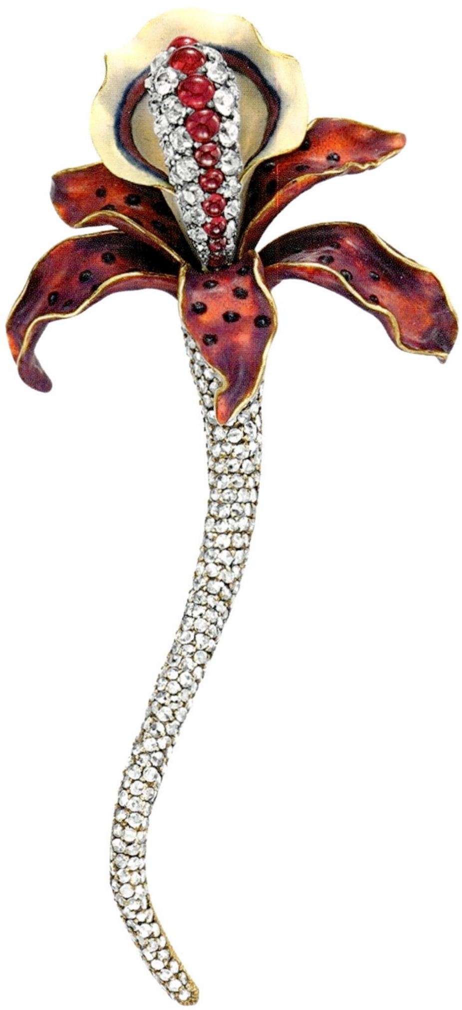

Orchid
Unknown jeweller
Mid 20th century

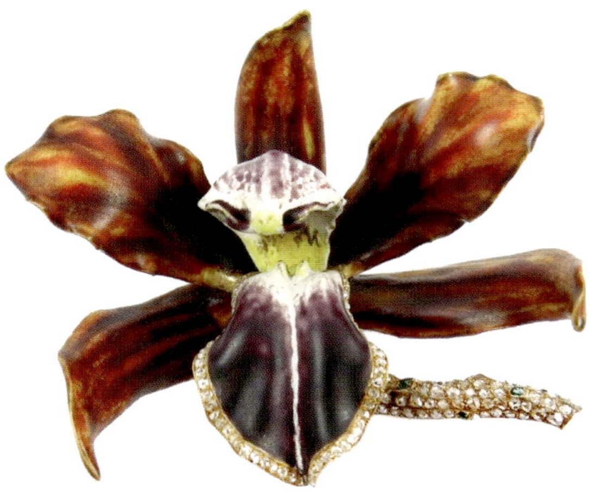

Orchid
Tiffany & Co.
c. 1900

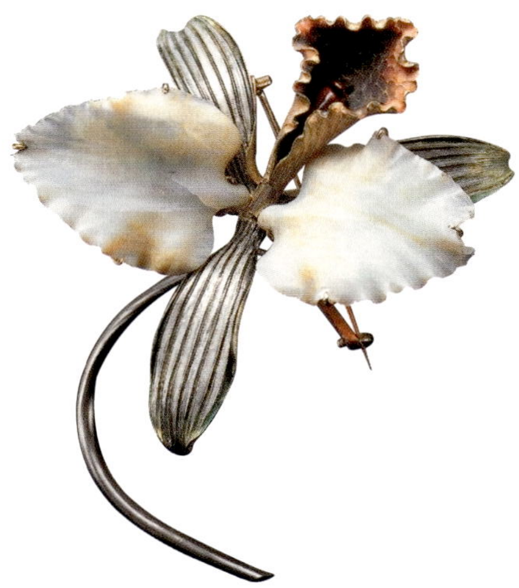

Orchid
Lalique
c. 1898–1902

Lalique preferred natural colours to simulate nature, favouring organic horn, earthy tones of *plique à jour* enamel, onyx, jade, carnelian and coral, never using precious stones such as diamonds prominently in a design, but rather to add shade, depth and define edges. His favourite stone was opal, being drawn to its mysterious flashes of colour, a look he sought with his use of frosted and enamelled glass.

> *How are we to depict the charm of these [Lalique's] flowers, this orchid, this curly chrysanthemum whose petals of green enamel are so right and so artistic in feeling, so fresh and so natural in appearance, these anemones with their exquisitely delicate corolla carved in opals of soft, iridescent hues? Is it not remarkable to see a hard gemstone interpret the delicate, velvety texture of a flower?*
>
> *French Jewelry of the Nineteenth Century*
> Henri Vever

Lalique used fluid goldwork, colour, texture and sinuous lines to depict forces of natural life: dynamic woodland scenes with shimmering carved opal lakes and gold trees entwined with green enamelled leaves, as if organically growing before your eyes. The atmosphere of each season was clearly defined in a particular piece, whether it was drooping glass and opal willow catkins, with spring light shining through the opals, casting a blue-green glow on the unfurling catkins, or an autumnal overripe grape- and vine-laden gold, horn, enamel, rock crystal and mother-of-pearl diadem.

When Japan opened its ports for trading in 1853, Europe became increasingly fascinated by their exotic arts and culture, and Japonisme became a major influence within the Art Nouveau movement. The style was identified by its whiplash curves inspired by the sinuosity and simplicity of oriental design, and painterly compositions displayed a heightened sensitivity to nature, as defined in Lalique's work, reaching its zenith of popularity around 1900. At the time there was also a vogue for plants of Asian origin in both English and French botanical gardens, where blooms such as the lacecap hydrangea, with abundant large pink and blue flowers, chrysanthemum, Japanese azaleas and orchids flourished. The unusual forms and intense hues of these species, more than Western flowers, made them an interesting subject for Lalique. In 1880, he studied for a time at London's Sydenham College, attached to the Crystal Palace and not too far from the greenhouses of Kew Gardens, the world's most renowned botanical garden at the time, bursting with sparkling inspirational Asian and tropical plants. The opalescent hues of his sculpted ivory orchid petals and silver, gold, enamel and glass Orchidée brooch, designed between 1898 and 1902, might well have been inspired by his viewing of the cattleya orchid at Kew Gardens.

Wild flowers appeal to me. Here [at Laurelton Hall] are the mountain laurel, the wild azalea, great masses of them.
Louis Comfort Tiffany

Another practitioner of the Art Nouveau movement was Louis Comfort Tiffany, the son of Charles Lewis Tiffany, founder of the Tiffany Glass and Decorating Company, later Tiffany Studios. The firm was famed for its lamps, 'favrile' glass, pottery and enamels. From 1907 it was also producing 'art jewellery', sold on the sixth floor of Tiffany & Co.'s Fifth Avenue store. Louis Comfort Tiffany has been described as a 'student of nature', spending time studying the forms of trees, flowering shrubs and wild flowers. Turning away from nineteenth-century interest in exotic Orientalism, he looked for inspiration in everyday species and humble wild flowers and grasses found in the American countryside. The flower of the wild carrot was one of his first designs for Tiffany, in silver enamel with green garnets, opals and diamonds. The Tiffany design department under his direction painted detailed studies of humble wild flora, such as Queen Anne's lace, weeds, vines, Virginia creeper and dandelions. He arranged loose-limbed long woodbine branches with five leaves in delicate twisted wirework, with translucent green enamel and one leaf partially covered by five milky opals, giving the appearance of a plant you might encounter in a woodland on a Long Island walk. Queen Anne's lace hair ornaments were wrought on silver and copper stems, white enamel, opal florets interspersed with demantoids and three red garnets at the centre and delicate networks of fine silver wire supporting white opals, to create a seed-ball blossom you might imagine dispersing on the merest whisper of wind.

Woodbine would have been ubiquitous throughout the Long Island landscape of Tiffany's country homes, climbing tree trunks, entwined over forgotten stone walls or along the forest edge, tenaciously adhering to its various supports.
Louis Comfort Tiffany and Laurelton Hall: An Artist's Country Estate
Alice Cooney Frelinghuysen

In 1879, the celebrated traveller George Frederick Kunz joined Tiffany's jewellery department, discovering and collecting American gemstones and minerals. This provided Louis Comfort Tiffany with a vibrant colour palette, enabling him to achieve a painterly effect in his work, akin to that of the Impressionists whom he admired. Kunz brought sapphires from North Carolina, beryls and tourmalines from Maine, garnets from Arizona, as well as quartz crystal, jet and amber. The gems allowed Tiffany to create contrasts between the sparkle of yellow diamonds and Montana sapphires, and opaque opals and moonstones. His pieces had a hand-wrought appearance, with a free organic naturalistic style, which suited his subjects of draped vines and sinuous curved clusters of grapes, representative of autumn in both his jewels and his Three Seasons leaded glass folding screen, displayed at the 1900 Paris world's fair.

The arts are witness to the changes in our landscape, flowers are subject to fashions, wild flowers and trees can disappear from one generation to the next.

As documenters of the natural world of their period, Lalique and Tiffany would have wrought a decorative jewel from a precious metal of the tapered branch of the humble ash, had they felt its future was uncertain.

> *Ash is laced through our hedgerows and woodlands and it will be a sad landscape without it. In spring its blue-black buds open into tiny mauve flowers ... like little bits of coral.*
>
> *Vogue*, March 2013
> Candida Lycett Green

During the Victorian age, the grandiloquent orchid was in fashion, captivating Charles Darwin who viewed them at Kew Gardens. 'I was never more interested in any subject in my life than in this of orchids', he wrote to Joseph Hooker, the director of Kew Gardens, from whom he had borrowed a book on orchid species while researching his 1862 work *The Various Contrivances by which Orchids are Fertilised by Insects*.

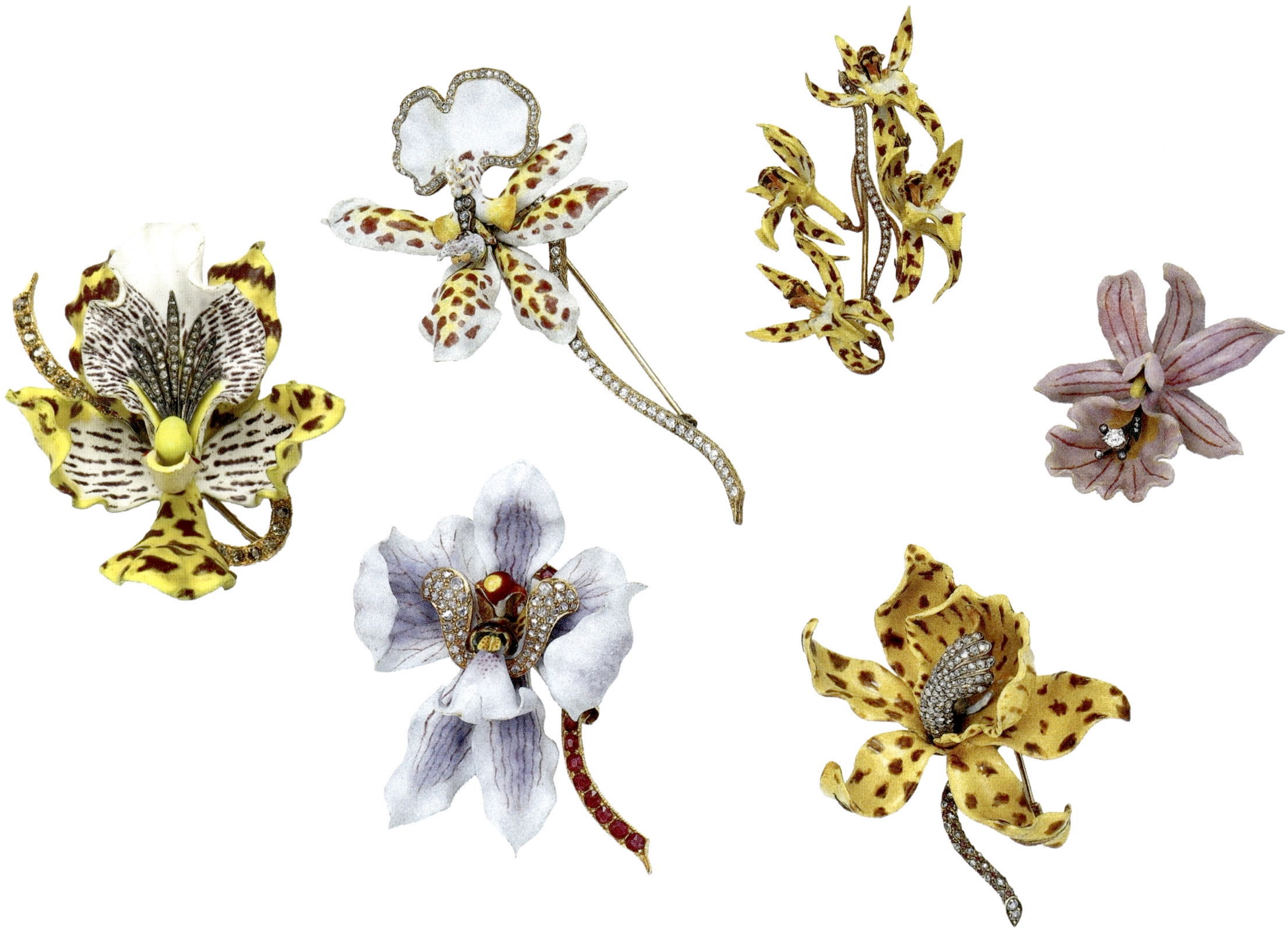

Orchids
George Paulding Farnham, Tiffany & Co.
c. 1889–96

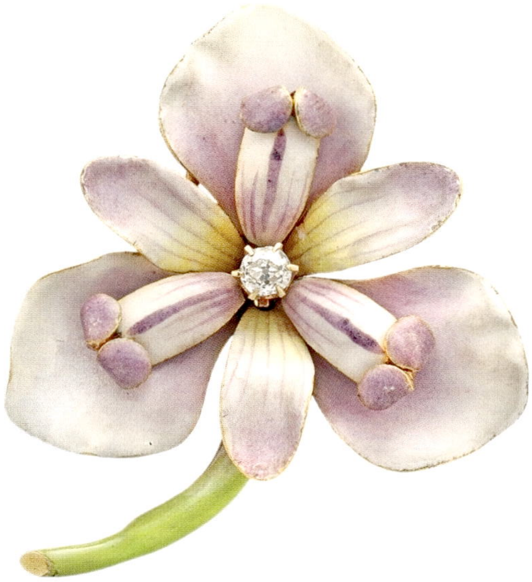

Orchid
Unknown jeweller
c. 1890

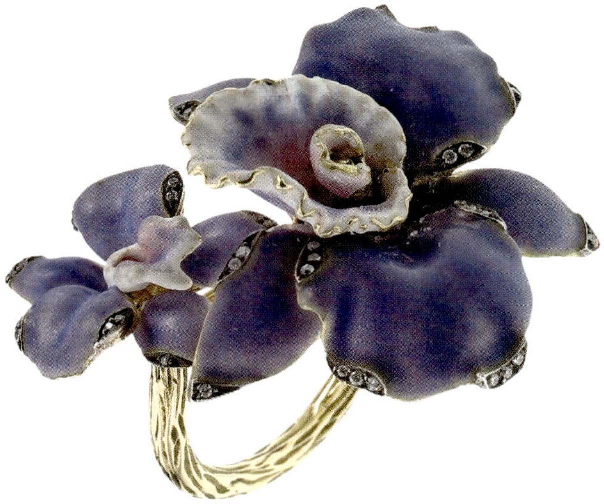

Orchid
Lydia Courteille
2008

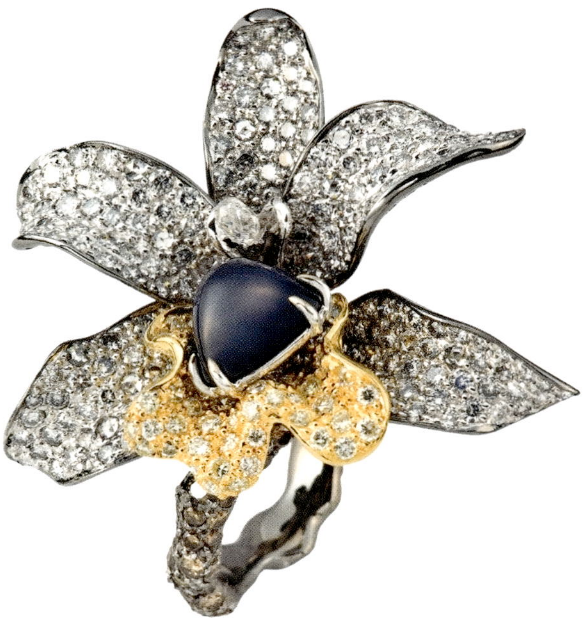

Orchid
Cindy Chao
2011

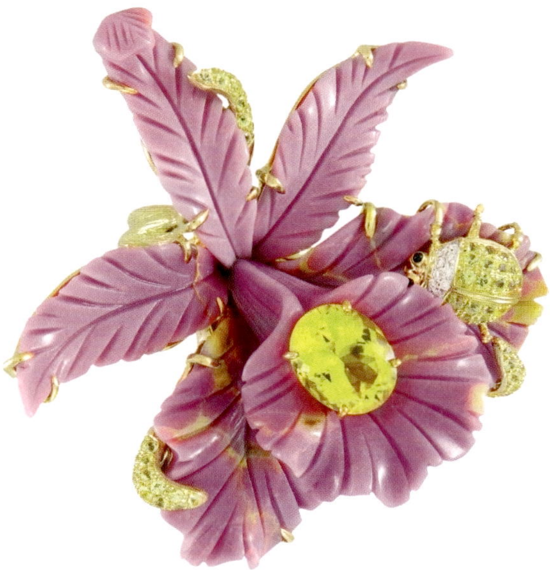

Orchid
Lydia Courteille
1997

There is fossilised evidence that orchids coexisted with dinosaurs during the late Cretaceous period. A bee trapped in a piece of amber from the Miocene era (fifteen to twenty million years ago) carried a piece of previously unknown orchid taxon on its wings. The richest concentration of the flower is in the tropics of Asia and Central and South America, where long graceful sprays can reach three metres in length. Darwin proved that the orchid had evolved to attract pollination with a labellum formed to look like the female body of a bee, as well as releasing a cocktail of chemicals mimicking the scent of virgin female bees. He also pointed out, thus providing a classic example of coexistence, that there must be a moth with a proboscis long enough to reach the nectar of the 35cm-long Christmas star orchid: an idea posthumously proven to be correct by the discovery of the hawk moth in Madagascar in 1903. The American painter Martin Johnson Heade produced small jewel-like paintings, featuring botanically accurate portraits of orchids, inspired by Darwin's writings.

Deeply glamorous, orchids are hauntingly beautiful flowers that conjure up an image of tropical paradise. Since the time of Confucius, the orchid in China has been a plant of great refinement and virtue, revered for growing modestly in inaccessible places. However, it also has earthier associations: its name in ancient Greek means 'testicle', due to the shape of the plant's root, and the flower is equated with female genitalia.

The orchid became a fashionable accessory during the nineteenth century, when new species brought back to England were acquired by horticulturists for extravagant prices. One orchid was reported to have cost £1,500 in 1890. Reacting to this desire for novel orchids, nurseries began employing intrepid 'orchid hunters' to track down wild plants in remote areas of South America and ship them back to Europe. Many plants perished en route, adding to the rarity of the flower.

By the 1880s, orchids had become highly prized status symbols. The New York financier Jay Gould lavished hundreds of thousands of dollars on the plants, as well as the installation of heating systems in greenhouses to aid their cultivation. There was a form of orchid mania amongst wealthy collectors, such as Empress Eugénie, who spent 18,000 francs on a rare orchid species (*Cattleya trianae*), and King Leopold II of Belgium, who had a series of greenhouses built in Laeken to house his exotic orchid specimens.

At Tiffany, botanical specimens were regularly brought to the so-called 'Tiffany School', one of the first US design schools, where meticulous pen-and-pencil watercolour studies were drawn by the student apprentices. One design student who spent years closely observing and painting botanical studies was George Paulding Farnham, who started to receive attention for his series of enamelled lilac, rose, heliotrope and trumpet vine jewellery around 1885. However, it was orchids on which he began to focus, using the watercolour sketches as the basis for the decorative enamelling of twenty-four life-like gold orchid blossoms, for which he won worldwide acclaim, as well as a gold medal, at the 1900 Paris world's fair.

Farnham's orchids were plated with copper to preserve the three-dimensional shape of the flower, enamelled on gold with stems encrusted with small semi-precious stones, creating a contrast to the fantastic realism of the petals. The shiny and matt enamelled surfaces illustrated perfectly the seductive colours of the exotic plant and the character of each individual species. The *Chysis limminghei* orchid, native to Brazil, is flecked with brown enamel, with white stamens and a diamond-set column protruding from the flower, whereas the soft sheen of the *Phalaenopsis schilleriana*, from the Philippines, is enamelled in white, purple, red, brown and yellow, with a Burmese ruby stem. Each flower is set with an extraordinary combination of the compelling beauty of nature, the fertile imagination of the designer and technical virtuosity. Although orchids are now widely found in the West, their tiger-spotted striped leaves, purple stamens and soft fragile cockleshell-pink soft curling and undulating petals with diamond tips remain intoxicatingly fresh and exotic.

At the 1925 Exposition des Arts Décoratifs in Paris, Cartier displayed its white orchid jewels on tortoiseshell combs. As *Harper's Bazaar* columnist and photographer Baron Adolf de Meyer explained, 'Equally charming, a circular comb for short hair, to be worn at the back on the head; each side it had two large bouquets of orchids in diamonds sprinkled with onyx, the flowers resting on the hair just above the ears.' Cartier played on the fragility and sensuality of the orchid in the delicacy of the forms and colours chosen, creating silken fabric petals, sepals and labella in stones.

The flower is always linked to sensuality and desire. For Marcel Proust in *Remembrance of Things Past: Swann's Way*, the orchid symbolised Odette, Swann's love: 'She had in her hand a bouquet of cattleyas, and Swann saw, under the veil of lace covering her hair, that she had this same orchid fastened to a plume of swan feathers.' Odette carried the orchids because they had 'the supreme merit of not looking like other flowers', reminding her of scraps of silk so delicate they could have been cut out from the lining of her cloak. In due course the flowers took on another significance, the expression 'to do a cattleya' becoming the code for Swann and Odette's intimate relationship.

Cartier created many jewelled orchids under the design directorship of Jeanne Toussaint, one example being the 1937 Orchidée brooch in aquamarines and amethysts, the stones faceted underneath with blue and mauve enamel to emphasise the colours. Although a flower lover, Toussaint never had blooms on table tops in her Paris apartment; instead, she had them in abundance in numerous vases dotted about on the floor, as she preferred to see them on the ground, exactly where they would be found growing in nature.

Orchids have had a reputation for being dark, mysterious and unpredictable, and wild orchids can still lure plant collectors into uncharted territory, but the moth orchid in particular is subject to industrial production techniques, so can be easily found. This has pushed Cartier into creating their own rare hybrid blossoms. 'We reinvent orchid colours and shapes', explains Pierre Rainero,

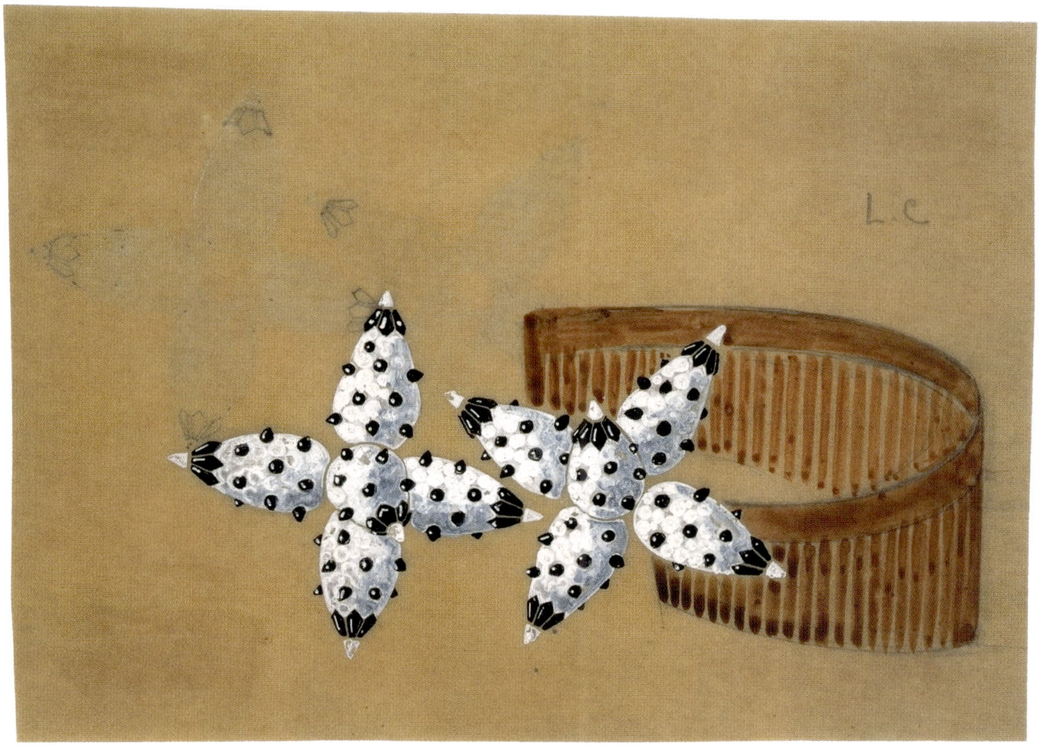

Orchids
Cartier Paris
1925

Cartier's image, style and heritage director. 'We feel there is more poetry in creating our own orchids - they are different and unique. You might recognise it as an orchid but you wouldn't know where it grows or where to find it.'

The visual representation of the flower has altered from stylised abstraction to naturalistic representation in the 'Caresse d'orchidée' collection, with complex cushion-cut purple tourmalines, *plique à jour* enamel and diamonds with exaggerated labella. Diamond petals are peppered with dustings of yellow sapphire pollen, on graduated garnet stems, with red rubellites making a provocative spilling gesture out of the central trumpet. Soft flowers are cut from a single morganite stone or piece of rubellite, with rounded voluptuous petals and brilliant round diamond labella.

> *How healthy, strong and rosy, a rosiness that moistens the lips of desire! How I love them! The border [of the orchid] is frizzled, paler than their throat, where the corolla hides itself away; a mysterious mouth, seductive sugar under the tongue, exhibiting and unveiling the delicate, admirable and sacred organs of these divine little creatures which smell so exquisitely and do not speak.*
>
> *The Divorce*
> Guy de Maupaussant

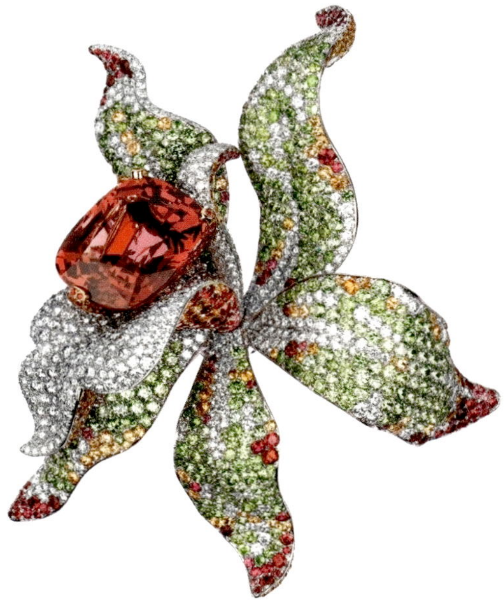

Orchid
Cartier
2005

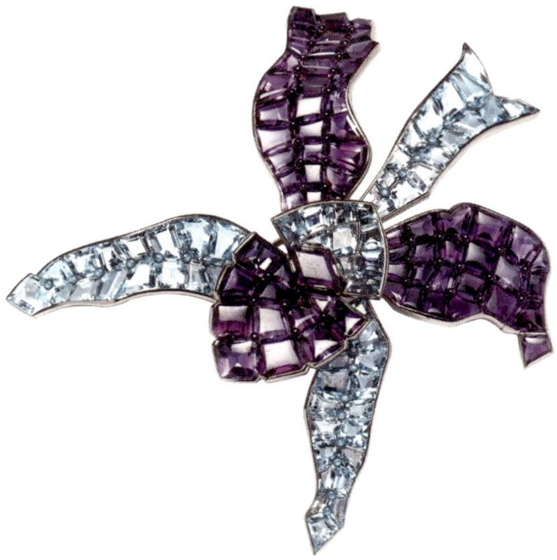

Orchid
Cartier Paris
1937

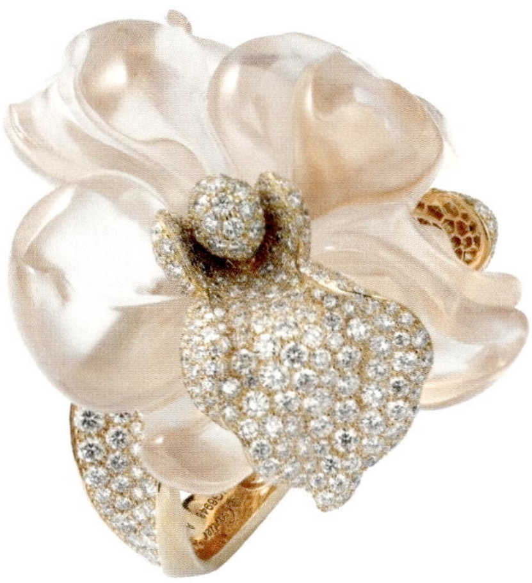

Orchid
Cartier
2012

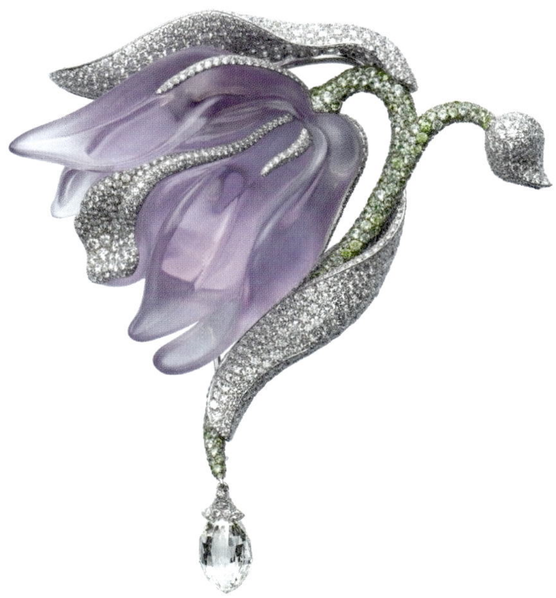

Orchid
Cartier
2010

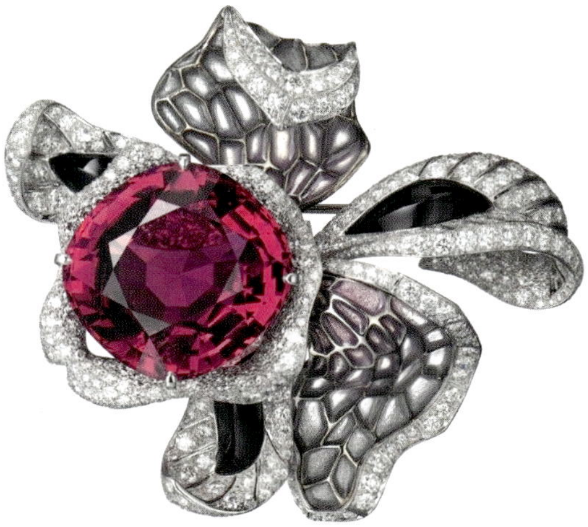

Orchid
Cartier
2012

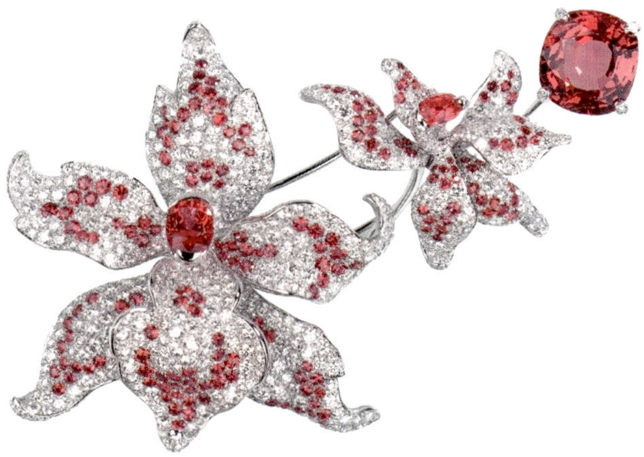

Orchid
Cartier
2005

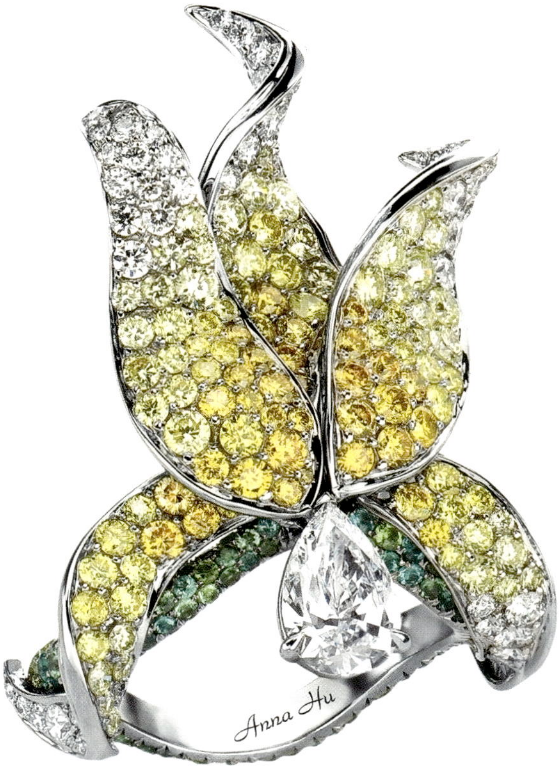

Golden Orchid
Anna Hu
2010

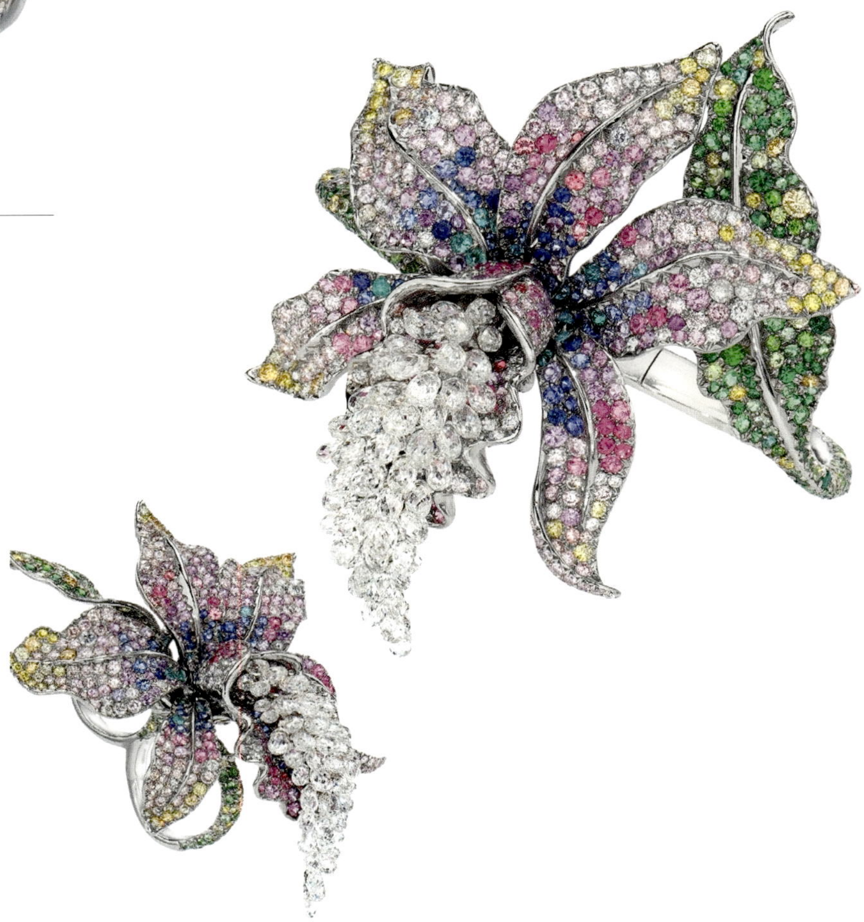

Orchids
Anna Hu
2011

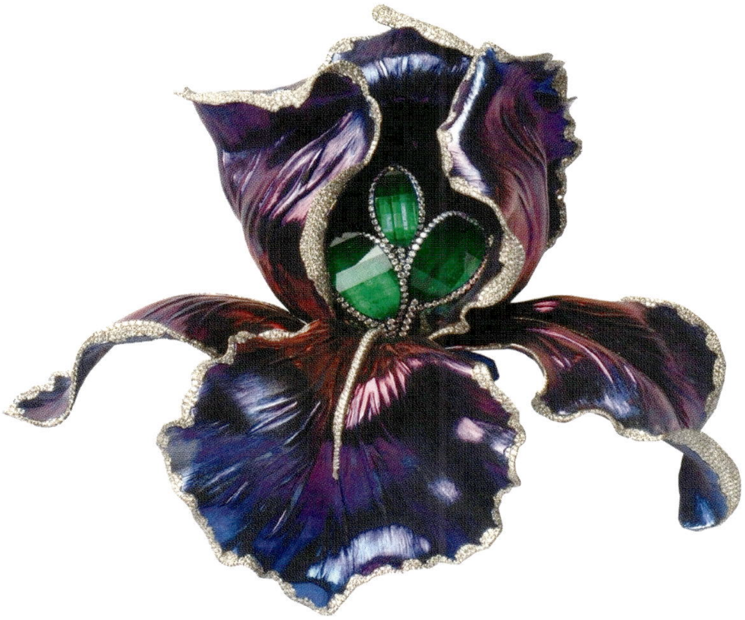

Orchid

Glenn Spiro
2002

French jeweller René Boivin had a great knowledge of botany and gardening through his membership of horticultural associations and subscriptions to gardening magazines. His favourite flowers were members of the Orchidaceae family, struck by the erotic baroque nature of their contours, and he timed the unveiling of his first orchid brooch to coincide with the June 1900 issue of *L'Atlas de l'orchidée*. Over the years, the house produced infinite varieties of orchid with ethereal realism, from startling yellow gold and diamond striped and spotted clips, to large imposing white and yellow diamond cattleya specimens.

Anna Hu 'paints' her orchids, aiming to blend Monet's impressionistic colour palette with elements of Chinese brush painting. Working from the actual plant, she makes blossoms of vibrant pink and golden yellow diamonds, with briolette diamonds cascading from the centre of the flower. The petals on her Golden Orchid ring, of pear-shaped fancy vivid yellow and white diamonds, Columbian emeralds, green tourmalines, demantoid garnets and tsavorites, appear wind-blown, the yellow diamonds graduating from deeper to lighter shades, with subtle green hues on the shank, alluding to the stem.

anemone • blossom • daisy • dandelion • lily of the valley • narcissus • pansy • violet • calla lily • foxglove • holly • lily • lotus • morning glory • poppy • rose • sunflower • sweet pea • thistle • hawthorn • wild oats • camellia

anemone • blossom • daisy • dandelion • lily of the valley

narcissus • pansy • peony • tulip • violet • calla lily • rose • anemone • daisy • dandelion • lily of the valley • narcissus • pansy • sunflower • sweet pea • thistle • hawthorn • wild oats • ivy calla lily • foxglove • heliotrope • iris • lily • lotus

anemone • blossom • daisy • dandelion • lily of the valley •

anemone • pansy • daisy • chrysanthemum • narcissus

• hawthorn • hydrangea • orchid

• vanilla flower • foxglove

• wild oats • camellia • heliotrope

heliotrope • iris • lily • lotus • morning glory • edelweiss •

hellebore • holly • ivy • mistletoe • snowdrop • winter plum • anemone

• blossom • daisy • dandelion • narcissus

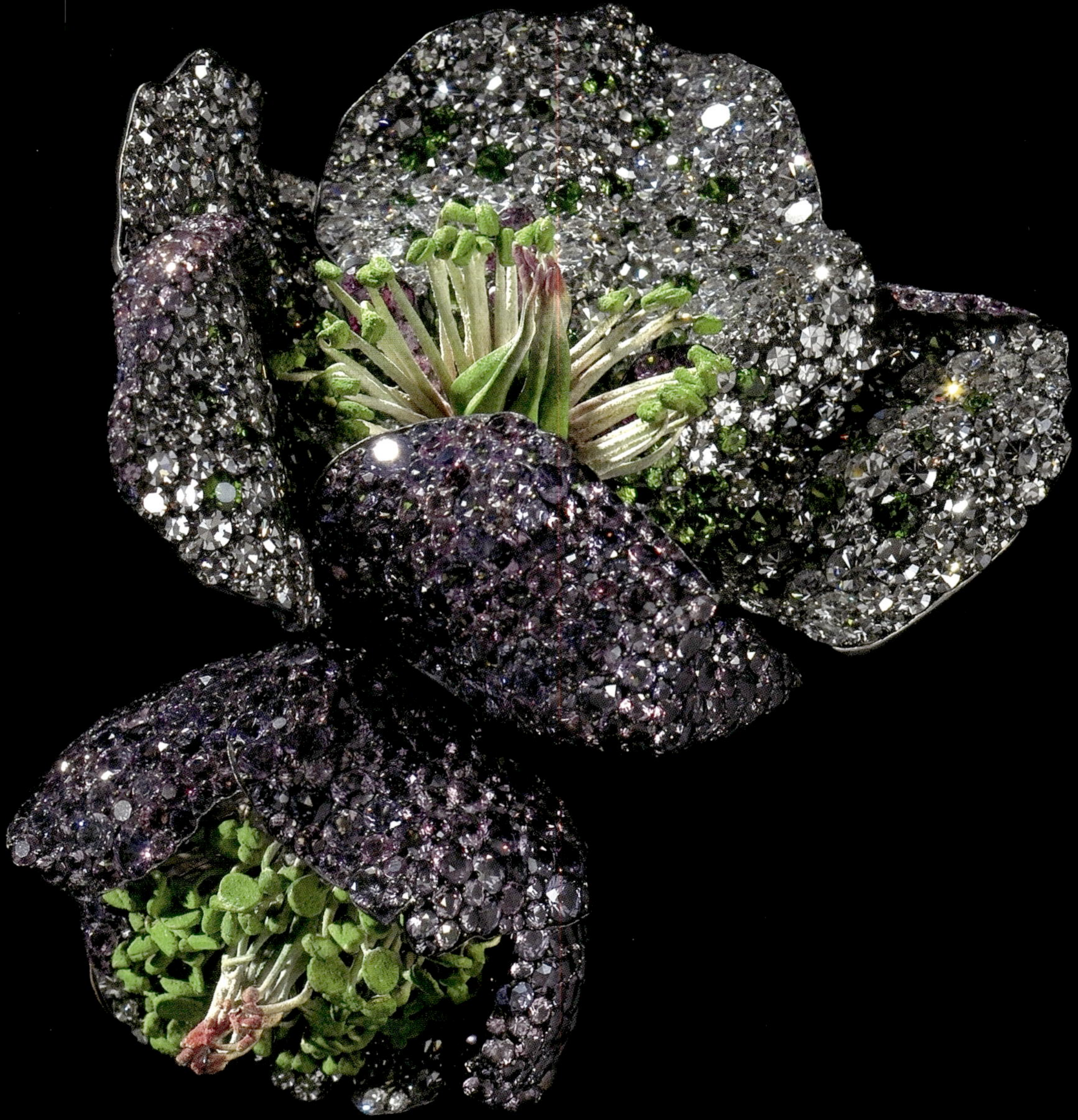

Hellebore
JAR
2002

Winter

In the sniffed and poured snow
on the tip of the tongue of the year.
Dylan Thomas

Winter is the still season when the ground spreads into a dazzling white sea of frozen foam, a vast monochrome horizon against which ruby-red berries and forever verdant emerald leaves sparkle like precious jewels in snowy hollows. Diamond is the stone of winter, the colour of dew and frozen water, sparkling in the winter sun as water turns to icy white, and glints through barren undergrowth like frozen glassy pools. Frost flowers grow in thin layers of ice, like jewelled icicles from long-stemmed plants, as water drawn up the plant stem oozes out and freezes into crystalline blossoms. The rock-hard ground is covered with a soft settling of frost, reflecting shards of light like crisply faceted diamonds, cladding the earth with a shimmery radiance. Each blade of grass, woody bough and forgotten spray bow under the weight of their snowy coat, which is slowly shed in single silvery drops, when warmed by the winter sun rising in the sky.

The diamond contrasts with all other stones, bringing their colours to life, much like flowers as they turn their faces towards the sun's rays. The diamond is a gem of light: when broken into a spectrum, it shimmers with rainbow colours, and, in turn, all the other shades in combination with one another shine with a brilliant white.

When the God of Mines called his courtiers to bring him all known gems, he found them to be of all colors and tints, and of varying hardnesses... He took one of each; he crushed them; he compounded them, and said: 'Let this be something that will combine the beauty of all; yet it must be pure, and must be invincible.' He spoke: and lo! the diamond was born, pure as the dew-drop and invincible in hardness; but when its ray is resolved in the spectrum, it displays all the colours of the gems from which it was made.

The Curious Lore of Precious Stones
George Frederick Kunz

Amid the frosted landscape you can catch glimpses of subtle pastel colours camouflaged in the snow, where large, white, flat-faced hellebores, lightly dusted with pink, lie with lime-green centres amongst deep green foliage. This is the snow rose, or Christmas rose, an innocent-looking white flower, whose purity belies its poisonous nature, grown from pitch-black roots used to ward off evil.

The legend of the Christmas rose is that a young girl called Madelon, weeping that she had no gift to bring the infant Jesus, was heard by an angel who touched the tear-splashed ground making white roses spring up for her to take. An ancient bloom, the Christmas rose was prescribed in small doses by Greek

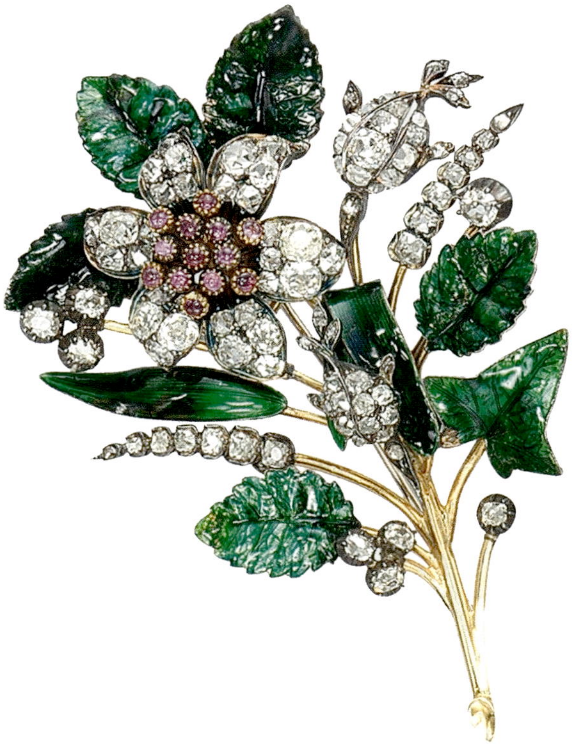

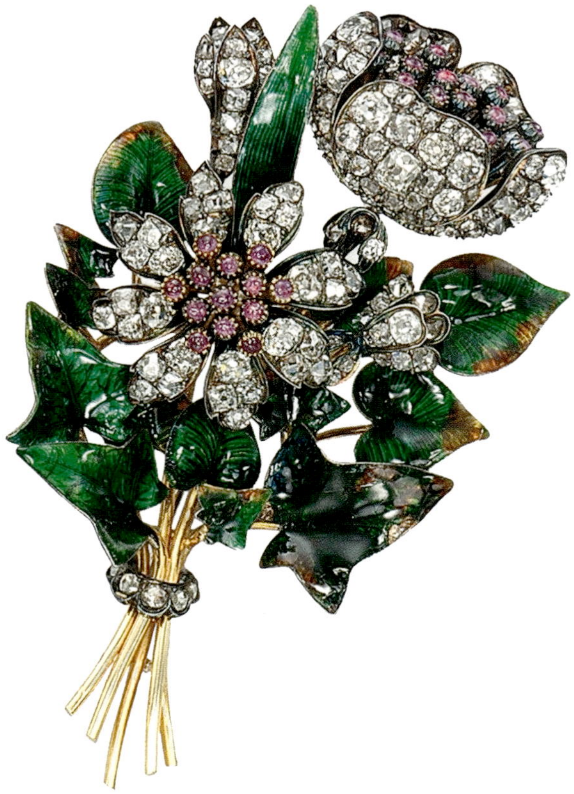

Christmas Rose
Unknown jeweller
c. 1850

physicians during the first century AD to cure mental disorders. During the Middle Ages, it was used to ward off witchcraft, so when the Christmas rose failed to bloom at Christmas it was taken as an ill omen.

Only the snow slides
Like gilded myrrh
From the rose-branches – hides
Rose-roots that stir.
...The snow amygdaline
Under the eglantine
Where bristling stars shine
Like a gilt porcupine.

When Cold December
Edith Sitwell

Icy diamond stalactite earrings, snowflake brooches and frost rock crystal and diamond bracelets herald the winter season at JAR's, where pretty violet sapphire, demantoid garnet and enamel hellebore flowers grow in snowball rock crystal and diamond boxes.

Stone-set Roses de Noël are the hardy perennial in the garden of Van Cleef & Arpels, which originally blossomed in France in 1968, following the political unrest, designed for a new modern woman looking for a less formal fine jewel. The diamond, winter-white coral and mother-of-pearl carved flower heads have gold wirework pistils and brilliant-cut diamonds nestled in the centre of curved petals. The flowers are an inspiration taken from nature; as opposed to mimicking the rose, the jewellery house's designers aim to capture the instant when nature's vital force and its intense fragility bloom simultaneously. Using poetic licence, Van Cleef's roses open their petals each year, bringing a fresh touch of colour to the winter landscape, with coral, turquoise, and chalcedony petals cradling hearts of diamonds.

Van Cleef's Cristaux de Neige, first designed in 1946, are tiny white frosted flakes with a crystalline structure, much like a diamond. At the centre of the star is a daisy-like icy stained-glass window, set with stones arranged tightly against one another to reflect the light, so that they glisten like frosty drops of dew. During the early part of the twentieth century, Fabergé designed rock crystal brooches set with tiny diamonds, which depicted the frost-like hairline cracks that would creep across the frozen Neva River in St Petersburg when the snow began to melt. Fabergé also added frosting motifs to large eggs of white topaz, using 1,508 rose-cut diamonds on a topaz base shaped like a block of ice, with rose-cut diamond icicles. 'Inside the egg is a small platinum basket decorated with 1,378 rose-cut diamonds, and in it white quartz snowdrops with nephrite leaves', wrote Fabergé himself in June 1913.

There is a small mountain flower called edelweiss, which blossoms in the snow at high altitude in rocky places, with dense protective hair making it like a fuzzy white star. It means courage and devotion for the brave man who would dare to pluck one for his sweetheart.

...It grows on the most inaccessible cliffs of the Tyrolese
mountains where the chamois dare hardly venture,
and which the hunter, tempted by its beauty and by
his love, climbs the cliffs to gather, and is sometimes
found dead at the foot, with the flower in his hand.

Eulogy for Thoreau, 1862
Ralph Waldo Emerson

The lucky girl whose suitor survived would press the flower, frame it and wear it as a jewelled pendant.

Where huge rocky buttresses bear up the clouds,
With all their floating reservoirs of rain;
Where the wide winding sheet of snow enshrouds
The glacier's sapphire clefts and glittering plain
This flow'r is found – the well nam'd Edelweiss.

Sonnet on an Edelweiss
Frances Anne Kemble

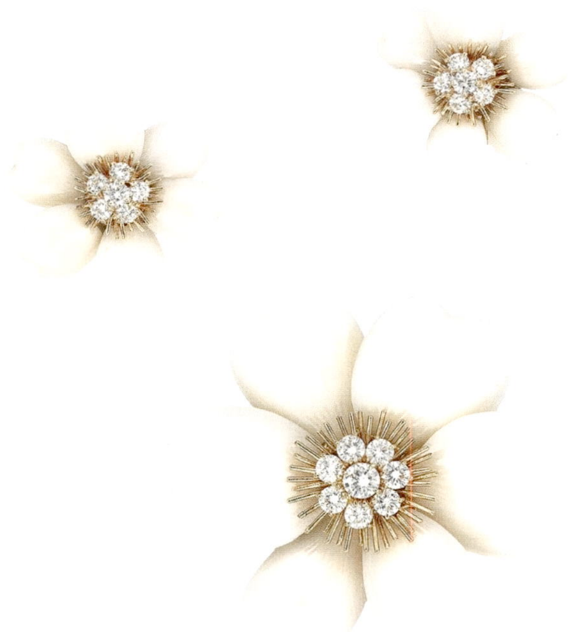

Christmas Rose
Van Cleef & Arpels
Late 20th century

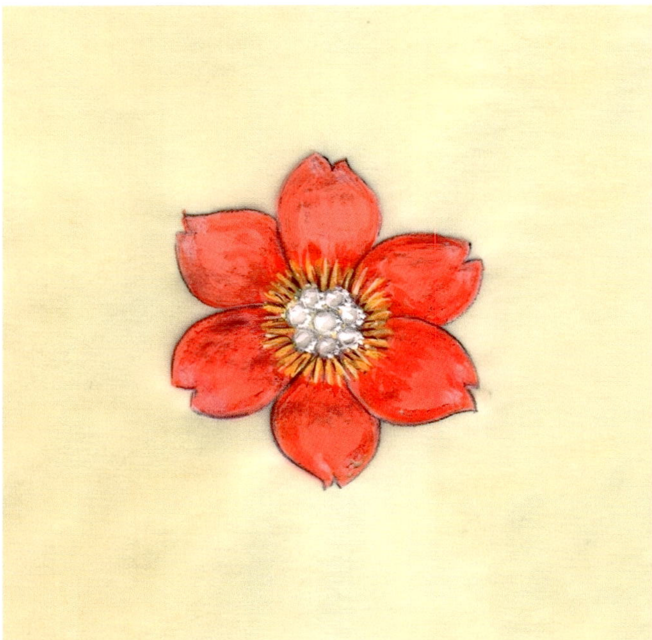

Christmas Rose
Van Cleef & Arpels
1970

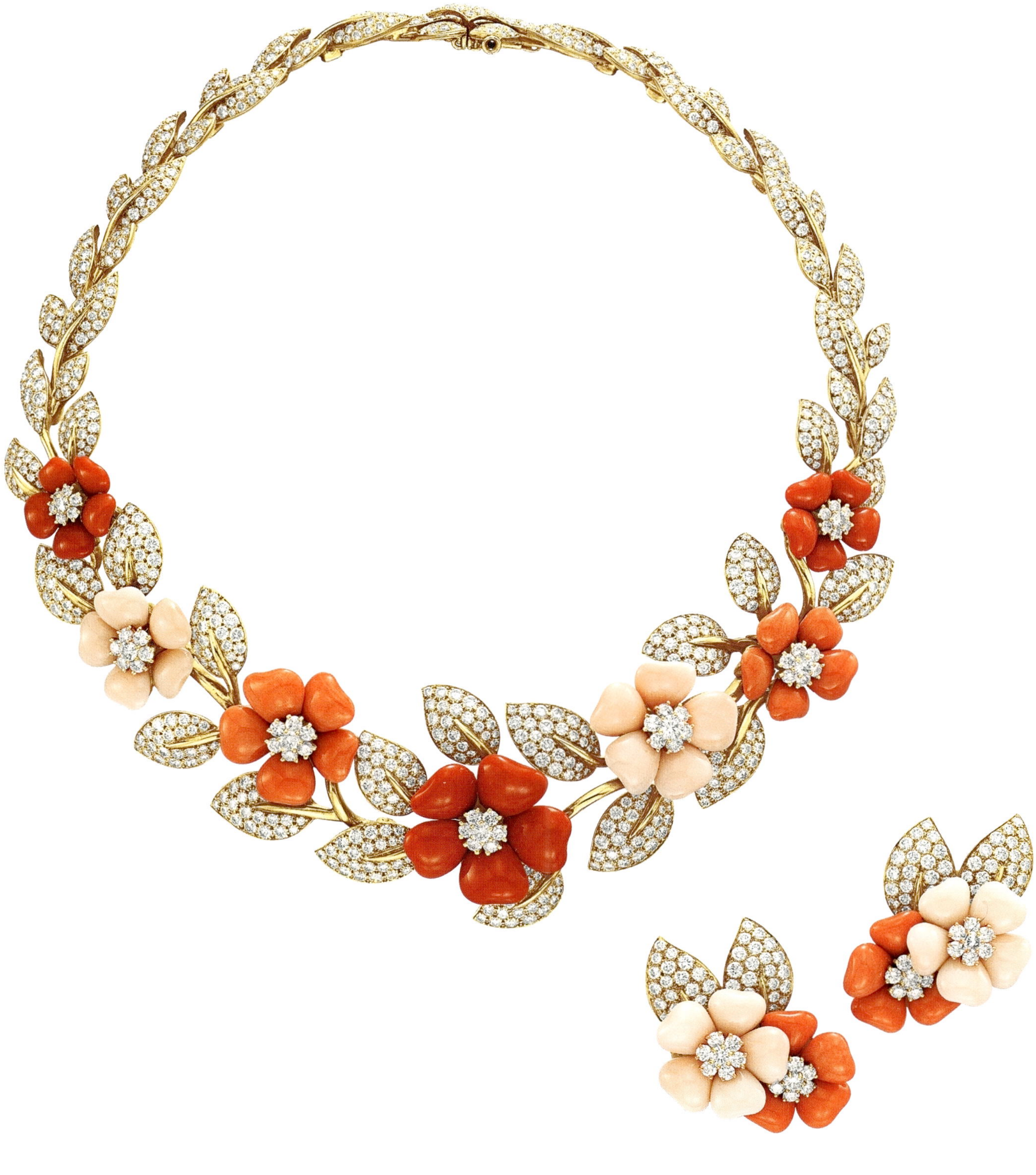

Christmas Rose
Van Cleef & Arpels
Late 20th century

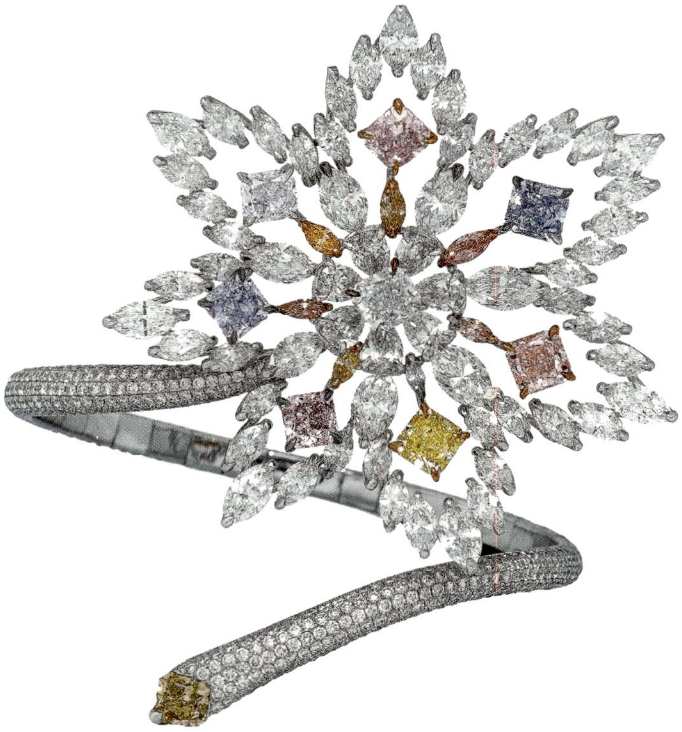

Frost Flower
Glenn Spiro
2010

Her Majesty the Queen received a 23.6 carat Williamson Pink stone as a wedding gift in 1947, from Canadian geologist John T. Williamson, which had been discovered in Tanganyika (now Tanzania). Cartier made this pale dusty pink diamond the centre of an edelweiss flower, set with marquise- and brilliant-cut diamonds, on a baguette-cut diamond stem. Van Cleef & Arpels also cultivate the tiny mountain flower, using frosty white diamonds and white opals to depict the rarity of its blossom.

Amongst the bare boughs and odd spires of red in a romantic English winter garden, the glossy evergreen triangular leaves of the ornamental plant ivy can be seen, which clings to trees, grows its creeping tendrils up brick walls and entwines in circles around porticoes. Ivy never leaves the trees to which it attaches itself, earning its representation in fine jewellery as a symbol of eternity. In ancient Greece, ivy was worn as a protective talisman by the god Dionysus and presented in wreaths for newlyweds to wear, whilst the Romans gave ivy vine crowns to victorious athletes. In the language of flowers, ivy's reputation for clinging meant it was associated with marriage and fidelity, making it a favourite with Queen Victoria. Over the course of the Victorian era, many diamond-set collet tiaras with emerald ivy leaves, or golden tiaras with ivy leaves and berries, decorated with enamel and cabochon chrysoberyls, were created for young brides, referencing wreaths of classical antiquity.

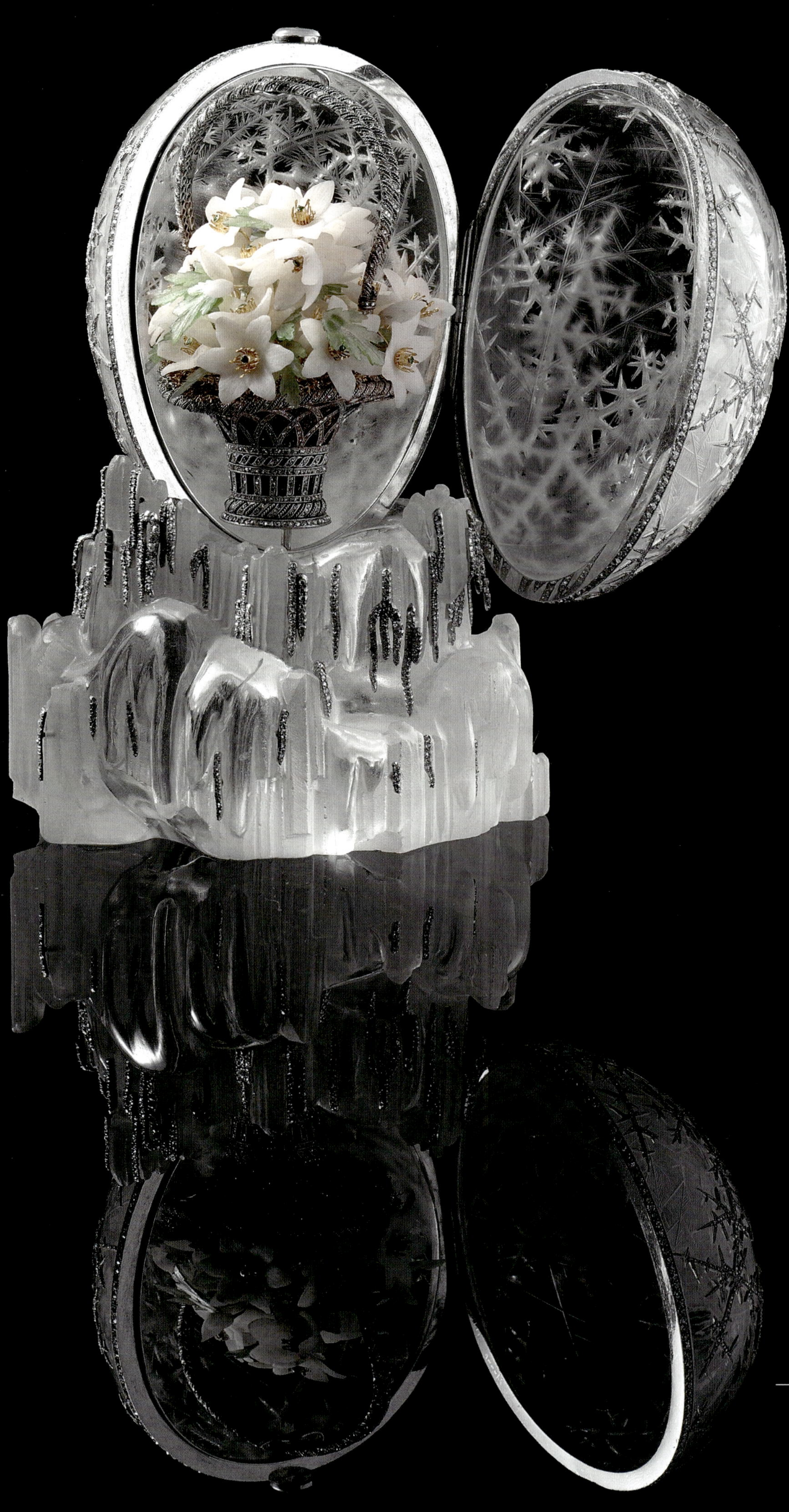

Snowdrops
Fabergé
1913

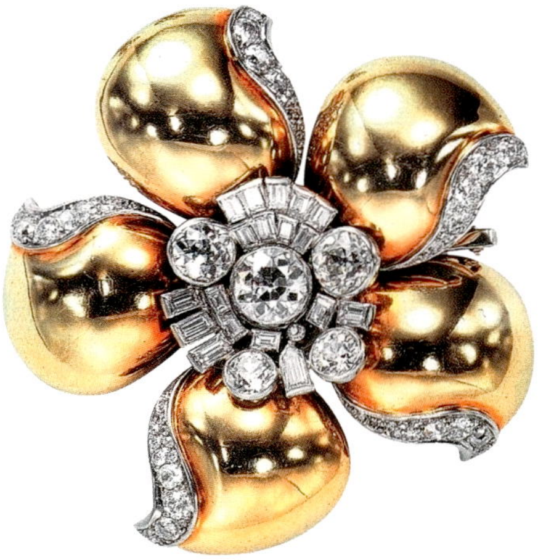

Edelweiss
Suzanne Belperron
c. 1935

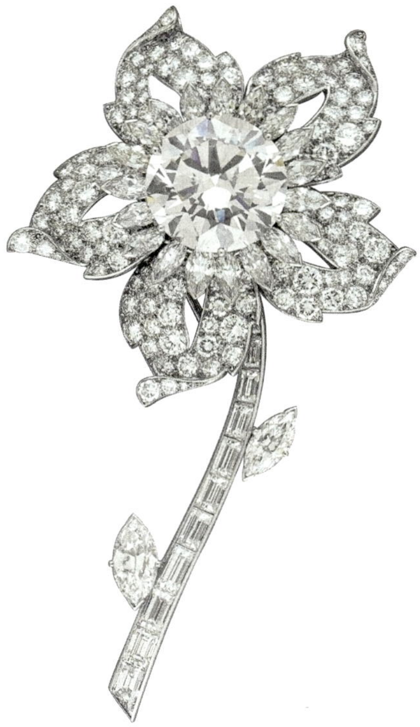

Edelweiss
Cartier
1947

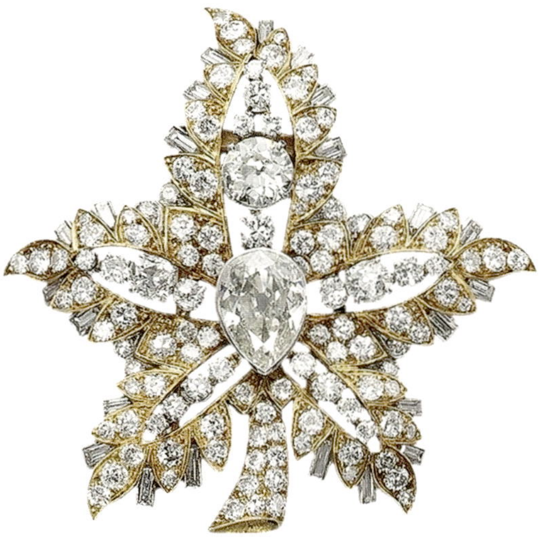

Edelweiss
Boivin
1948

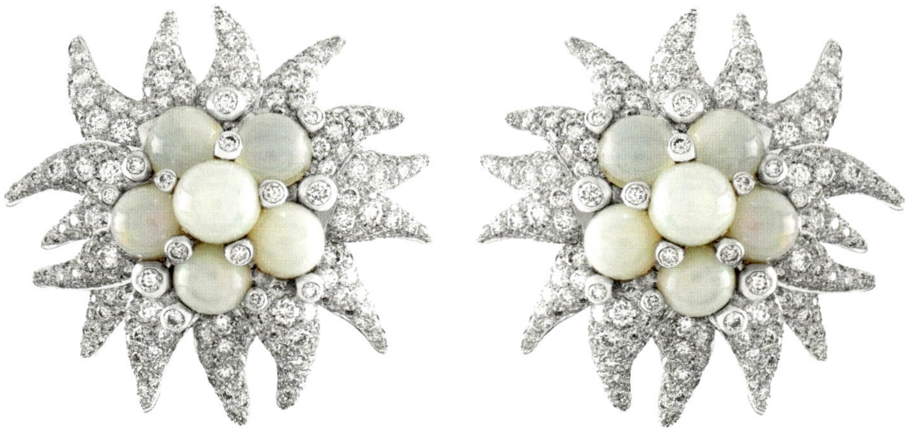

Edelweiss
Van Cleef & Arpels
2012

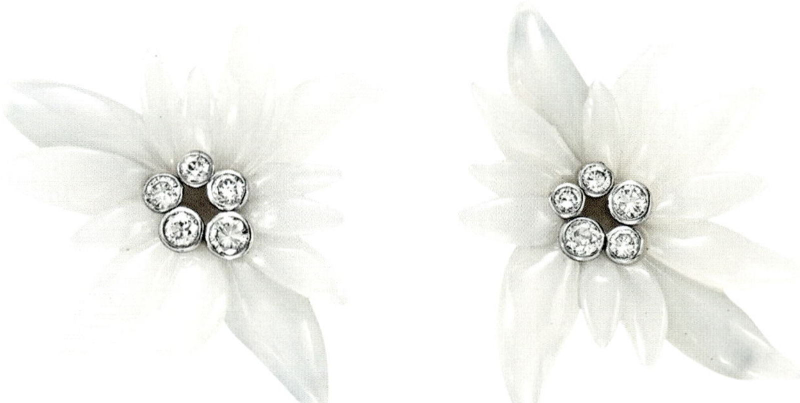

Edelweiss
Suzanne Belperron
c. 1950

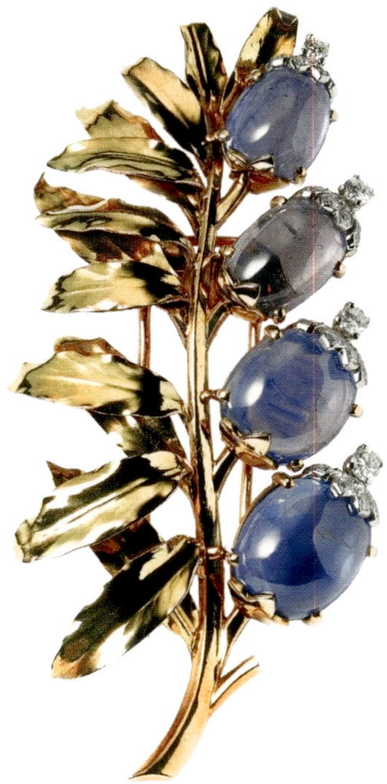

Mistletoe
Cartier Paris
1943

This old stone tower was very massive – and rather ruinous, too, for it was Roman, and four hundred years old. Yes, and handsome, after a rude fashion, and clothed with ivy from base to summit, as with a shirt of scale mail.

Merlin's Tower
Mark Twain

More recently, the role of ivy has come to be entwined with prickly ripe green-leafed and red-berried holly, the symbol of man; thought to bring peace to homes, it is used as decoration during the Christmas holiday. On one wintry night in 1940, when the legendary American diamanteur and jeweller Harry Winston was returning to his Scarsdale estate, he noticed a holly wreath hanging on his door coated with a dusting of December frost, which made the holly leaves glisten like diamonds. Winston became fascinated by the way the wreath's sculpted shape was created, not from branches, but by individual intertwining leaves. He designed a new diamond technique he called 'clustering', using pear-, marquise- and brilliant-cut diamonds together to create three-dimensional jewels, sparkling from all angles, like ice-covered holly and ivy in a decorative winter wreath.

The sun and moon shed one white light.

Love's First Fever to her Plague
Dylan Thomas

Designer Shaun Leane was inspired by Dylan Thomas's line to create a White Light brooch using thirteen flawless D-colour Forevermark pear-shaped diamonds. White diamond collets cascade like frozen icicles from branches laden with ivy-style opalescent leaves, the green leaves shimmering with frosted soft blue enamel, luminous in the soft ethereal winter light. 'I made it to encapsulate the first snow of winter,' says Leane, 'which falls reducing everything to zero, man eclipsed by a quiet cover of pure white. Snow crystals settling on leaves with light so pure that it cuts to the essence of what is precious.'

At Cartier during the 1950s, the ivy leaf was golden in colour, created with realistic chased vein details running through the leaf, as if it had been picked and pressed from nature and mounted on a scrolling diamond-set stem. Designs at the house of René Boivin, by the 1930s, were increasingly naturalistic, based on fruits and flowers, with lush emerald leaves, which also featured pronounced veins. Brooches were created as winter leaves, falling with baguette- and circular-cut diamonds, centring on a pear-shaped diamond. Other foliate motifs were to be found in a yellow gold and calibre-cut emerald and 'Pampilles' necklace, with each crisp leaf set with moss-green peridots.

During the Belle Époque, the fashion in Paris was for formal *jardins à la française*, but jeweller Frédéric Boucheron admired the wild ivy that grew spontaneously under the arches of the Palais-Royal, and he took the green foliage of the plant as inspiration for diamond-set corsages and brooches *en tremblant*, with quivering tendrils and leaves. Boucheron set a new trend with designs featuring plane tree leaves and rustic bouquets of flowers, pinned to the front of gowns and worn as chokers. During the 1940s, he created a new 'high kicking' style, for mounting stones on different leaves, resembling knots or pistils of a flower

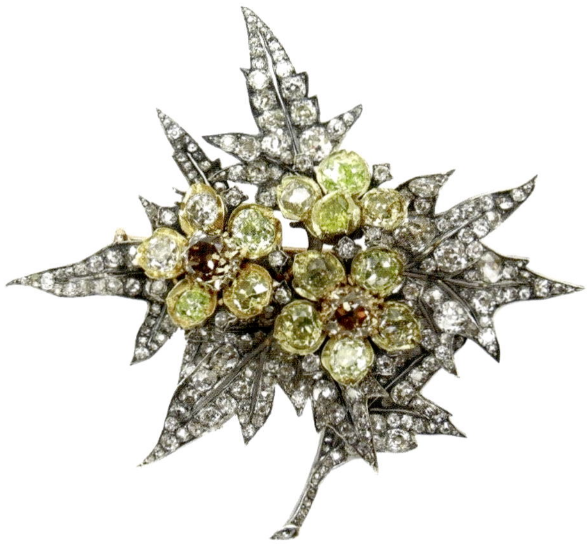

Holly
Unknown jeweller
c. 1880

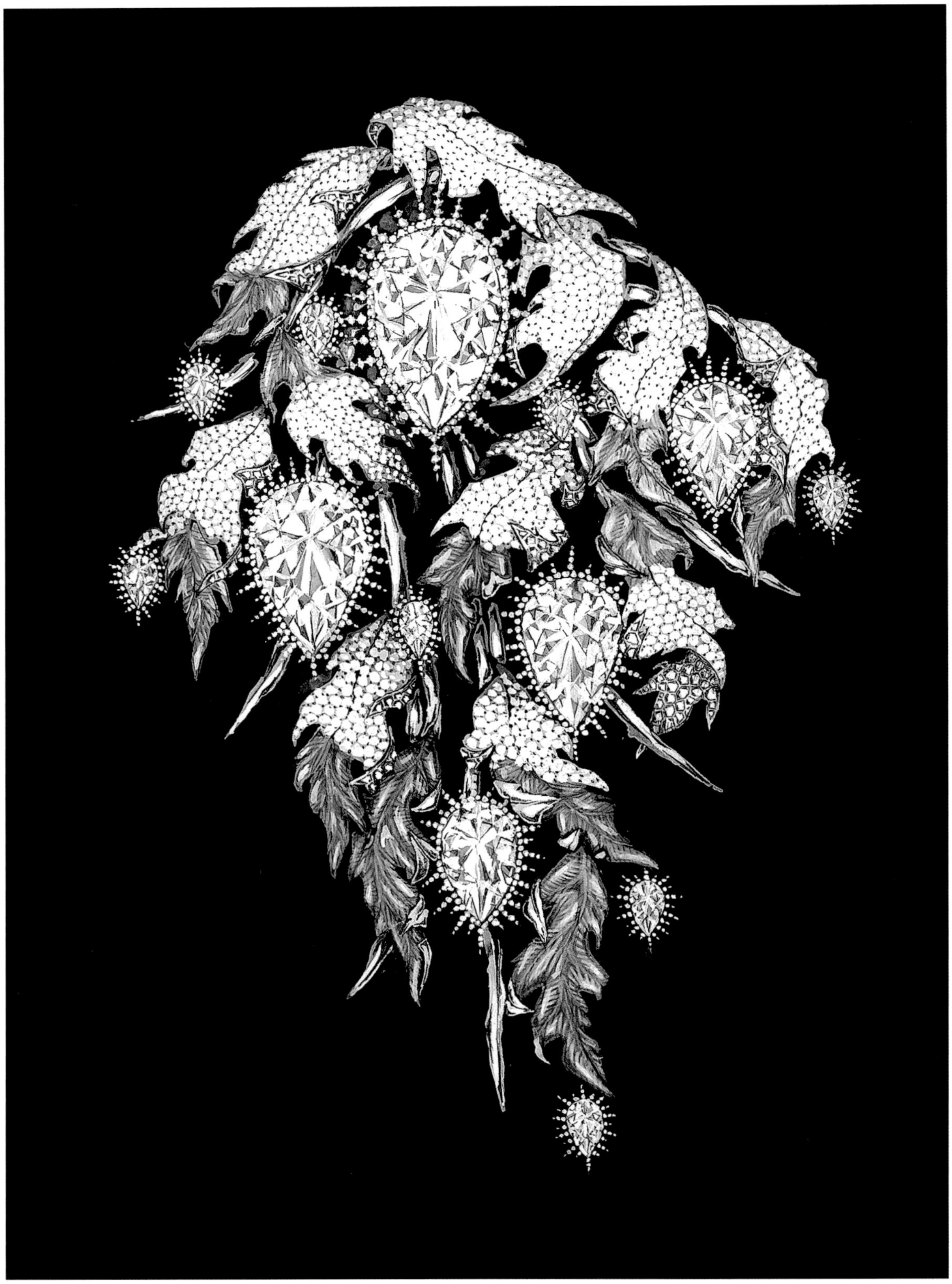

White Light
Shaun Leane in collaboration with Steinmetz
2009

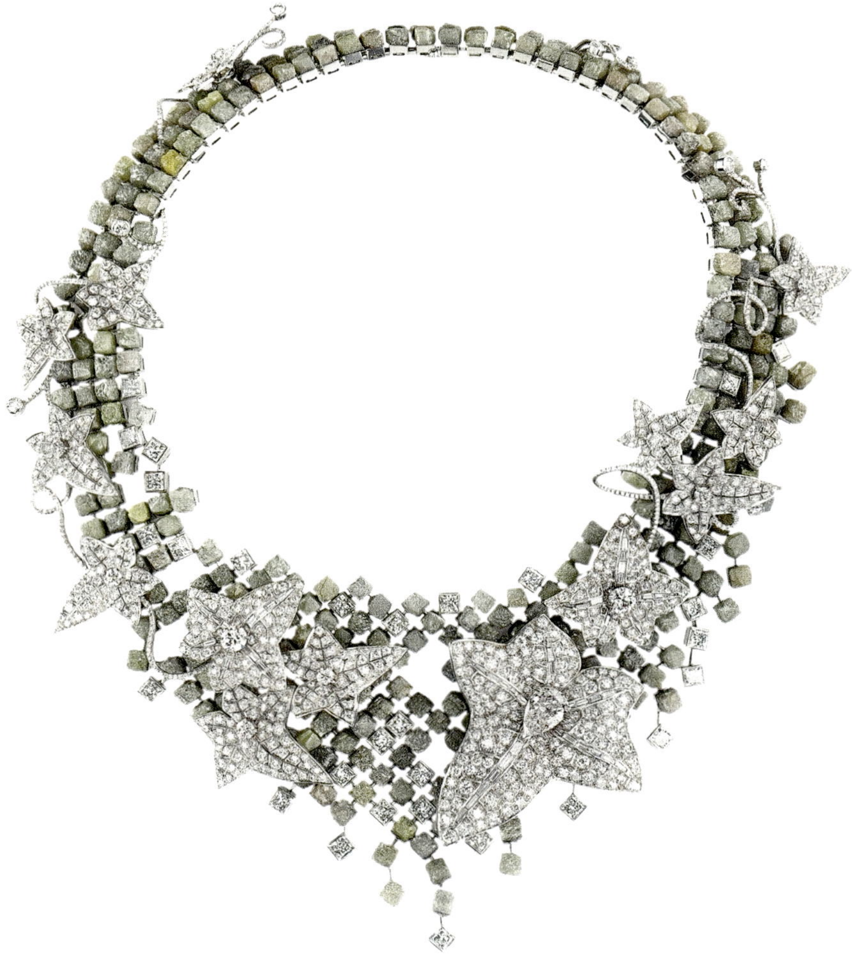

Lierre de Paris
Boucheron
2012

clustered together to create a sense of depth, or diamond sprays of flowers with stems so supple that they quivered with every movement. In 2003, Boucheron's creative director Solange Azagury Partridge, with a nod to antiquity, designed an ivy leaf tiara in black gold, entirely set with emeralds, which was worn by Queen Rania of Jordan. Proving that ivy remains a constant motif for the firm, the recent Lierre de Paris necklace, unveiled at the 2012 Biennale des Antiquaires, has three-dimensional diamond ivy randomly growing over rough-cut diamonds to make the foliage appear as if it were springing up from the Parisian cobblestones.

The rugged trees are mingling
Their flowery sprays in love;
The ivy climbs the laurel
To clasp the boughs above

The Serenade
William Cullen Bryant

In 1893, searching for an exclusive address, Frédéric Boucheron was the first French fine jeweller to move to the Place Vendôme, choosing the façade of No. 26 in the noble neoclassical square for the way the building captured the sun's rays, throwing light on the stone pavings throughout the day. At the time, one apartment in the building was occupied by the reclusive Countess de Castiglione, famed for being a femme fatale in her youth. For the firm's 150th anniversary, designer Shaun Leane created a necklace that drew upon the countess's nocturnal meanderings around Paris. Inspired by the queen of the night, a flower that only blossoms fleetingly during the night time, the eleven blue sapphire buds were created with mechanisms to enable them to flower after dark, transforming themselves into delicate diamond-set and ruby flowers, which wrapped themselves around the neck like dark romantic clinging ivy. The blackened gold necklace gleams with pavé-set brown diamonds, masking prickly thorns with a swirl of movement, protecting a magnificent pear-shaped 15-carat lilac sapphire.

Victoire de Castellane created a flower-like fairytale ivy necklace for Dior, called Je m'attache ou je meurs. Three thousand diamonds twinkle in the form of a creeping ivy motif, entwining around the neck, with the ivy symbolising a vampire in plant form as the necklace's name suggests: 'I am attached', like ivy, and will stay for eternity. 'I like playing with the names used in botany to

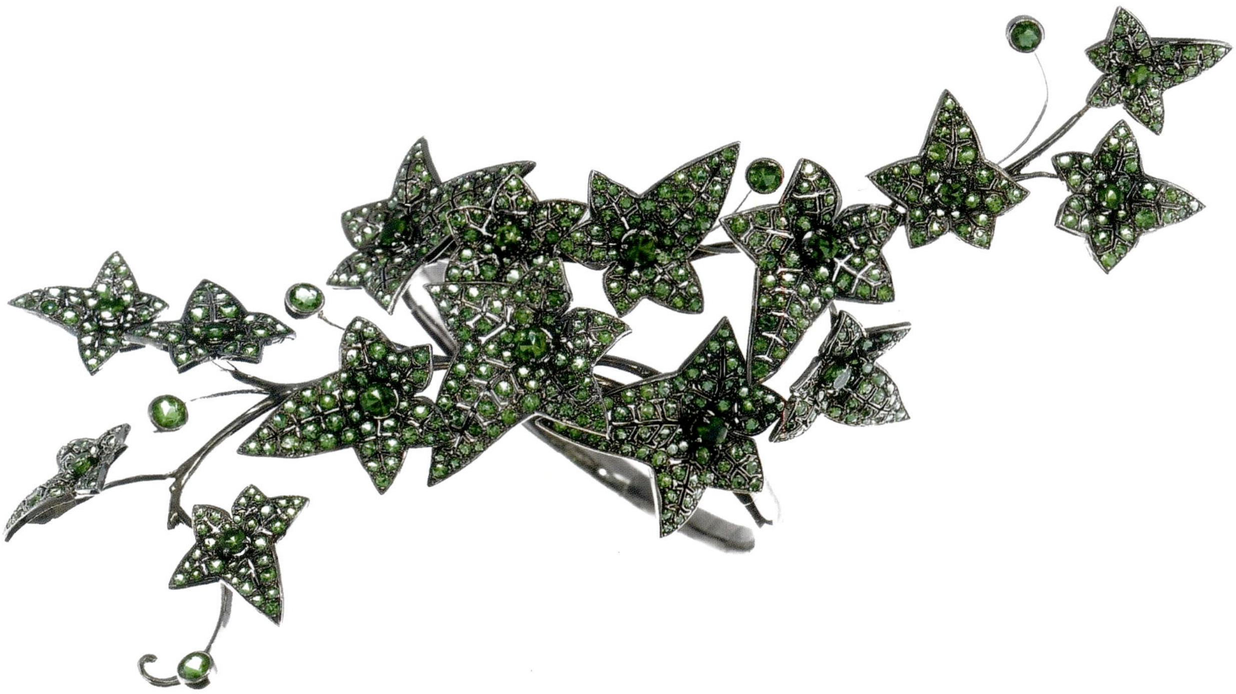

Ivy
Boucheron
2002

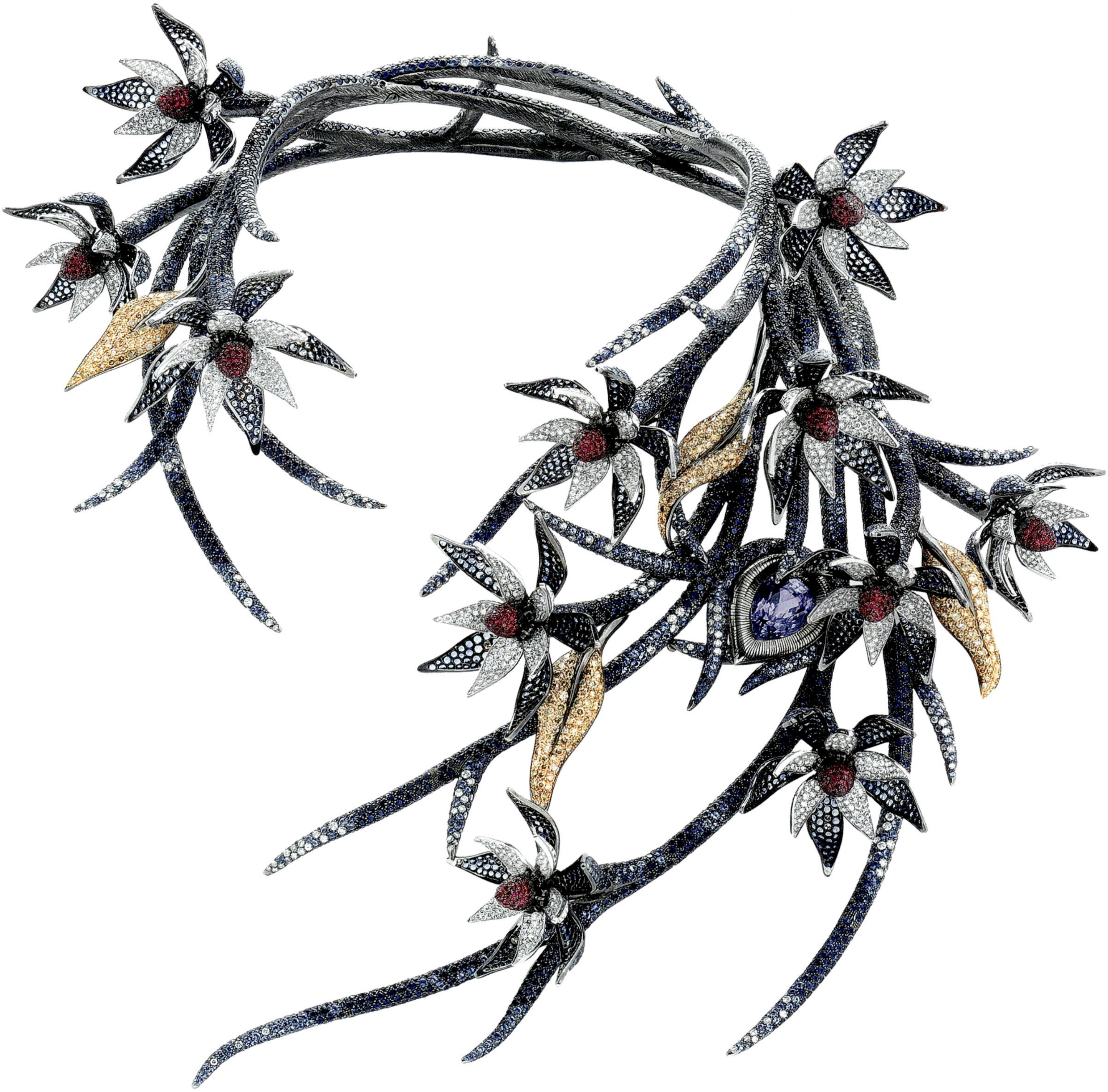

Queen of the Night
Shaun Leane for Boucheron
2008

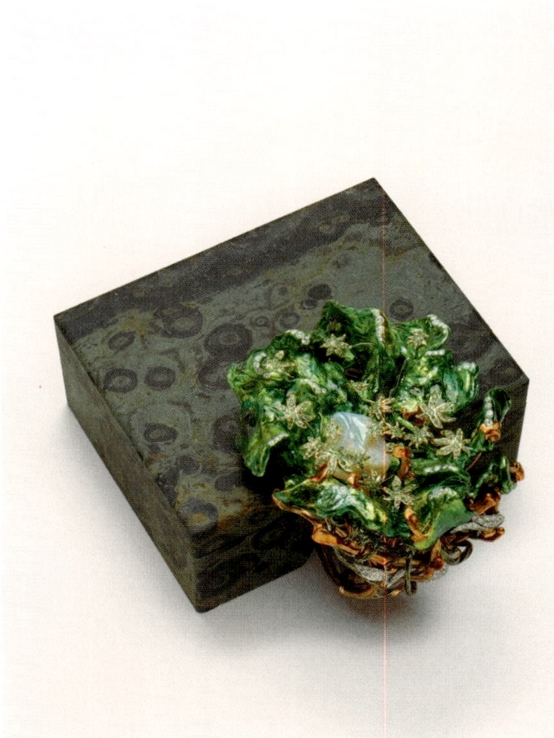

Cana Bisextem Now
Victoire de Castellane
2010

designate species', she says of her Cana Bisextem Now from the 'Fleurs d'excès' collection. This large imaginary ivy-coloured flower was created with lacquered silver, yellow and white gold, diamonds and garnets. A closer look reveals that the delicate ivy-shaped leaves formed from emeralds and cucumber jasper, like curling smoke rings, are actually cannabis flowers, camouflaged in brilliant acidic green lacquer.

Within the infant rind of this weak flower
Poison hath residence and medicine power.

Romeo and Juliet
Shakespeare

Plants can have the dual role of being both medicinal and poisonous. We kiss underneath the mistletoe, but some species can be toxic and deadly. Women of the Italian Renaissance knew the powers of belladonna – deadly nightshade – which they used to dilate their pupils, giving them a dark, come-hither appearance. Indeed, it was in tribute to Italian women that deadly nightshade was named 'belladonna', which translates as 'beautiful woman'.

Victoire de Castellane imagined the island of Belladonna, where seventeen poisonous flowers, also given pseudo-botanical names, seductively blossom with a hint of menace. The flowers act as a metaphor for the female species, with long, limb-like stems; they are brilliant, fluorescent, toxic, man-eating

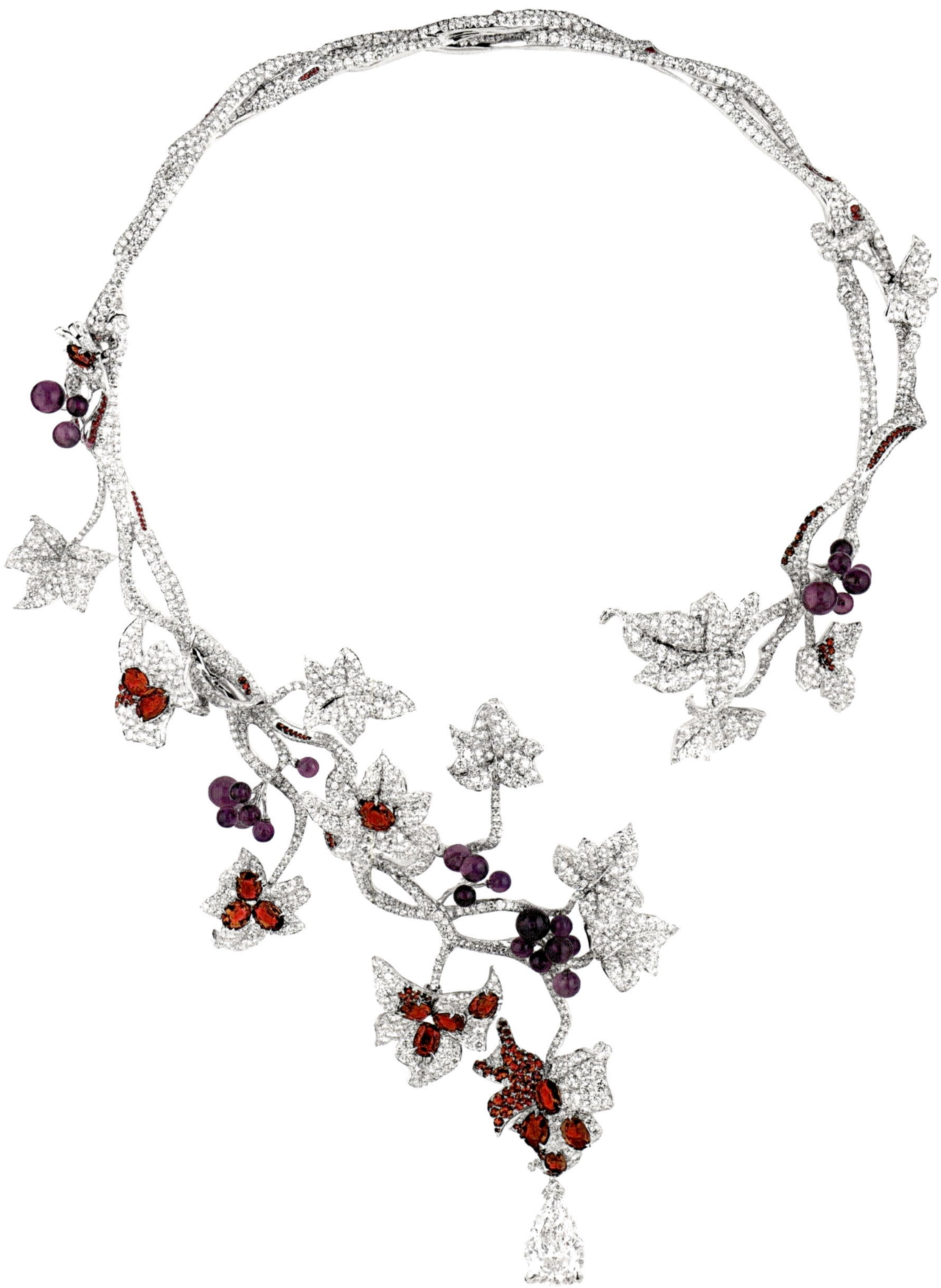

Je m'attache ou je meurs
Victoire de Castellane,
Dior High Jewellery
2008

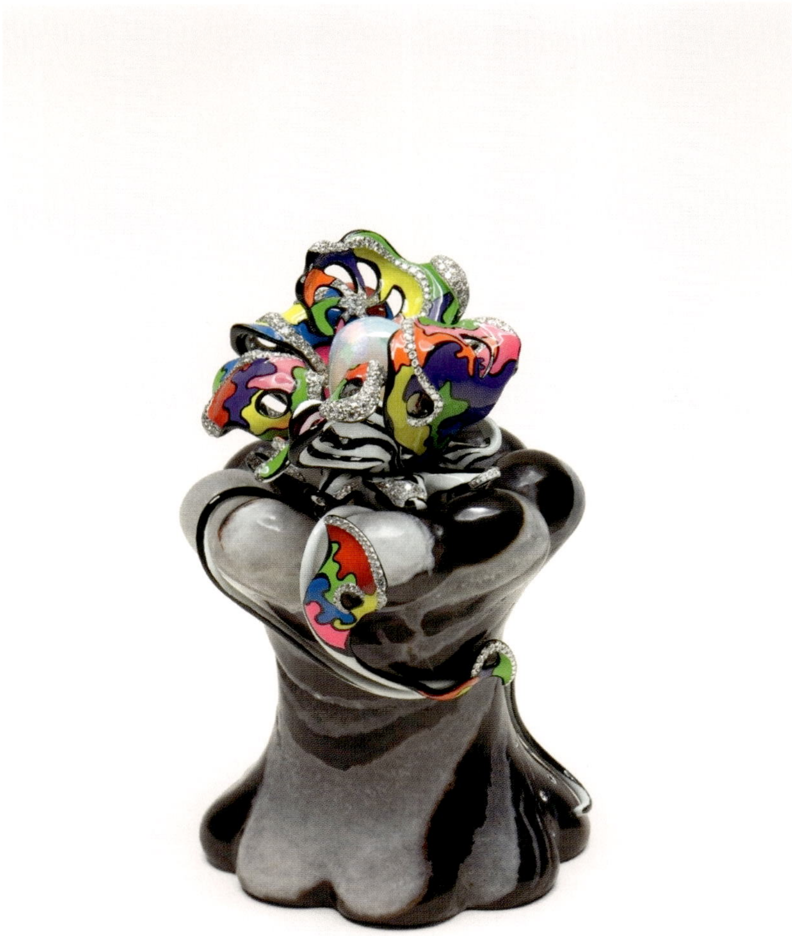

L.Es Delirium Flash
Victoire de Castellane
2010

carnivorous flowers. Some blooms were designed with a monochrome colour palette, echoing winter colours, such as the poisonous necklace in white gold, diamond and glitter lacquer, whilst others have vibrant extravagant colour palettes of hand-painted neon lacquer colours, with gemstones including tanzanite, amethyst, herb-green tsavorites and rubellites. Reina Magnifica Sangria has rich green emeralds, intense blue Paraiba tourmalines, and red-, pink- and black-tinged lacquer on the petals, set with 70-carat turquoise tourmalines, the bright colours denoting danger, whilst the diamonds create mirror centrepieces to lure in their prey.

Winter dawn is the colour of metal,
The trees stiffen into place like burnt nerves.

Waking in Winter
Sylvia Plath

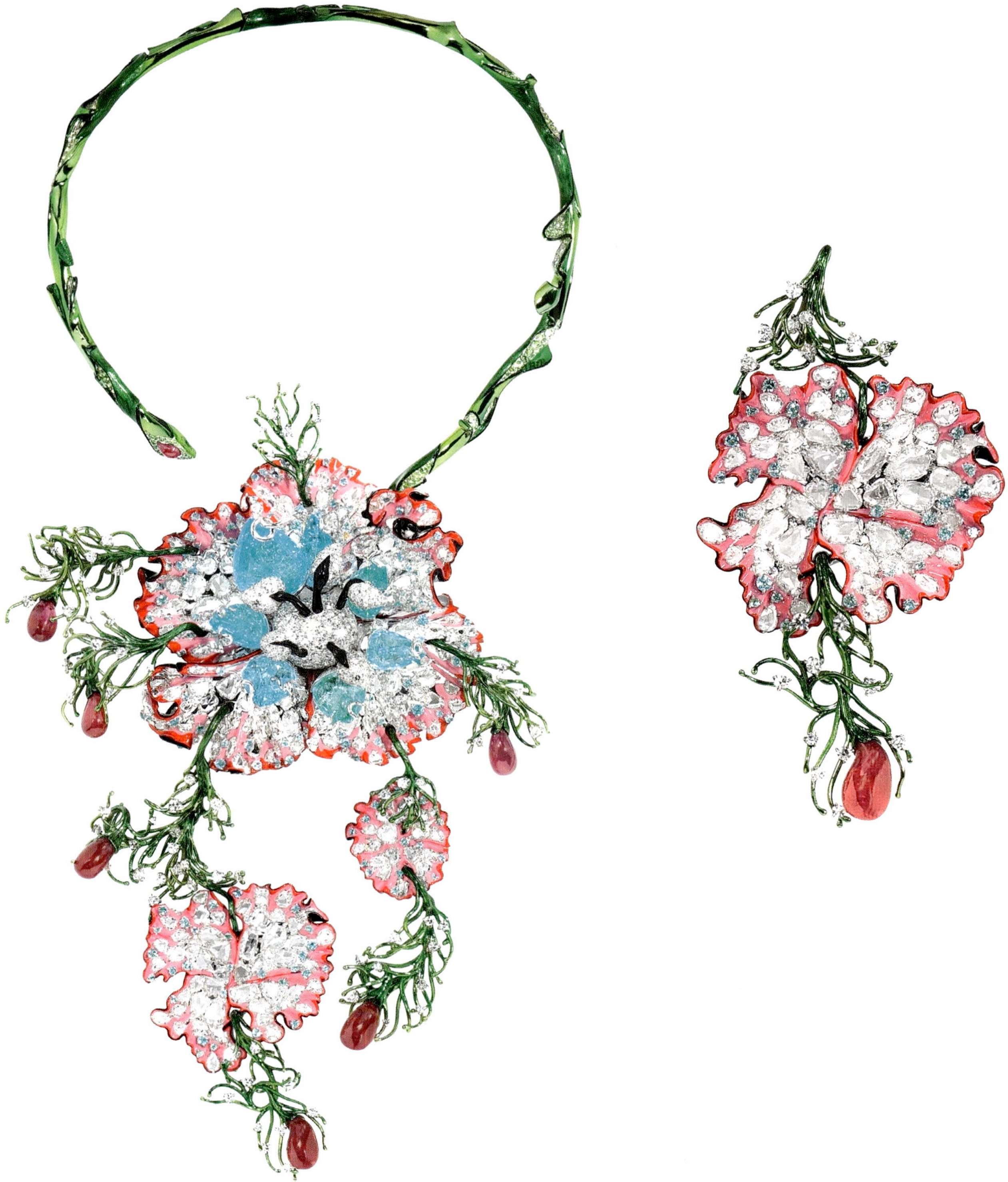

Reina Magnifica Sangria
Victoire de Castellane,
Dior High Jewellery
2007

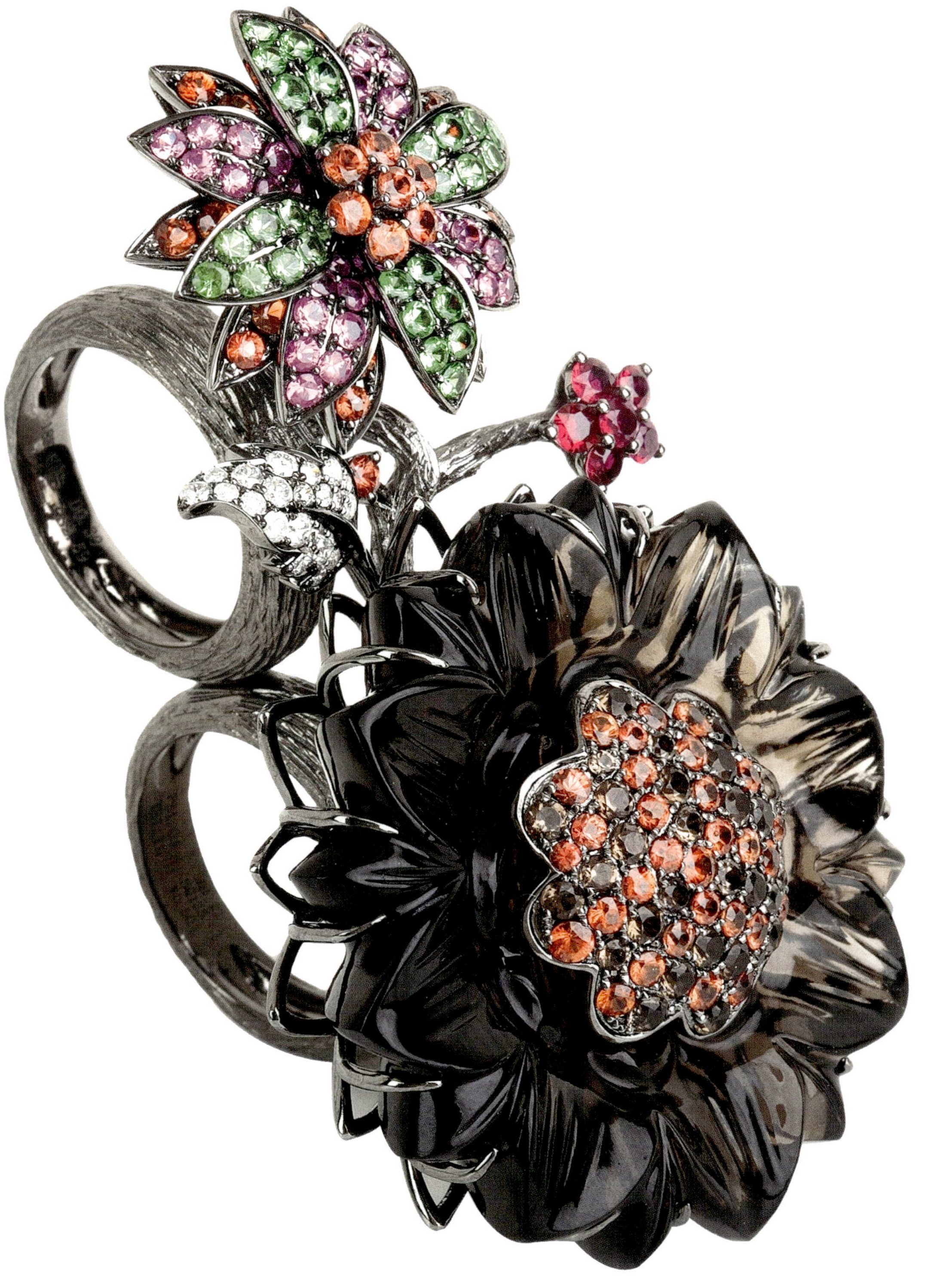

Poisonous
Bochic
2014

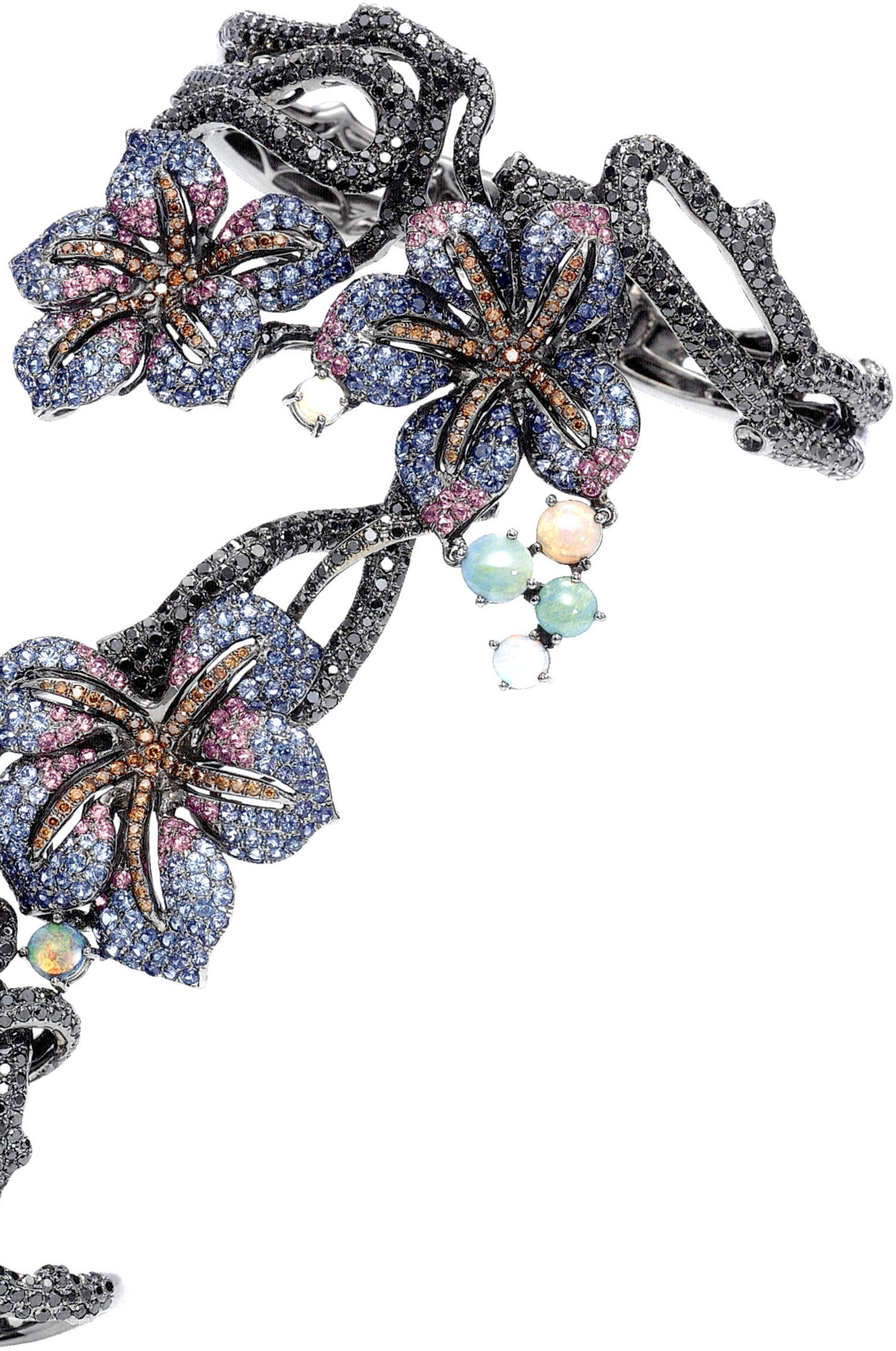

Poison Ivy
Wendy Yue
2013

Winter is the time when poisonous berries are most attractive, there being little else to entice the hungry. Like an extravagant surreal hybrid, the Ancolia Veneinosa Pop, with its hypnotic red berry spinels, yellow-orange and pink sapphire crimson pistils, and Mexican fire-opal bead-set corolla, makes an intoxicating flower, which is dangerous due to the poison it secretes. Black stamens and menacing pistils are mounted on high-tension settings like antennae, with diamonds creeping around necks and hands like verdant ivy. The flowers open at dawn, with a mechanism to reveal alluring trappings, and close at nightfall, each petal delicately sculpted by hand, every curve featuring a dewy smattering of coloured diamonds, silvery white gold, opals, sapphires and pistil-like prongs with gleaming diamond-studded centres.

The cold camellia only, stiff and white,
Rose without perfume, lily without grace,
When chilling winter shows his icy face,
Blooms for a world that vainly seeks delight.

The Camellia
Honoré de Balzac

The exotic Asian camellia symbolises grace and harmony in Japan, but for the samurai it represents death and the transience of life. The flower was introduced to Europe by the botanist Georg Joseph Kamel, after whom it was named,

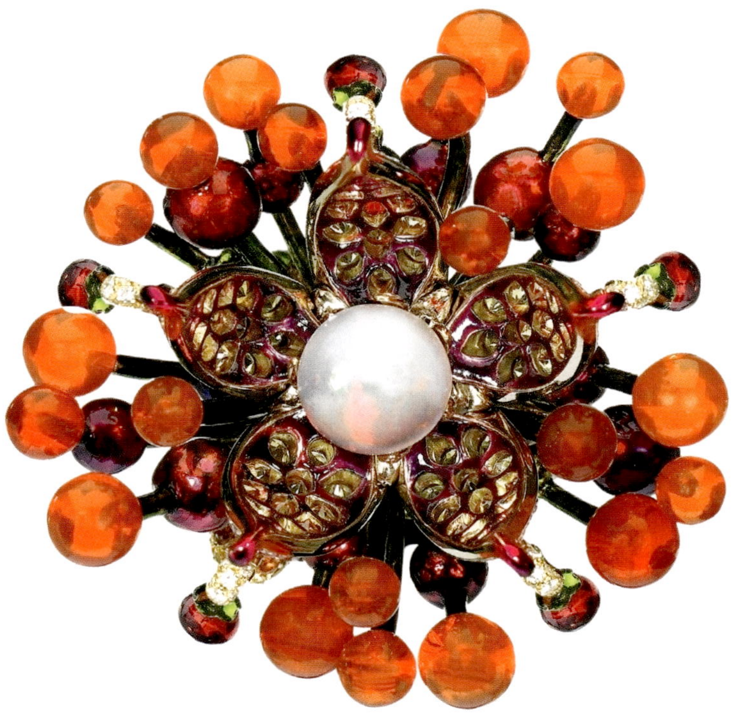

Ancolia Veneinosa Pop
Victoire de Castellane,
Dior High Jewellery
2007

the perfectly symmetrical white petals standing for perfection and the red and pink for love and longing. The camellia quickly became the most fashionable, and expensive, flower of the nineteenth century, carried by women in bouquets and worn in buttonholes by men. In Charles Dickens's novel *David Copperfield*, the hero finds himself alone in a room with Miss Larkins: 'She admires a flower (pink camellia japonica, price half a crown), in my buttonhole. I give it her...'

The flower was used by courtesans as a subtle signal of their availability. In the novel *La Dame aux camélias*, written by Alexandre Dumas in 1848, the courtesan Marguerite was never seen at balls or the theatre without a camellia bouquet, white flowers for twenty-five days, followed by red when she would be favourable to proposals.

Gabrielle 'Coco' Chanel was deeply touched by Sarah Bernhardt's performance in *La Dame aux camélias*, at the Théâtre de la Renaissance in 1913, and later that year she was photographed for the first time on the beach at Étretat, with a white fabric camellia decorating the belt around her matelot-style jersey top. It was the first flower given to her by her lover, Arthur 'Boy' Capel, and she liked the fact that the flower was worn equally by men and women, androgyny having a life-long appeal for her. She never wore real flowers, disliking the idea that they might fade and die on her, choosing instead to use fabric replicas, with soft curves and rounded petals in her buttonhole or hair, having them engraved on the buttons of suits, pinned on garments or embroidered as lace motifs: in this way the camellia became a key element of her style and a recurring motif for the fashion house. For the 1998 Chelsea Flower Show, Karl Lagerfeld, with gardener Tom Stuart Smith, created the imaginary garden of Coco Chanel, with antique statues dotted around central interlaced letter c's, in a formal *jardin à la française*, bursting with camellia-like blossoms of snow-white jewels against the eighteenth-century-style vivid green box hedges and topiary.

Fresh flowers were important to Chanel, 'All I want from you are fresh flowers picked by your own hand', she said to another of her lovers, the Duke of Westminster, whose conservatories and greenhouses she raided to decorate her villas in the South of France. 'She has built for herself one of the most enchanting villas that ever materialised on the shores of the Mediterranean', wrote US *Vogue* of her garden at La Pausa in 1930, commenting on her orchard and garden, which abounded with figs, grapes, olive trees and fragrant lavender. Her favourite camellia has remained a constant motif on the runway of Chanel, as well as in the firm's 'Jardin de camélias' fine jewellery collection.

During the 1930s, René Boivin created camellia brooches designed as a series of overlapping diamond-set petals, accented with calibre-cut rubies. Suzanne Belperron, on the other hand, had her camellia petals carved in chalcedony, with centres of old mine-cut diamonds, emerald leaves and each stem finished with an emerald drop. Hong Kong-based jeweller Michelle Ong makes contemporary camellias with breathtaking combinations of white rose-cut diamonds, drawing

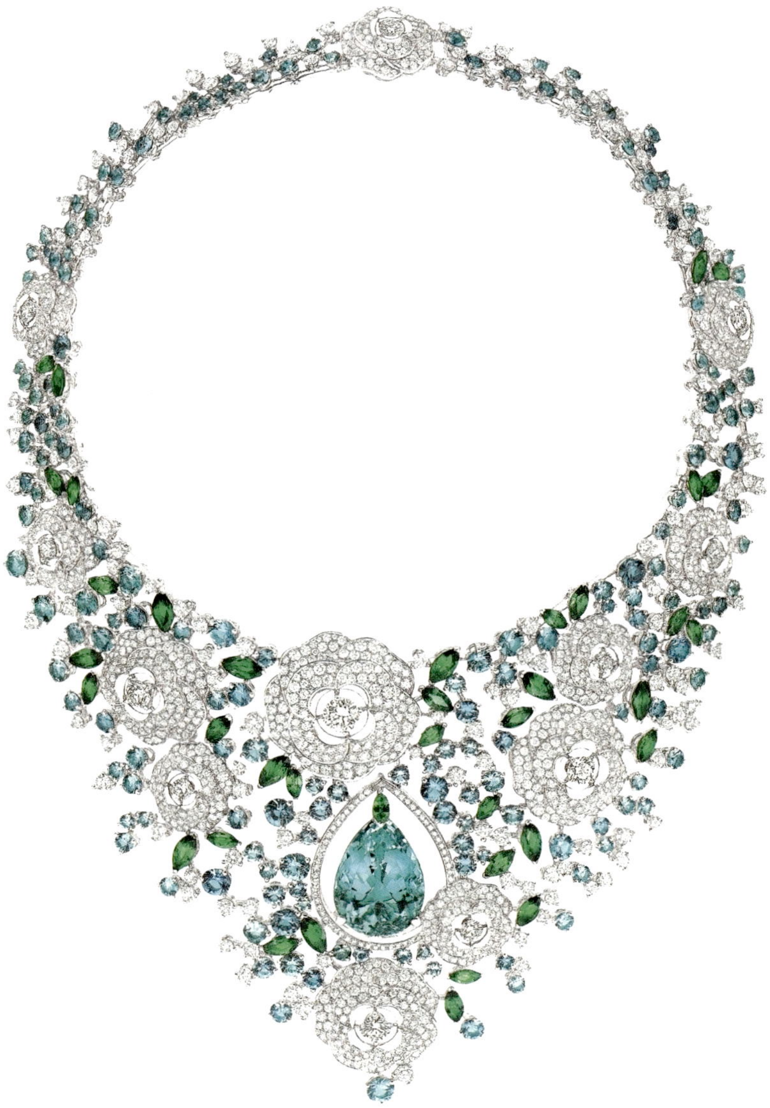

Camellia
Chanel
2013

the viewer into a black diamond centre that serves to highlight the purity and whiteness of the blossom itself. Chanel use abstraction and geometric styles in their designs as liberally as voluptuous organic round shapes, with a freedom of material from multicoloured sapphires and Mandarin garnets to snow-white shimmering diamonds and opals, to make luxurious bouquets of Coco Chanel's favourite flower.

Sculpted hard stones mimic alabaster petals, diamond-set white camellias are trimmed with black diamonds, cultivated around a 35-carat rare Paraiba tourmaline centre, scattered over bib necklaces of rubellites, tourmalines, mandarin garnets, shimmery opals and white South Sea pearls, or in gold worked into light and lacy blooms, almost like broderie anglaise, similar to the first fabric petals of the camellia that Chanel jauntily attached to her belts.

One camellia *objet* has its strong green waxy leaves fashioned from dazzling white diamonds, whilst the bloom is sculpted in shiny forest-green emerald stone, reversing the colour codes of the flower. Another black lacquer contemporary-style brooch has a patchwork of white and yellow diamond stones, mimicking the Coromandel Chinese screens collected by Coco Chanel to use as wallpaper to decorate the walls of her apartment in Paris. The folding wood screens emerged in the Ming Dynasty (1368–1644), with dark lacquered backgrounds covered with intricate patterns, painted and decorated using ivory, mother of pearl, gold and precious stones.

> *I've loved Chinese screens since I was 18 years old. I nearly fainted with joy when, entering a Chinese shop for the first time, I saw a Coromandel for the first time. Screens were the first thing I bought.*
>
> *Chanel Solitaire*
> Claude Delay

The screens took their name from India's Coromandel Coast, from where they were shipped to Europe in the seventeenth and eighteenth centuries. The screens often depicted scenes of nature, with floral borders and Chinese winter landscapes of hanging mists on mountain tops and clusters of snow-bowed pines. The hardiness of the evergreen pines rooted in the icy winter ground makes them a symbol of longevity in China, and their use as a motif in Chinese decorative arts is a sign of noble endurance in the face of adversity.

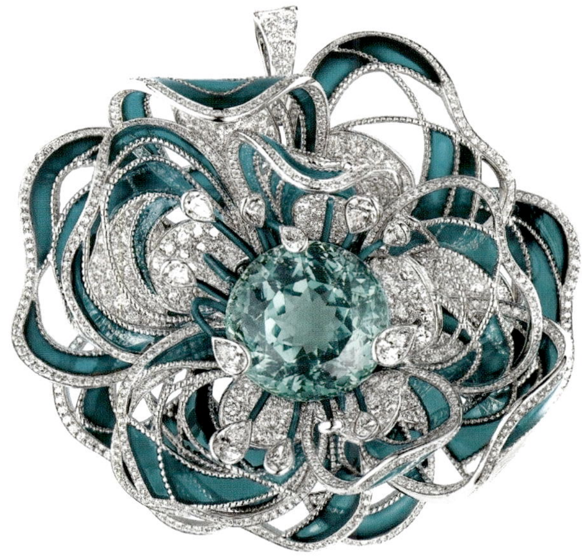

Tourmaline Paraiba Camellia
Lorenz Bäumer for Chanel
2008

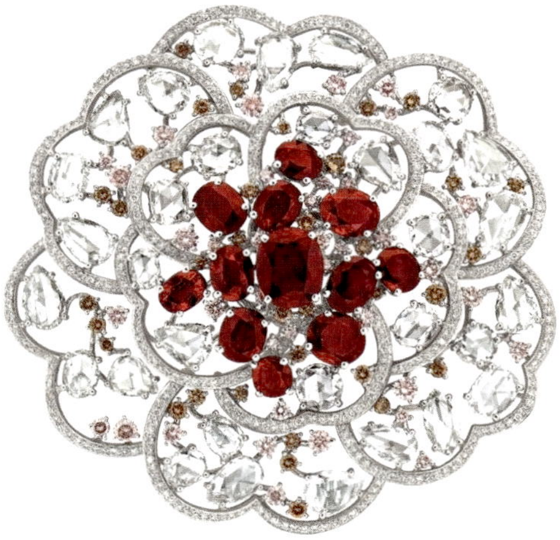

Camellia
Chanel
2010

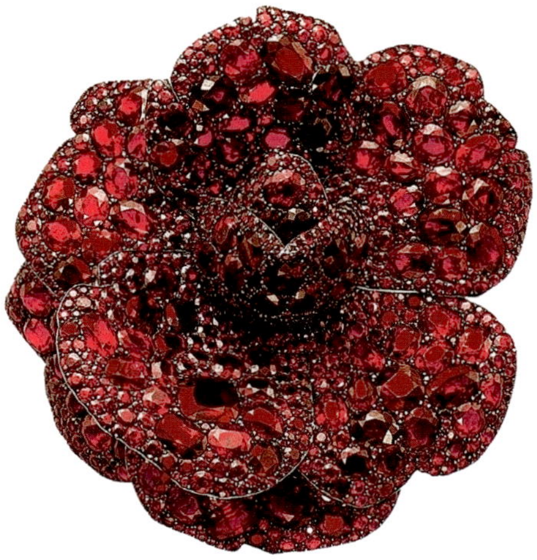

Camellia
JAR
2003

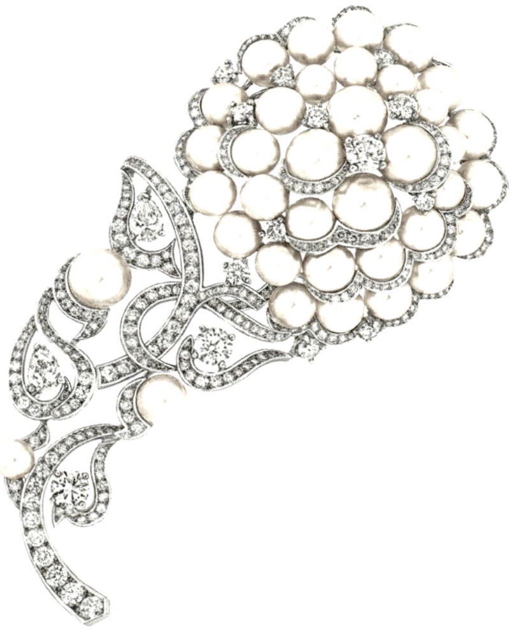

Camellia
Chanel
2014

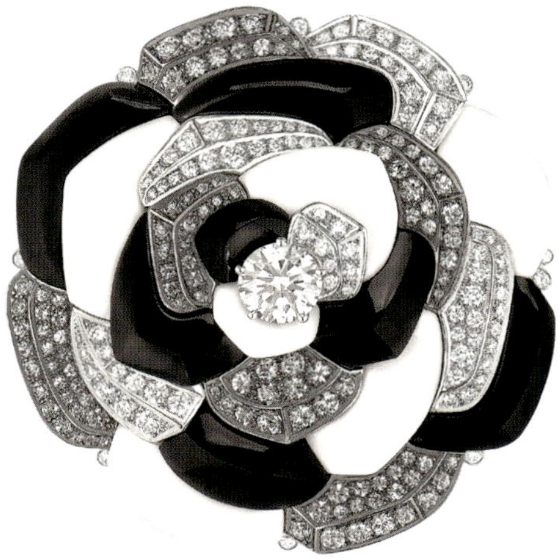

Camellia
Chanel
2013

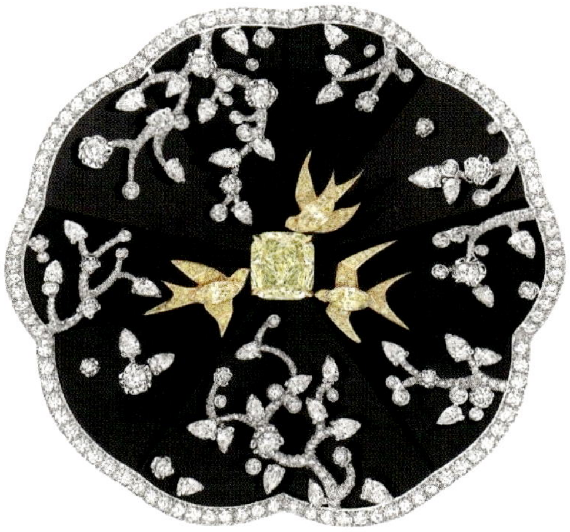

Coromandel Camellia
Chanel
2013

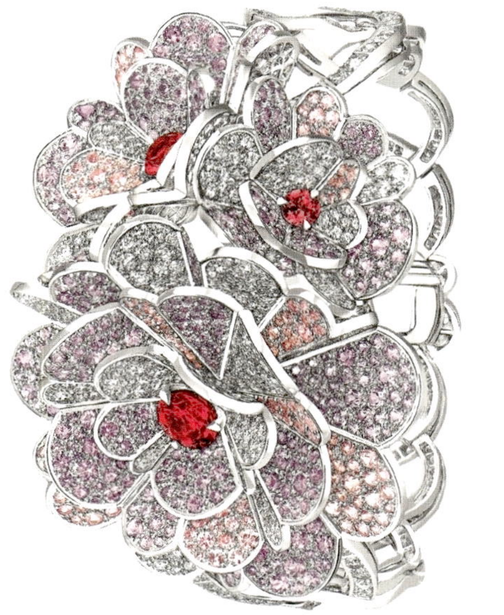

Camellia
Chanel
2013

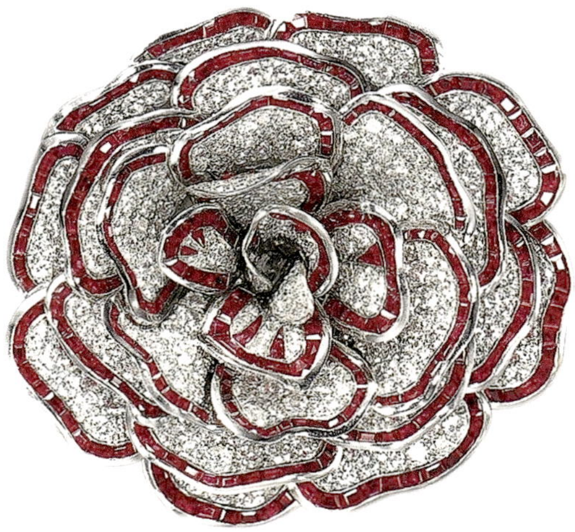

Camellia
Boivin
c. 1938

One must have a mind of winter
To regard the frost and the boughs
Of the pine-trees crushed with snow.

The Snow Man
Wallace Stevens

Creating evergreen flowers with an oriental colouration, Cindy Chao uses jadeite and emeralds in new buds, ready to burst into full bloom when the diamond snows of winter have disappeared. 'When I design a unique floral piece,' explains Chao, 'I go out and buy actual potted flowers. The cycle of life – nurturing and caring for the flora, observing various stages of blossom and full bloom, and even withered leaves – is my inspiration, allowing me to express the force and spirit of life.' Although the jadeite and emerald pieces have the look of winter evergreen, they are influenced by Chao's favourite white lilies and moth orchids.

'There's always a pot or vase of them at all times in my office', Chao says, 'so perhaps traces of these two kinds of flowers are hidden in my work'. She carves out the exact form she would like to present in the final work, sculpting numerous different leaves or petals at once, before putting them aside for weeks; they only become part of the final jewel if she can still feel the life she wants to capture when she returns to them. Her evergreen colours are inspired by the cypresses planted in 1640 amongst the Roman statues and sculptures of the Boboli Gardens in Florence. She chooses jadeites to look as if they have just emerged from water, moist, fresh and transparent, with rose-cut diamond leaves, to create a frosty scene, as if the plant is surviving an icy winter, ready to welcome the new awakening.

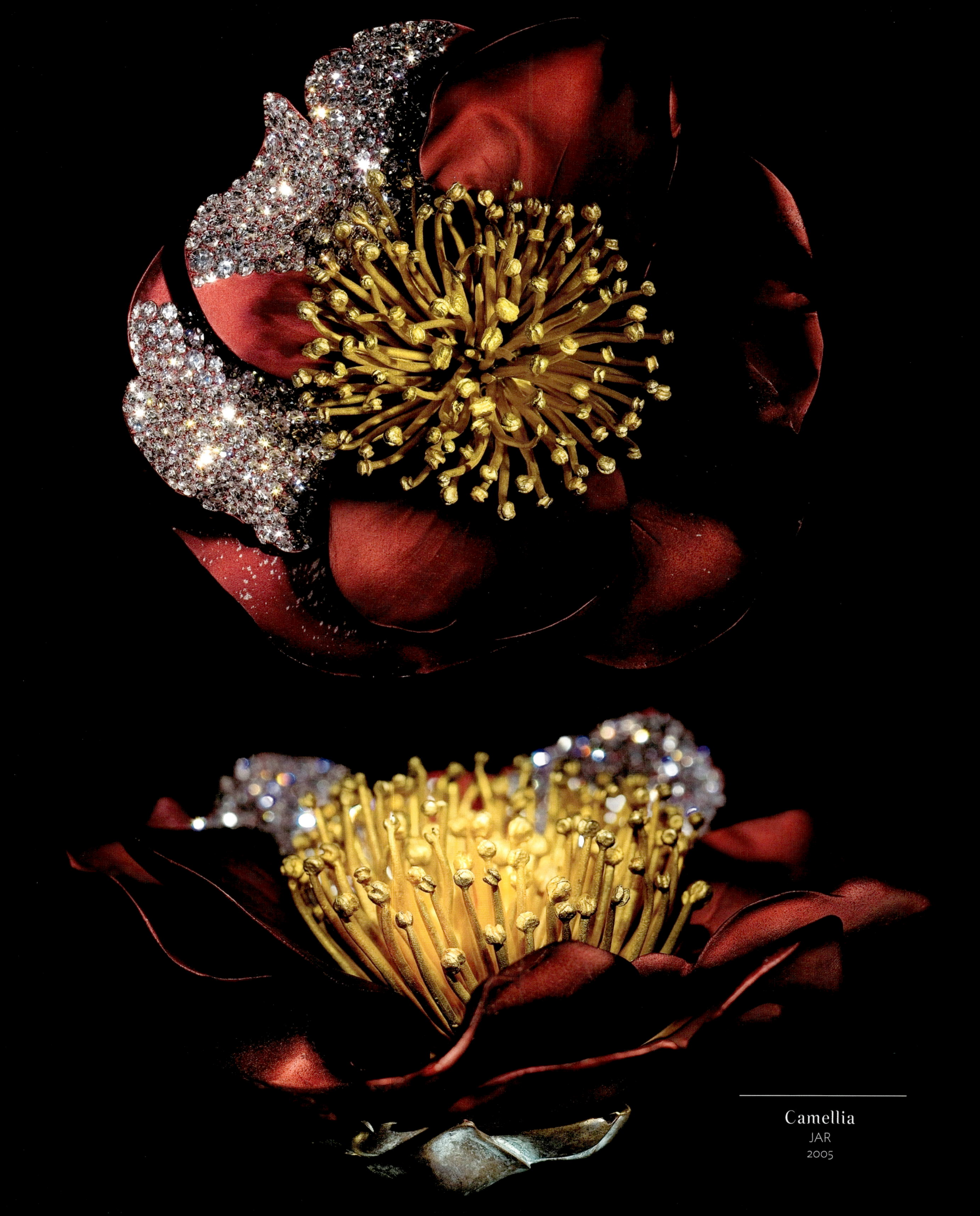

Camellia
JAR
2005

The Colombian emerald centre stone of Chao's floral brooch has a rare hexagonal cut, giving it a geometrical shape, with straight, rigid lines. The flower petals, by contrast, are velvety, smooth, soft and undulating. She also contrasts the petals, which are meticulously paved with round, brilliant-cut diamonds, with the stem, which is simply coated with black enamel, giving a minimal opulence to the winter bloom surviving on the last ebbing light of the year.

Inspired by the four seasons, which have been known as the 'Four Gentlemen' for over one thousand years in traditional Chinese ink-and-wash painting, and represented by plum tree blossom, orchid, bamboo and chrysanthemum, Anna Hu uses winter plum blossom for her bangles. Janet Zapata describes a visit to Anna Hu's studio thus: 'Amid the jeweller's tools and machines are plants and flowers, many grown from seeds. This trove of flora provides an endless source of inspiration for metal and gemstone design.'

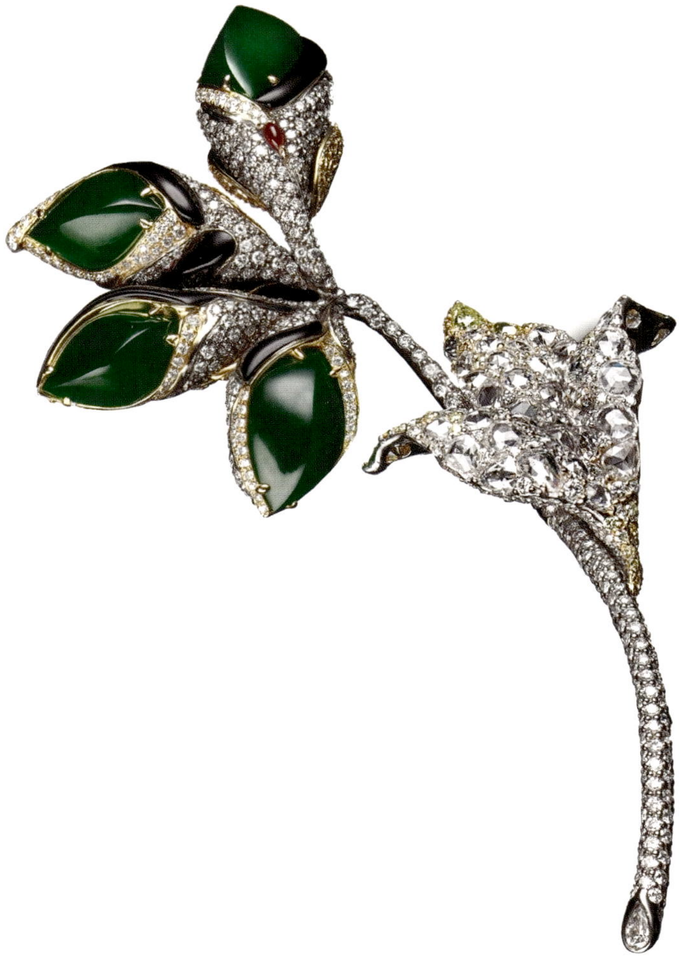

Evergreen
Cindy Chao
2008

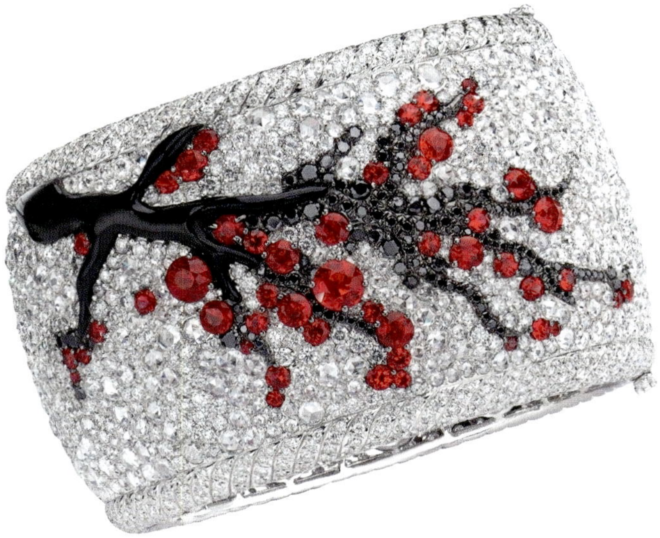

Winter Plum
Anna Hu
2011

The winter plum blooms late in winter, its fragrance detectable even in breaths of freezing wind. Symbolic of courage and humility, its branches are cut and brought inside with wishes for a fruitful new year. Its presence, when stalks of flowers are firmly rooted in ice, is seen as remarkable, and a metaphor for inner beauty. Hu has depicted the plum with stark black branches; the perfectly matched Burmese ruby plum blossoms stand out against their snowy wind-swept diamond landscape.

Looking out of her turret at Sissinghurst Castle on the surrounding snow-clad paths, Vita Sackville-West's thoughts turned to her famous White Garden: 'All the same, I cannot help hoping that the great ghostly barn-owl will sweep silently across a pale garden, next summer, in the twilight – the pale garden that I am now planting, under the first flakes of snow.' As the sun dwindles, using the same brush of imagination, a jewellery designer plants the seeds of jewels in sketches for pale stones, dreaming like a gardener of the tall diamond-white flowers that will come to life, ready to bloom the following season.

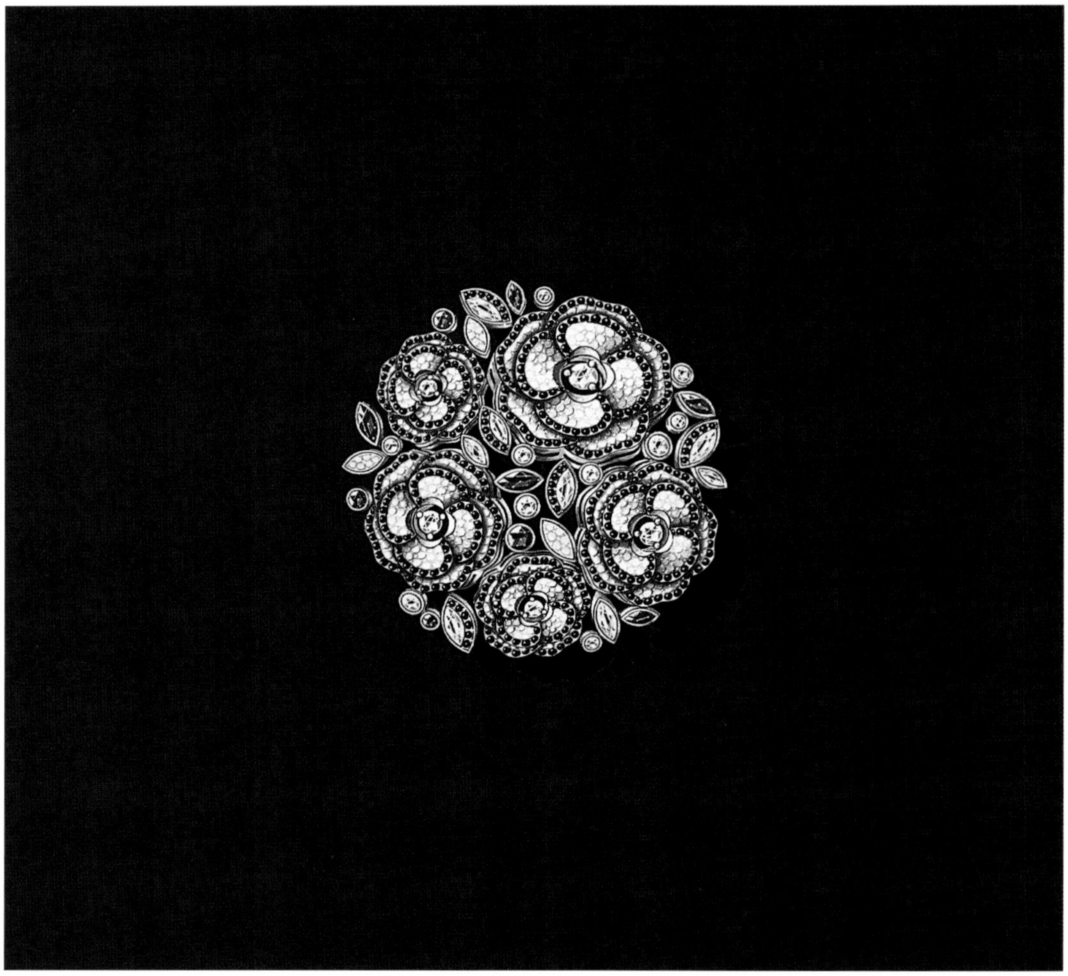

Camellia
Chanel
2013

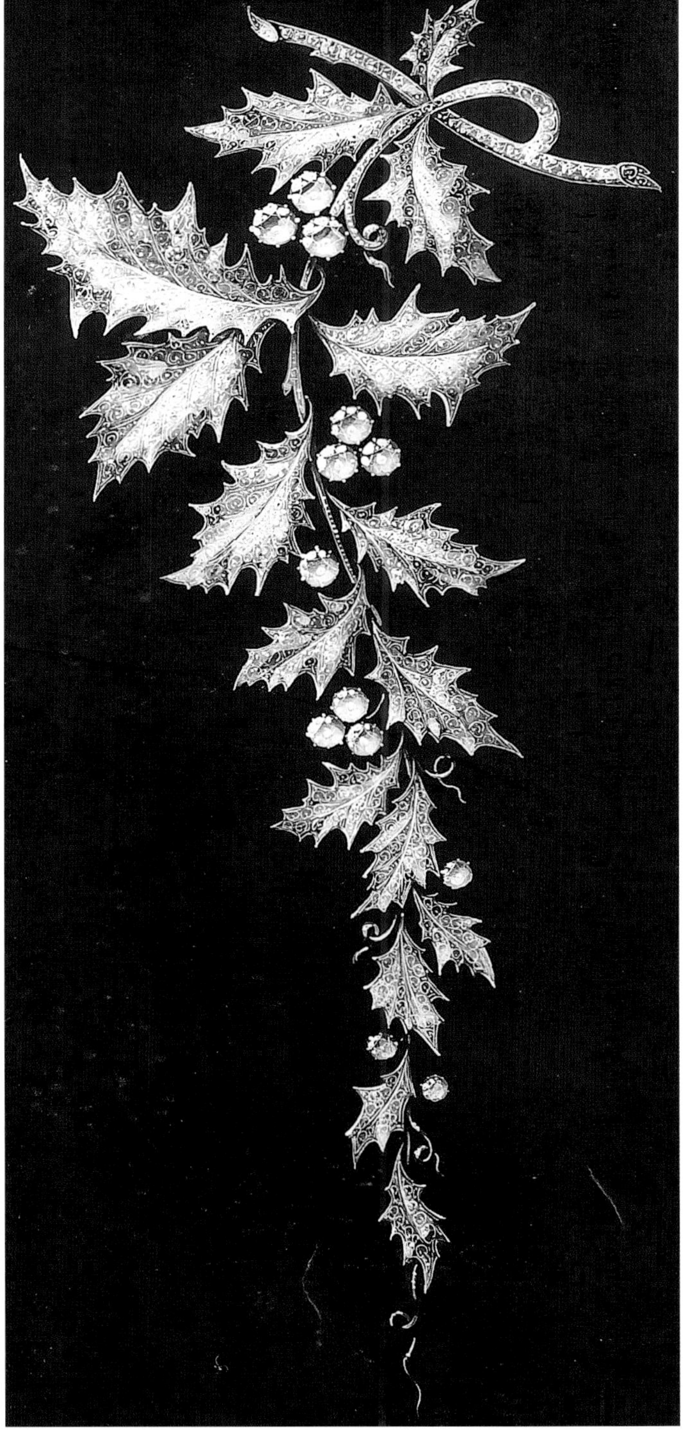

Holly
Chaumet
c. 1890–1900

Picture Credits

4
All credits SABBA Paris 2014.

14
© Lorenz Bäumer.

16
left Image © Bentley & Skinner.
right Image © Bentley & Skinner.

17
LALIQUE S. A. Collection.

18
Fleur du Jour necklace © Boucheron.

20
left Pansy ring flat finish – Demantoid garnet and diamond pansy brooch c.1900, adapted as a ring by Eliane Fattal for S. J.Phillips 2013. Image courtesy S. J.Phillips Ltd, London.
right Originally created for Mrs. John Hay Whitney in 1945 © Verdura. All rights reserved.

21
Image courtesy S. J.Phillips Ltd, London.

22
left © Christie's Images Limited (2004).
right © Christie's Images Limited (2004).

23
left Graff Diamonds.
right © Christie's Images Limited (2009).

24
Claude Lalanne, Anemone necklace, 2013, Galvanised copper, Unique. Image courtesy of Louisa Guinness Gallery.

25
© Adler.

26
top N. Welsh, Cartier Collection © Cartier.
middle © Verdura. All rights reserved.
bottom © Christie's Images Limited (2010).

27
top Graff Diamonds.
middle © Christie's Images Limited (2010).
bottom Designed by Jeremy Morris © David Morris London.

28
left Courtesy of Wartski, London.
right Image © Symbolic & Chase.

29
Cherry blossom clip © Van Cleef & Arpels.

30
Japanese cherry blossom necklace © Suzanne Syz Art Jewels.

31
© Wendy Yue.

32
© Gimel Trading Co., Ltd.

33
Photo credit: Philippe de Givenchy.

34
Study for a white and red tulip brooch, gouache on paper, Joseph Chaumet. Collection Chaumet Paris.

38
Pivoine Mystérieuse necklace © Van Cleef & Arpels.

39
top left Lady Peony ring © Anna Hu.
top right N. Welsh, Collection Cartier © Cartier.
bottom left © Carnet Jewellery.
bottom right Graceful Peony © Carnet Jewellery.

41
left © Verdura. All rights reserved.
right © Christie's Images Limited (2009).

42
top Drawing of the lily-of-the-valley diamond and enamel tiara created for Béatrice Ephrussi de Rothschild, gouache on paper, Joseph Chaumet. Collection Chaumet Paris.
bottom Drawing for a lily-of-the-valley clip, Van Cleef & Arpels Archives © Van Cleef & Arpels.

45
top Photo: Katharina Faerber.
bottom Photo: Jozsef Tari.

46
© Christie's Images Limited (2013).

48
© Christian Dior couture.

49
Courtesy of Wartski, London.

50
Courtesy of Wartski, London.

51
Cartier Archives © Cartier.

54
Mellerio dits Meller.

56
© Gimel Trading Co., Ltd.

57
© Christie's Images Limited (2010).

59
Victoire de Castellane, Opiom Velourosa Purpra, 2010. Lacquered silver, white gold, rubies, diamonds, rhyolite. Necklace: 19 x 19 cm; with base: 13 x 22 x 21.5 cm. Ed. unique © Victoire de Castellane. Courtesy Gagosian Gallery. Photography by Erwan Frotin.

60
Victoire de Castellane, Heroïna Romanticam Dolorosa, 2010. Lacquered silver, white gold, diamonds, jonquil diamonds, rubies, white gold, rock crystal. Necklace: 26.5 x 14 cm; with base: 9.8 x 27 x 16.2 cm. Ed. unique © Victoire de Castellane. Courtesy Gagosian Gallery. Photography by Erwan Frotin.

62
bottom left © Carnet Jewellery.
bottom right Photo credit: Philippe de Givenchy.
top left Garance clip © Van Cleef & Arpels.
top right © Moussaieff.

63
Poppy necklace from the Red Carpet Collection © Chopard.

65
Photo: Katharina Faerber.

66
top The Moira Collection © Moira.
bottom © Christie's Images Limited (2012).

68
Flower brooch, graphite and gouache on buff tracing paper, Cartier Archives © Cartier.

69
Flower brooch, graphite and gouache on buff tracing paper, Cartier Archives © Cartier.

70
top N. Welsh, Cartier Collection © Cartier.
bottom left N. Welsh, Cartier Collection © Cartier.
bottom right N. Welsh, Cartier Collection © Cartier.

72
Photo credit: Tiffany & Co.

73
left Photo credit: Tiffany & Co.
right Photo credit: Tiffany & Co.

74
top left © Buccellati London.
top right © Buccellati London.
bottom left © Gimel Trading Co., Ltd.
bottom right N. Welsh, Cartier Collection © Cartier.

77
top left © Christie's Images Limited (2010).
top right N. Welsh, Cartier Collection © Cartier.
centre Brilliant Thistle brooch © Carnet Jewellery.
bottom left Thistle brooch © Boucheron.
bottom right Tahitian pearl and thistle brooch © Shaun Leane.

78
left Retail card for a thistle clip. This clip was owned by the Duchess of Windsor, Van Cleef & Arpels Archives © Van Cleef & Arpels.
right Originally created for the Duchess of Windsor in 1947 © Verdura. All rights reserved.

79
© Glenn Spiro, G London – www.glennspiro.com

80
© Christie's Images Limited (2007).

82
Drawing of a diamond and ruby orchid brooch, gouache on paper, Joseph Chaumet. Collection Chaumet Paris.

83
top © Lorenz Bäumer.
bottom left Conch pearl lily ring, Four Seasons Collection © Cindy Chao THE ART JEWEL.
bottom right Photo by Thibaut Rondoni and Guillaume Benoit © Lydia Courteille.

84
Photo credit: Tiffany & Co.

85
Mellerio dits Meller.

86
left Calla lily bangle © Asprey.
right Photo by Thibaut Rondoni and Guillaume Benoit © Lydia Courteille.

87
© Wendy Yue.

88
Celestial Lotus necklace © Anna Hu.

90
Enchanted Lotus brooch from De Beers Diamond Jewellers.

91
© Gimel Trading Co., Ltd.

93
Tiara composed of seven brooches, graphite and gouache on buff tracing paper, Cartier Archives © Cartier.

94
Wondrous Diamond Woodrose © Carnet Jewellery.

96
top left Image courtesy S. J.Phillips Ltd, London.
top right Photo by Thibaut Rondoni and Guillaume Benoit © Lydia Courteille.
bottom Yellow diamond rose ring, Four Seasons Collection © Cindy Chao THE ART JEWEL.

Picture Credits

97
© Christian Dior couture.

98
Vanilla Dream Ring.
Photo: Fabien Cruchon © Piaget 2014.
All rights reserved.

101
top left N. Welsh, Cartier Collection © Cartier.
top right © Christian Dior couture.
bottom left © Lorenz Bäumer.
bottom right N. Welsh, Collection Cartier © Cartier.

102
Garrard designed and created the Burmese ruby and diamond tiara in 1973 for Her Majesty Queen Elizabeth II. The image is reproduced here by kind permission of Her Majesty the Queen.

103
© Christian Dior couture.

104
top © Christian Dior couture.
bottom Image © Symbolic & Chase.

105
Photo by Thibaut Rondoni and Guillaume Benoit © Lydia Courteille.

106
Photo: Jozsef Tari.

107
© Wendy Yue.

110
© Gimel Trading Co., Ltd.

112
© Chatila.

113
Photo: Katharina Faerber.

114
Oak tree necklace from the Animal World collection © Chopard.

115
left Drawing for a Mystery-set chrysanthemum clip, Van Cleef & Arpels. Archives © Van Cleef & Arpels.
right Photo credit: Tiffany & Co.

116
left Drawing of a gold and diamond hydrangea brooch, gouache on paper, Joseph Chaumet. Collection Chaumet Paris.
right Drawing of a diamond hydrangea bunch brooch terminated by a bowknot, gouache on paper, Joseph Chaumet. Collection Chaumet Paris.

117
© Chaumet.

118
© Christie's Images Limited (2010).

119
N. Welsh, Cartier Collection © Cartier.

120
left Daisy heritage aquamarine ring © Asprey.
right © Verdura. All rights reserved.

122
Photo: Reinaldo Viegas.

123
Photo: Jozsef Tari.

124
top © Christie's Images Limited (2013).
bottom left Private collection.
bottom right Photo: Shoichi Kondo.

127
Assorted orchid brooches designed by G. Paulding Farnham. Photo credit: Tiffany & Co.

128
top left Image © Bentley & Skinner.
top right Photo by Thibaut Rondoni and Guillaume Benoit © Lydia Courteille.
bottom left Sapphire orchid ring, Four Seasons Collection © Cindy Chao THE ART JEWEL.
bottom right Photo by Thibaut Rondoni and Guillaume Benoit © Lydia Courteille.

131
Orchid head ornament, graphite, Indian ink and gouache on buff tracing paper, Cartier Archives © Cartier.

132
top left K. Riou © Cartier.
right N. Welsh, Cartier Collection © Cartier.
bottom left V. Wulveryck © Cartier.

133
top right V. Wulveryck © Cartier.
left © Cartier.
bottom right K. Riou © Cartier.

134
left Golden Orchid ring © Anna Hu.
right Enchanted Orchid ring and bracelet © Anna Hu.

135
© Glenn Spiro, G London - www.glennspiro.com

138
Photo: Jozsef Tari.

140
© Christie's Images Limited (2012).

142
top © Christie's Images Limited (2013).
bottom Drawing for a pink coral Christmas rose clip, Van Cleef & Arpels. Archives © Van Cleef & Arpels.

143
© Christie's Images Limited (2012).

144
© Glenn Spiro, G London - www.glennspiro.com

145
Courtesy of Wartski, London.

146
top left © Christie's Images Limited (2003).
right Cartier Archives © Cartier.
bottom left © Christie's Images Limited (2012).

147
top Edelweiss earrings © Van Cleef & Arpels.
bottom © Christie's Images Limited (2013).

148
N. Welsh, Cartier Collection © Cartier.

149
Image courtesy S. J. Phillips Ltd, London.

150
White Light by Shaun Leane in collaboration with Steinmetz for the Forevermark Precious Collection © Shaun Leane.

151
Lierre de Paris necklace © Boucheron.

152
Ivy bracelet © Boucheron.

153
Queen of the Night necklace, designed by Shaun Leane for Boucheron. Image © Boucheron.

154
Victoire de Castellane, Cana Bisextem Now, 2010. Lacquered silver, yellow gold, white gold, diamonds, emeralds, garnets, cucumber jasper. Bracelet: 8.4 x 8.8 cm; with base: 8 x 13.1 x 10.9 cm. Ed. unique © Victoire de Castellane. Courtesy Gagosian Gallery. Photography by Erwan Frotin.

155
© Christian Dior couture.

156
Victoire de Castellane, L.Es Delirium Flash, 2010. Lacquered silver, white gold, diamonds, opals, zebra agate. Ring: 4.8 x 5.3 cm; with base: 10 x 6.3 cm. Ed. unique © Victoire de Castellane. Courtesy Gagosian Gallery. Photography by Erwan Frotin.

157
left © Christian Dior couture.
right © Christian Dior couture.

158
Double Flower ring © Bochic.

159
© Wendy Yue.

160
© Christian Dior couture.

162
Camélia Aquatique necklace, Jardin de Camélias collection © CHANEL Fine Jewelry.

163
Camélia Tourmaline Paraiba © CHANEL Fine Jewelry. This piece was created based on a design by Lorenz Bäumer.

164
top left Camélia Exquis brooch © CHANEL Fine Jewelry.
top right © Christie's Images Limited (2012).
bottom Camélia Perlé brooch, Les Perles de Chanel collection © CHANEL Fine Jewelry.

165
top left Contraste de Camélia brooch, Jardin de Camélias collection © CHANEL Fine Jewelry.
top right Camélia Coromandel brooch, Jardin de Camélias collection © CHANEL Fine Jewelry.
bottom Camélia Origami bracelet, Jardin de Camélias collection © CHANEL Fine Jewelry.

166
© Christie's Images Limited (2000).

167
Photo: Jozsef Tari.

168
Jadeite floral brooch, Four Seasons Collection © Cindy Chao THE ART JEWEL.

169
Winter Plum bangle © Anna Hu.

170
Camellia brooch drawing for the Jardin de Camélias collection © CHANEL Fine Jewelry.

171
Drawing of a diamond holly corsage ornament, gouache on paper, Joseph Chaumet. Collection Chaumet Paris.

174
Drawing of a diamond, ruby and emerald nasturtium brooch, gouache on paper, Joseph Chaumet. Collection Chaumet Paris.

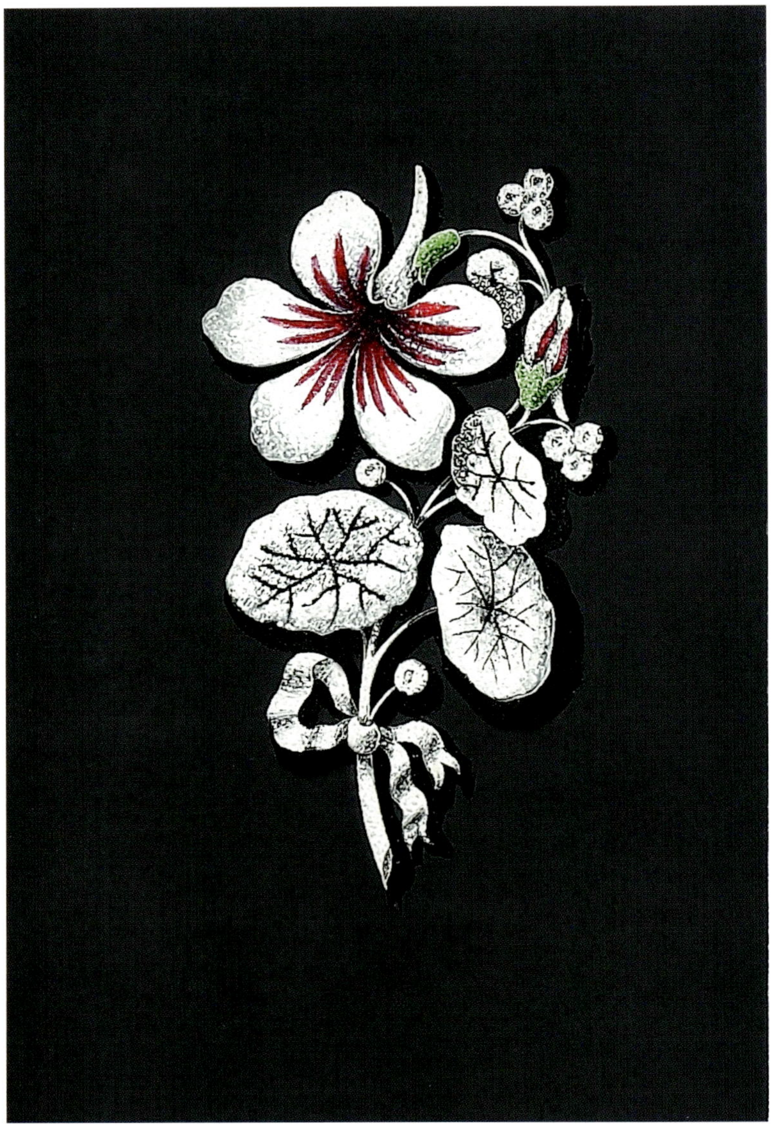

Nasturtium
Chaumet
c.1890–1900

Biography

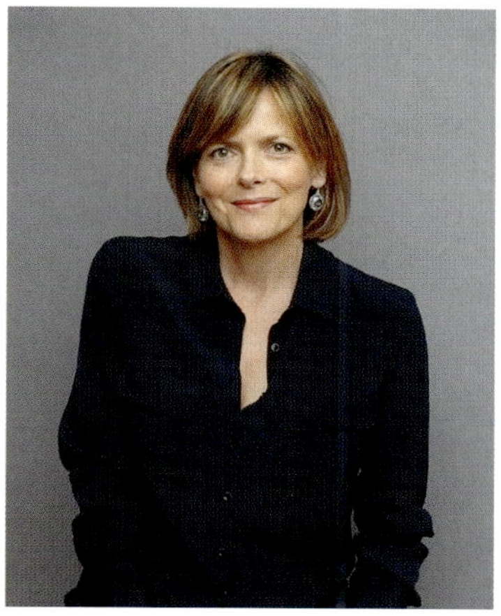

Carol Woolton is jewellery editor of the British edition of *Vogue*. She is a leading authority on jewellery and has written widely on antique and modern jewellery for publications and newspapers such as *The Financial Times, The Times* and *The Daily Telegraph*. She is the author of two other books by Prestel, *Fashion for Jewels: 100 Years of Styles and Icons* and *Drawing Jewels for Fashion*.

Acknowledgements

I would like to thank my friends and colleagues around the Place Vendôme in Paris, New York's Fifth Avenue, central Hong Kong and of course my home turf along Bond Street and the environs of London in both jewellery and fashion houses for their unfailing support with glorious imagery of their creations as well as their precious floral inspiration.

And Joel Rosenthal and Pierre Jeannet for their incomparable bejewelled botany, planting in my head some years ago the seed of an idea which has blossomed into this book.

© Prestel Verlag, Munich • London • New York, 2014.
© for the text, Carol Woolton, 2014.
© for the images, see Picture Credits, page 172.

Front Cover: Morning glory necklace, Jean Schlumberger, Tiffany & Co., c.1963
Back Cover: Reina Magnifica Sangria, Victoire de Castellane, Dior High Jewellery, 2007

Prestel Verlag, Munich
A member of Verlagsgruppe Random House GmbH

Prestel Verlag
Neumarkter Strasse 28
81673 Munich
Tel. +49 (0)89 4136-0
Fax +49 (0)89 4136-2335

www.prestel.de

Prestel Publishing Ltd.
14–17 Wells Street
London W1T 3PD
Tel. +44 (0)20 7323 5004
Fax +44 (0)20 7323 0271

Prestel Publishing
900 Broadway, Suite 603
New York, NY 10003
Tel. +1 (212) 995-2720
Fax +1 (212) 995-2733

www.prestel.com

Library of Congress Control Number is available.
British Library Cataloguing-in-Publication Data: a catalogue record for this book is available from the British Library; Deutsche Nationalbibliothek holds a record of this publication in the Deutsche Nationalbibliografie; detailed bibliographical data can be found under: http://dnb.d-nb.de

Prestel books are available worldwide. Please contact your nearest bookseller or one of the above addresses for information concerning your local distributor.

Editorial direction: Lincoln Dexter
Editing: Sarah Kane
Graphic Design: Amy Preston and Amélie Bonhomme
Production: Friederike Schirge
Origination: Repro Ludwig, Zell am See
Printing and binding: TBB, a.s., Banská Bystrica

Printed in Slovakia

Verlagsgruppe Random House FSC® N001967

The FSC®-certified paper Condat matt Périgord has been supplied by Papier Union, Germany

MIX
From responsible sources
FSC® C022120

ISBN 978-3-7913-8114-5